An
Oriental Mission
for
Global Vision

First Published, 2021

Published by

GenNext Publication
5, Ansari Road
Daryaganj, New Delhi-110002
Phone: 9811692060
E-mail: gennextpublication@hotmail.com

Printed at: Gyan Press, Delhi.

Cataloging in Publication Data--DK
Courtesy: D.K. Agencies (P) Ltd. <docinfo@dkagencies.com>

Mishra, Subhash Chandra, 1953- **author.**
An oriental mission for global vision / Dr. Shubha Chandra Mishra (Ph.D).
pages cm
Includes bibliographical references.
ISBN 9789353249311 (HB)

1. Philosophy, Asian. I. Title.

LCC B121.M57 2021 | DDC 181 23

THE SPOT LIGHT

In digital dogging, ADD (Attention Deficit Disorder) or ADHD (Attention Deficit Hyperactivity Disorder) – like mania or hypomania upsets B.P, Mood ease and efficiency. So do open the treasure chest of global classics on the clues of life philosophy to relax sulky mood and tackle all challenges of brooding melancholy of your mortal life. Further such Catholic Enterprise to steer the East- West interwheels would serve as an angel to collate universal harmony and hilarity against Bio- hazard.

So feel its feature or beauty of 24 theme- petals of the lotus-work on Axiology for the Ultimate Reality through Oriental Mission and flow with focal felicity of the Global Vision. Each theme enriches and radiates multi-pollen of viable perception which tends to humanize aspirations and ambitions of life with two- ply (East- Western) tenets under cosmopolitan Spirit.

– Anonymous

The Reader

I owe a deep sense of gratitude to the Reader-Cum-Communicator being advised to entertain the holy work with global attitudes and impressions cherished in it. It is brimful of ultra-modern devices more than inventions to ease stress and strain in bio-life. Its mission is to boost up crystallized cognition and fluid intelligence to solve global problems under specific system of life. It would change our whims of thoughts to blossom into positive Consciousness under holy horizons. It would act as a shower of self-serenity and sanctity. As an advisory on human life, it would turn and control the aura of the community under pristine propensity. The work may be treated as the Cyclopedic Digest of the oriental and modern conflux of knowledge prone to global humanity and harmony.

Here 05 chapters of the work correspond to 05-Gross-Elements (Matters), 05 senses of wisdom, 05 senses of Action and 05 Looks of Lord Shiva as Global Savior. As 05 qualifiers are inevitable for proper origin and orbit of human life on global level; So 05 chapters in the work have been explored for Bio-bonanza as-

1. Ths 1st chapter rotates round the sheer materialistic view of Education-System, Human nuisance, oriental senses of Human Rights and Havocs in material life on global level-all amendable on oriental devices.
2. The 2nd chapter rotates round micro-Mechanics & Hexa-Philosophy of oriental geniuses, globo-oriental view on mankind and democracy of cult, religion, culture and Industrial Re-enforcement-all amendable under oriental tenets.
3. The 3rd chapter rotates round Nature-human harmony, Mono-Metaphysical Concept. Anatomic Amplifier of 'AUM' & Zero (0) zenith, and oriento-healing tips for women harrying on global level.
4. The 4th chapter rotates round holistic treat of ailments, Vedic rites for Eco-care, Lord Shiva character for global Savior & human plight on Karma-Philosophy.
5. The 5th chapter rotates round Vedopnishadic tints & tips for terror-war aversion and post-mortem life-soul appropriations or provisions.

Thus the theme of the work-Oriental potentials to gear the Bio-globe

Moreover, the holy work was penned to let celebrate the conjugal lives of the billions under spiritual spotlight. The work intends to illumine the Globe at the special cause or event of the Half-Century Autumn of my conjugal life as oriental seers of yores illumined the multiverse with their mindoscope. Further its contents might tune up the Morpho-lute in amity & felicity perceivable through the holy device. The Work on Globo-Axiological Philosophy (Metaphysics + modern Science) for Bio-bonanza could be finished by virtue of single covalent-Energy No-63 oriented to global commission and confluence in the teeth of global havocs due to the new Coronavirus (covid-19).

Any suggestion to optimize the work is solicited on E-mail-drscmishra6@gmail.com

Because - "to err is human
to mend is divine"

The Author

Acknowledgement

I acknowledge the academic awareness & acumen of Acharya Sarita Choudhary to keep up the work with available measures. So I cherish her cozy and calmy life.

I feel felicitation to testify the mosaic mind of Kavita Jha, Educator, to manage the work with utmost devotion and fervour. Her prompt painstaking beggars description to note that she and her consort of melody could shoulder the MSS- work for final display with corporeal & cordial measures. So I owe her onus and wish her glamour in life.

I feel the know-how concerns of Er. Gangesh Kumar to step-up the work. So I wish him brighter future.

I credit the possible support of Er. Neha in completion of the work. She might attain the pitch of life.

I cheer the technical knowledge of Shashwat who could harness the work with his wide learning. So he is, also, liable to be blessed for his promising career. He bids fair to be a versatile figure.

Blessed are Shivangi & Shreya to have shared digital problems of the work promptly. They, also, bid fair to get on the land with digital minds.

My heart leaps up to coddle,
Darsha Kumaram to grace the work,
My heart springs up to cuddle
Ṛcha Nilānchal to hem the work,
The child is Father of the man
As stress-busters in long run
Fate of buds hope of a man
Into dreams of feat & fun.

The Author

ज्ञान–विज्ञान–तृप्तात्मा

Jnāna-Vijnāna-Tṛptātmā

Gyāna-Vigyāna-Tṛptātmā

Cognition-Cosmic science to sate the Inner Self

Contents

MEGA-NOBLE-MAXIM

1. समानी वः आकूतिः समाना हृदयानि वः
   समानमस्तु वो मनो यथा वः सुसहासति।
   ऋग्वेद–9 or 10/191/14
   (included Article- 14th-18th in The Constition of India)
   "Samāni vaḥ AAkutiḥ Samānā Hrdayāni Vah
   Samānmastū vo Mano yathā vaḥ Susahāsati
   Rigveda.9or10/191/14
   "Eulogist!
   Your will power and wish be common to all
   Your state of heart & feeling be common to all
   Your mind and conscience be common to all
   Your objectives & enterprises be common to all
   Your accord and acme be common to all."
2. पुमां पुमांसं परिपातु विश्वतः
   "pūmān pūmānsam paripātū viśwataḥ:
   "Let human beings be rescued on all sides."
3. इज अ–खज्ना मीसाककुम् ला तसफिकू–न
   दिमा अकुम् व तुखरिजू–न
   अन्फुसकुम् मिन् दियारिकुम् सुम्–म
   अकरर्तुतुम् व अन्तुम् तशहदून।
   कुराण–संत वकर–1/2/84
   "Ija A-khaganā misākakum Lā Tasfikū na
   Dimā Akum va Tukhariju-NA
   Anphaskum Min Diyārikum sum-Ma
   Akarartutum va Antum Tasahaduna-Quran St Bakar-1/2/84
   "The Almighty made you pledged
   Not to combat or kill among yourselves
   And not to banish them from the Land
   You are the witness of such pledge." ---Quran St. Baker (1/2/841)
4. Thou shall love thy neighbour
   But I say unto you love your enemies. ---The Bible (1:1:43-44)
5. Bless them that curse you
   Do good to them that hate you---The New Testament-XII:14:60

The profile

Name – Dr. Shubha Chandra Mishra
Father's Name –
Vidyavācaspati Late Babu Mishra

Postal Address –
Dr. (prof) Shubha Chandra Mishra
Ward No. 10
P.O. Jhanjharpur Bazar.
Dist. Madhubani (Bihar)-847404
Designation - Principal

M – 9939984914 / 7667921138
Email – drscmishra6@gmail.com

1. Academic qualification – M.A. Acharya. Ph.d.
2. Professional Qualificatioin –
   a. U.G.C Sponsored R.C. Programme — Kurukshetra University Kurukshetra (Harayana) — Qualified- 1991 Qualified- 1991
   b. Do (Auditions performance) — Lucknow university Lucknow (U.P) — do - 1991
   c. do — University of Calicut Kerala) — selected 1992
   d. do — Poona university, Pune (M.S) — Qualified 1995
   e. Professional Development Programme (Officers) — University of Hyderabad, Hyderabad (A.P.) — 2009
3. Seminar/Workshop/Webinar
   a. Bharvi's principle of life (Dais lecture) — -A partial fulfilment of R.C. programme -Poona University Pune (M.S.) — 1995
   b. National ability in Chhatrapati charitam (Dais lecture) — Do — 1995
   c. Workshop on Manuscriptology & Palaeograpy (3 weeks) by Indra Gandhi National Centre for the Arts, New Delhi — In collaboration with Poona University Pune (M.S) — 1995
   d. Research Methodology in Indology — Mithila Institute of P.G. studies & research in Skt. Learning, Kabaraght (Darbhanga) Bihar — 2004

e.	National Seminar sponsored by U. G. C on post-Independence Skt. works on Indian Democracy	B.B.A. Bihar university Muzaffarpur (Bihar)	2007
f.	Learned speech on the great use of social service	Spl. Camp at Dr. J.M.S. College, pastan Navtoli (Madhuban) Bihar	2014
g.	Learned speech on Swami Vivekanand Jayanti & National Youth Day	Kalptaru Cultural Evolutional Trust, Ghaziabad (U.P)	2020

4. Project work/Research project

a.	Skt. teaching method	A partial fulfilment of the R.C. programe, Lucknow university, Lucknow (U.P)	
b.	An oriental approach to human globe	Indian institute of Advanced Study Rashtrapati Niwas, Shimala (H.P) The project appreciated and fellowship award constrained to limitation-	1997
c.	Minor U.G.C. research project-Supervisor	On Distingguished women in Krishna literature in Mithila Region.- a perception by Dr. Ravindra Nath Jha	2013-14

5. Article published/underwork

a.	Chhatrapati charitam parichayah	Vishwamaniṣa Bulletin under K.S. D.S.U Darbanga (Bihar)	1981
b.	suddhādwet Ke pravartaka Acharya Ballava ka pustivāda	Mathureshwar jee Felicitation volume Raipur (M.P)	1994
c.	Common culture of Mithila & environment	Mithila institute of Skt. P.G. studies & Research, Darbhanga (Bihar)	2006
d.	Kalsarpayoga Mimānsā	Do (Śastrartha technical Journal)	2008
e.	Research on Sanskrit Literature-Time mandate	"Dainika Jagaran" News Paper (MUZ.) Edition	10-09-2009
f.	Vidyāvācaspati pt. Baba Mishra-A commemoration	Esteemed Journal 'Sāstrārtha' M.I . skt. studies & research Darbhanga(Bihar)	2012
g.	Wine-shun in oriental opinion	Pratibimaba (Hly Journal) M.R.P.L. Manglore (Karnatak)	2015
h.	Awareness compaign for wine-shun	Suggested to Govt. of Bihar	2017

6.	**Extra-curricular Activities**		
a.	Chief guest at Education & Cultural Conference on Yuva Avam Loktantra	Under the auspices of Nehru Yuva Kendra, Jhanjharpur (Madhubani)Bihar	1981
b.	Programme officer	Dr. J.M.S College pastan Navtoli (Madhubani)	1994-96
c.	As a Spl. Guest to deliver learned speech on Rastrapitā Gandhi & Village panchayāt	Inaugurated by Hon'ble M.P. (R.S.) M.L. Mandal at P. Raj. Ganauli Andharathadhi Madhubani (Bihar)	2004
d.	Nodal officer (C. unit) (NMEICT)	National Mission for Education through Information & Communication Technology, MHRD, New Delhi.	2010-11
e.	Analyst (Swot & Rusa)-Institutional Development planning & 20-point theme for NEP, MHRD, New Delhi	To the State of Bihar (Educational Deptt.) Patna & MHRD, New Delhi	2014-15
f.	Ex-officio member in University Selection Board. K.S.D.S. University, Darbhanga	Constituted to Dr. R.K.T.J college. Ekahari (Ladania) Madbhubani	2014-16
g.	Ex-officio member (Counselling Committee)	NAAC Peer Team, Banglore for K.S.D.S.U (Darbhanga), Bihar	2016

Chapter - 1

Cosmo-Human-Corner & Oriental Care

1(A)-Justification

I am the scion of the scholar dynasty renowned for philosophers, thinkers and scholarly stalwarts. I was brought up in a gazetted but fairly earned family with traditional tint at victory land of vill-Harina (Jhanjharpur), Bihar. I, being the eldest of the gross family, had to abide by estate affairs as a relief to the helm of the family. Hardly I spared my time for my academic adhesion. In my student life I used to be engaged in harvesting and procuring the landed property at distant places for years together. At the same time I had to tackle the complications of my gross family who cared a fig for my regular studies. In the mean-time I was united into a wed-lock in early teens. So I could not enlighten my intelligence and propel perseverance in a pastoral life. But my genetic quality of learning and logic paved way for completion of my studies in loitering steps. Somehow or the other my intuitive intelligence was let confined to the grave of rustication. So I could not display my mindscope for want of proper platform & environment. Luckily I happened to pull on my academic career in the vicinity of legends whose scholarly talks and techniques left an indelible effect on my mind. Anyhow I sailed my voyage of life with my spouse's engineering till retirement of service.

It is worthwhile to note here that stay-at-home persons are also born genius. They do have spruce personality and tactful skill to highlight the name and fame of the land. But sometimes they fail to give vent of their valuable conception amidst depression and barred environment. This idea is manifested in the following stanza of English poet Thomas Gray in "Elegy"-

"But knowledge to their eyes her ample page
Rich with the spoil of time did never unroll
Chill penury repressed their noble page
And froze the genial current of the beat."

Tenor-extreme poverty has a freezing effect on the vast scroll of wisdom to be gathered by experiences and suppresses the growth of their genius and checks the flow of noble, warm and joyous feeling in their hearth. Further the poor rustics buried in the neglected part of the churchyard might have earned great fame by virtue of divine gift (genius) as spiritual leaders of the world. Some of them might have held the sceptre (sign of royal power) in their hands and ruled the Empire. Whereas some have earned fame as musician who produced extremely melodious music of rapture by playing on the lyre.

Consequently precious ideas of my fertile brain are compelled to be subsided amidst barred environment and as such I fear the line of Lord Tennyson-

"Man may miss and man may gain
But I keep on missing guiltlessly for good."

In a retired life my intent to enlighten my mindscope gave vent to this literary pursuit reposed in my mind for decades together; and the lamenting panorama of English poet, Thomas Hardy inspired me much to reify my intellectual endowment despite extinguishing gemo-intelligence and inner fire in grave rusticity as follows:-

"Full many a gem of purest ray serene
The dark unfathom'd caves of ocean bear
Full many a flower is born to blush unseen
And waste its sweetness on the desert air
Perhaps in the neglected spot is laid
Some hearts once pregnant with celestial fire
Hands, that the rod of empire might have sway'd
Or wak'd to ecstasy the living lyre."

Remember that we do live in Aryavart which commanded the deepest reverence in every nook and corner in the world. The intuitive knowledge and spiritual light that had been emanated from the virgin land, illumined the different parts of the sub-continents for thousands of years. The splendour of light that had been diffused by her had no parallel in the entire domain of the human race. To secure universal welfare, Shree Adi Shankar, great Advait scholar underlined the essential unity of traditions and sects to save Hinduism from disruption.

But with the advancement of the Iron Age beginning since 3102 B. C. onwords, changes of purpose, mind, and form have been sliding down in the human race as forecast in **SHREEMADBHAGVATMĀHAPURĀNA** - 12/12/1-16/. Wherein sanctity, patience, pity, longevity, strength and memory would be dropping. The rich would be deemed to be of high descent, of high dictum and of high virtues. The powerful person would manage to manipulate justice favourably. Marriage would be set up on the mutual will & pleasure of the partners and not on supervision of their abode's inclination. Seldom it would be celebrated through traditional rites.

The fraud would be deemed to be expert in behaviours ignoring the honesty and the truth. The basic facility of the male and female folk would be coition and not moderate character.

The Brahmins would be known by sacred threads and the ascetic would be known by saffron attire and staff. Only the trick-spoken Brahmins and heretic ascetic would be deemed to be more learned and honourable personalities. Bathing would be done with combing and designed apparel. Distant ponds would be places of pilgrimage and the nearer ones or reservoirs or pious rivers and parents would be neglected. The emblem of physical grace would be snaky hair, and the biggest principle of life would be appeasing nuclear appetite of own nuclear family under wed-lock. Service to religion would be for name and fame. Political leaders would impose undue burden of taxes ruthlessly and the public would flee to Himalayan forest for fear of being kidnapped and caressed. The public would be vexed with calamities like heavy rain-falls, drought, chilly climate, fierce floods and deadly epidemics.

The maximum life of human beings would be 20-30 years of age. Human body would be dwarf, tiny Lilliputians, slender and sick-ridden. Persons would live on lie, theft, excessive violence and many criminal activities. Cows would give little milk naturally as she-goats. The plants of paddy, barley, wheat and the like would not produce corns and trees would be tiny and thorny. The Vedic track of human life would be distracted and houses would be vacuum due to non- hospitality, avedic recitation and diminishing population (shortlivedness).

So in order to reinstate peace or proper life we would follow the footprints of our seers, philosophers and social thinkers hoping to look for divine benediction in the last episode of life.

Now such forecasting events in the universe are being proved to be true and I am grieved to mention here that the world falling to pieces under the spell of techno-moral avalanche, humanity is being teased by utter selfishness and sheer materialistic view of life. The present world is engrossed with eroding elements which might cause near-total eclipse of human beings. The entire atmosphere has been polluted with continual operation of sophisticated nuclear missiles. The air is pregnant with envy, strife, jealousy, malignity, suspicion and deceits. It is a tragedy of our time that injustice masquerades justice. Hypocrisy and ceaseless quest for supremacy have queered the pitch for harmonious set-up; direct and indirect wars are still being fought in various parts of continents. The continents are passing through extremely dangerous and trying period. The entire world seems to be in a great turmoil; unhealthy individualism has come up to the surface. Our well – deservedly reputed administrative mechanics has been deteriorating also and is ceasing to be apolitical and non-partisan. As a sequence of which we have been aloof from our cultural and spiritual heritage geared to Vasudhaiva Kutumbakam (cosmopolitan spirit).

Besides these negativities, most corroding elements in our body are casteism, communalism and regionalism. So a clarion call be given to root out such evils eating into the vitals of humanity.

Trivial parts of our life are stressed while the paramount ones are neglected. Among children there is juvenile delinquency. Courts themselves are on trial and losing the credibility. Law makers and other power wielders are the cynosure of public criticism.

Such malicious instinct and villainous design ingrained in devilish nature are, indeed, a great menace to human world. As Shakespearean Villain IAGO managed to kill the prettiest and most innocent creature – Desdemona. Because such dangerous ideas are just like a poison which in the beginning, is not distasteful but when it is swallowed to work on the blood it burns like Sulphur as a mine in Act-III Scene-III of Shakepearean Tragedy "Othello".

"Dangerous conceits are in their nature's poisons
Which at the first are scarce found to distaste
But with a little act upon the blood
Burn like the mines of Sulphur."

Destructive competitions, mutual distrust are reckless drive to pull one's rivals down instead of joint endeavour to ensure global welfare are rampant.

Political assassins, Hi-jackers, Guerillas are rampant. Thus we live in a violent and disorderly world marred by mafia culture. Vices of many brands and corrupt life style are geared to debased material –all add up human torture & injustice on global level.

The entire world seems to be in a great commotion. Countries are broken into pieces of Forward, Backward, Harijan, Hindu, Muslim, Bodoland, lingua sovereignty and the like.

Joint family is breaking into pieces, families or parties in small groups; religion in cult; atom in EPN and so on and so forth.

This process of disintegration is going on rapidly without hurdles. The slogan-I am proud, I am destroyer or killer is at the climax. Human sensibility, itself, has been splitted into trivial matters. Despite Herculian efforts there are yet terrible mood pieces in every corner of the world and even the Nature has not been spared.

Despite making partial victory over Nature to provide practical amenities with satellites, these scientific discoveries have put a red mark on the very existence of life on the earth.

Different kinds of bombs and artilleries-powerful and destructive beyond imagination- have compelled-their inventors to pass sleepless nights. The safe moment of our lives is rare and the next moment is war like horrors. Consequently murder, crime, riches, greed and the like have covered the whole world to inches. Men and women want to attain human integration in parts and not in full. Because the integral quality of a person is lost.

The city of Los Angeles (in America), being the crown of ultra-modernity, has become the greatest city of crime in the world. The rate of murder, rape, robbery, kidnapping and the like is at the highest in the world. Even in India the news of rape with innocent girls is common. The chief officials responsible for law and orders, are red-handed arrested for making homo-sexual relation with juveniles. Some saints and preachers lead their pilgrimage in luxuries and Tantriks are brokers in share markets. The crown authorities of legislative power namely national leaders are busy at the bigger scandal amounting to billions. The film on a man who has shot dead hundreds of innocent citizens, proves to be super-hit under consideration of Oscar Award. The big terrorists with arms and ammunition succeed to explode the palaces of cities at midnight, loot passengers' trains and hijack aero-planes.

The lives of freedom fighters in India could have hardly imagined that Indian Independence would be broken into so many pieces and those pieces on their own parts would be bent on divorcing "Indian Freedom itself". So I am grieved to say-what was irrigated in the blood of martyrs is treading India's freedom into forward sovereignty, backward sovereignty, Alpha sovereignty minority sovereignty, lingua sovereignty and the like.

Cash nexus has been the motto of life and market has been the alternative of everything; Mohallas, Villages and towns are rapid – race of business. Every home is changing into a shop. Fathers are hopeless of their children only because they are not fit for money minting affairs.

Housewives are divorcing their husbands because they are not crooked and crafty cash-drawns. So we get managed to lead a chaotic life in Bazar.

Thus the whole arena is burning into the whirl of mental fire, life is at sixes and sevens and it is too hard to live in the world.

The society is lamenting under casteism, communalism, terrorism. There has been rapid downfall of human values. The itch to display one's bossism has acquired epidemic proportion.

On the other-hand Science and Technology have made a commendable command over the lifestyle of the living beings in the universe. Their accomplishments are observed in almost all the concerned spheres such as agriculture, biotechnology, engineering, medical, electronics and space science programmes. Further in the Nuclear Age, Atomic Energy was looked upon as a big hope in view of vast potentialities for development in multi – dimension such as –

- Nuclear medicine or therapy to cure deadly diseases by supersonic rays emitted with radioactive Isotopes.
- Nuclear communication to propel ships, buses, railways, T.V., Radar, aero-planes and intelligent Satellites.
- Agricultural field by energy released through nuclear fission to enhance genetic qualities of seeds and crops.

So it was but natural that human beings, in general, found a deep solace and relief in the strides of science being the substitute of God.

I cannot help saying that 'faith' is the experienced truth while' Science' is the experimented truth. At normal situation each is rejecting the other on solid arguments viz Galileo's experiments made question mark on the Bible's conception; Charles Darwin put question mark on the longevity of the earth. John Dalton's further analysis of the Atomic theory and hypothesis of Avogadro suffered further analysis and observation with tools of scientific researches. It does not mean that science is a fraud. To my views both physical and metaphysical science can jointly free us from the grip of evil craving as well as culminating into total ruin.

It is worthwhile to note here that we, today, boast much of our scientific achievements made by the least numbers of personalities destined to mental agonies of the largest number of the society. The large number of the society remains absorbed in striving every nerve to make worldly demands towards a complete wreck. Because the largest section remains whirled in illusionary trap.

It is owing to the fact that mere intellectual know-how is destined to hanker after the avarice of life of the individual who is suffocating out of endless wants for transient pleasure. Whereas orientalists laid much stress on the metaphysical obligations in the perception of the Self for eternal bliss. So all should attune their soul for the harmony of love with one another. So better to husband material gains and heap up immaterial ones. Such idea to make the world understand the feasibility of orientology (Sanskritology-Integral science) in modern life is put up through this work. Apparently men of letters of the smart society treat Sanskrit as a language (dead language) only. Whereas it is the repository of at least 18 branches of scientific knowledge with socio-technical devices of which the current teaching curricula are bereft.

In ancient times the medium of common parlance and class-rooms was through Sanskrit language only. So it was but natural that all disciplines for global care were penned in Sanskrit language only. So we happen to learn those terse topics and theories in formulas which are needed to be dealt sincerely and lucidly as the westernists have done with joint venture of the oriental and modern scholar.Hitherto whatever researches have been done are the outcome of the substantial or theoretical touch in orientology; And whatever researches are yet to be done are reposed in the vast vagina of Sanskrit lexicon being the mother tongue of Indo- European languages including German, English, Latin, Spanish, Italian, French and etc.

Now it is the fitness of thing to quote that our powerful oriental brains under innocence were interrupted and later on enticed by alien forces who happened to have crowned with championship. Let the matter be hushed up with Shakespearean proverb in 'Macbeth' – "fair is foul and foul is fair."

Somehow or the other our taste for knowledge might vary with floating spin of interests for centuries. Today the smart society does not recognize the lore and locus of sanskrit pandits. They are deemed to perform ritual services only. They have to embrace hardship of life on meagre gifts for pious works at random against regular perks and packages. It is irony to note here that we, the people, are destined to celebrate many sacraments or ritual sacrifices since birth to death somehow or the other. Yet we do not give them much weightage for their theosophical themes as we do with the technocrats or the Elites or the Statesmen or the Consultants or the Intelligentsia or the likes. They, pundits or orientalists, are deemed to be strangers to share our nuclear thoughts and throbbings. That is why I have tried to rectify such latent notion through the literary work which might cast a comprehensive conatus to its credibility.

So absurd to say that the whole oriental learning is obsolete and the learned pundits are destined to sarcasm. So much so they are used to pocket social satire and are treated as off-stream of emerging educational drives. On the other hand we boast much of Gandhian view of education in 3H formula (hand, heart & head) which is off-shoot of our oriental learning. The reason for such discrimination is to have confused with brain-drain of the cash spinners who succeed to cope with their accumulative interests. Consequently we, the people, are left to lament for brain balance and buoyancy. So I am to outline my views haunting on my mind for decades together to mesmerize the global gamut.

So let me narrate the current abnormalities towards wreck and risk, and their remedial measures through Indo-European devices. Further in order to dilute with the above running problems I opine to take resort to our metaphysical pioneers and fathomless seers who have suggested valuable measures to make our life smooth, sublime and soft as a reward. Because life is a punishment and reward as well. It is subject to birth, old age, diseases, death and mistaken to gratify material senses as its ultimate goal in terms of inner pains and punishment. But life's ultimate goal is benevolence and bliss as a reward in terms of fitness and freedom from the whirl of birth and death. It should be borne in mind that Hinduism, Islamism, Buddhism, Christianism, Zoroastrianism, Sikhism and the like served and saved the life on the earth and that of human beings in particular in their own ways. Though quite different in character and same in spirit, their tenets shared a common pivot of "faith" which was misused by modern misinterpreters for personal ends. Such misinterpreters with fissile spirit got the better of the multiplicity of "faith" to create a common hatred against one another. And we get entangled in ismic fever as the by-product of their poor or narrow advocacy. So we should come forward to thwart such misinterpreters and follow the footprints of our celebrated seers of yores to avert envy, strife and tumult on the earth. At the same time the shallow intellectuals or the sciolist are prone to adopt biased views on spiritual or ritualistic pattern of life outwardly. But they connive at the scientific faults and boast much of their immediate benefits. It was not natural on the part of human beings to envy spiritualism or asceticism due to falling prey to horrors and huntings by terrible sovereigners. The material mongers challenge the concept of the Vedas, the Quran and The Bible. Consequently the whole world is let burnt unto flames of fatal fuss. That is why we do come forward to thwart such evil doers and draggers.

In view of the above topsy-turvy situation, the moment entails Herculian Courage and zeal to foil human fissure in order to reserve and save the integrity and amity of human race by getting the schism abridged with entente cordiale.

There was a crisis in the battle of Britain when Churchill appealed to the United States – "give us the tools and I will finish the job". So in order to bridge human fissures causing tensions, riots, bloodshed, moral debacle, emotional starving, ismic fever, ethico-cultural crisis, metaphysical disharmony and human avarice, I would like to furnish here, a literary fulcrum around which 5 techno-tools as contents would finish such global fission with the cultivation of relevant canons of the Vedas. the Upanishads, the Smritis, The Puranas, The Indo-hexa-philosophy, yogic science, the Quran, the Bible, the Tantras (occult power), the Epics and other Applied Science of the celebrated thinkers and seers of the world under the techno-contents –

- Cosmo human corner & Oriental care
- Oriental Brains & Creedal culture
- Micro-metaphysical feature & she-state
- Holistic care & Lord- Testament
- Global Terror and Oriental canon

So it has been imperative to undertake microcosmic studies in entirety and undergo such literacy device of integral discipline in human philosophy dealt through this piece of work. It would enrich the mind of human race with cosmopolitan spirit and enhance the breadth of vision. Further it would mould to grow into Ultimate Reality to bestride the destiny of the human life to perfection. I have laid on the social and practical aspect of Sanskrit towards integral elevation of humanity in a logical manner. Besides the book is penned to serve as therapeutics to increasing social ailments on global forum.

The book deals with traditional and pristine theories to crystalize oriental interests seconded by ultra-modern exposition to entertain the readers of all trades and origins. It would tend to trim the problem-free philosophy of life on global level. Lastly such literary enterprise is to usher a renaissance in the domain of perennial delight and cohere physico – metaphysical Science for global power, peace, perfection, poise and prosperity in one hamlet, as it were-

इमा रुद्राय तवसे कपर्दिने क्षयद्विराय
प्रभरामहे मतीः
यथा शमसद् द्विपदे चतष्पदे विश्वं पुष्टं
ग्रामेस्मिन्ननातुरम्–ऋग्वेद–1/114/1

"Eemaa rudraaya tavase kapardine kshyadwiraay
Prabhramahe mateeh
Yatha shamsad dwipade chatuspade vishvam pustam
Grame sminnanaaturam- Rigveda-1/114/1"

Tenor-

"Let our wisdom be lodged
With sin expiator & hair matted
Of heroic lord Rudra
All creature biped & quadruped
Be powerful and perfect
Dwelt in a global hamlet
To avert terror and torture
For life of sweet lyre"

Thanks to my destiny to have completed the work by virtue of retentive tenacity which could tear through all terrible tempest in life.

Now I ought to offer my flowery homage to civil image of Late Adya Devi and classical legend Vidyāvācaspati Late Babu Mishra, Director, Mithila Skt. P.G. Studies and Research Institute, Darbhanga (Bihar). His intellectual endowments, sparking speculations and logical expositions could auto-enhance my skill and scanning power. I cannot help expressing my sincere heart with partner & Patron(Mission) Mrs. Kalpana Mishra Alias Bachi, "Shastri", whose commendable cooperation to accomplish the work on global diameter is ever hailing.

1(B)- Educare & Digishālā

To me our prevalent education policy is responsible for fissiparous trends in society. It is not catering to our social needs. It does not train the people to think and act spontaneously in response to full potential of Natural law which plays vital role in increasing an armour of coherence, fraternity and congruity - that invite felicity and avert trouble before it arises –

"हेयं दुःखमनागतम्"
Heyaṃ dukhmanāgatam

It makes us highly competitive and not cooperative; it makes us simply think about oneself. It prepares students as a disintegrate personality. On completion of courses & semesters, the passed out students get indulged in fissiparous activities causing mutual distrust, human atrocities and ritual conflicts on international level. The existing education policy based on alien curricula has severed our emotional ties. It teaches us to lead a false co-life with missiles and arsenals; further it does not cater to our luminant knowledge and spiritual needs. It is responsible for human crises only. As a push for carnal pleasure and egoism we fail to utilize the precious resources of the Nature. Such detached notion of education forbids us to think of mass interests; and so we are confronted with repercussions of modern competitive systems to vie with one another. At the same time I would like to save humanity from electro-nuclear conflagration.

While addressing at the Bombay Presidency Association in 1885 – Md. Badruddin Tyagi Jee said, "The current system of education is meant for caste feeling and fissile trends which have distracted us badly". So we have brimful of learned citizens. But they are made to hanker after their own interests by hook or by crook.

Contrary to intuitive wisdom of our seers, knowledge, today, acquires from teachers and books is preparative, imitative and derivative. The alien policy is subject to students' dissatisfaction. Because it is intentionally unfulfilling. It fails to satisfy the thirst for knowledge of the Self. Because there is no existence of the Self in human psychology in the eyes of the Colonist. In other words there is no room for sense of values. Whereas German scientist Albert Einstein observed – "The student must acquire an understanding of and a lovely feeling for values he must acquire a vivid sense of beautiful and of morally good; otherwise with this specified knowledge more closely resembles – a well-trained dog than a harmoniously trained person".

So our seers of yores formulated invocation to evade eroding consequences in learning between the teacher and the taught as KATHOPNISAD (Katha branch of KRISNA YAJURVEDA) states-

सहनाववतु सहनौभुनक्तु
सहवीर्यं करवावहै
तेजस्विनावधीतमस्तु
मा विद्विषावहै–2/3/19

"Sahnāvavatu sahnaubhunaktu
Sahviryam karvavahai
Tejaswināvadhitmastu
Mā vidwiṣāvahai –2/3/19"
Tenor- "Co-defend learning light
Co-enjoy mundane sight
Co-enhance energy might
Co-cultivate lustrous height
Co-avoid malign fight".

Such collective recitation does nurture flowery felicity of knowledge – product in an adorable atmosphere. Further such mutual understanding would help the learning youth to serve bio-beings unanimously. We must know that we have come in the space-world for all mankind as the ATHARVA VEDA Commands –

सर्वा आशा मम मित्रं भवन्तु–19/15/16
Sarvā Āshā mam Mitram Bhavantu – 19/15/16
"Friendship be pervaded in all directions".

Today, on the contrary, "Education" means how intelligent enough to know on which side the bread is buttered. Unfortunately lessons given in schools or colleges are only to enable students to qualify in examinations which are, often, confused with the term "Education" itself. It is only mistaken as a licence to obtain employment -

"या विद्या सा नियुक्तये"
"Yā Vidyā sā Niyūktaye".
But the U.G.C. has logo mark.-

"या विद्या सा विमुक्तये"

"Yā Vidyā sā Vimuktaye". –

"Knowledge or learning for salvation or emancipation".

Of course, one cannot ignore the need to earn one's livelihood but does a person live by bread alone? Is it not his duty to cultivate his own personality too?

Meseems that such question may crop up owing to the fact that we have wrong conception of the term "Education". Here "Education" is derived from Latin term "Educare – means to educe or draw forth the latent gifts of the individual". In brief it is drawing out of the best qualities of a person – to educate, encourage and enlighten the Self or spiritual values as the bee who collect nectar whenever they go. So seek for goodness that is found in everyone. When things change inside you, things change around you. Christian St. Andrew Gide wrote- "there are admirable potentialities in every human being, believe in your strength and in your youth, learn to repeat endlessly to yourself; it will depend on me". We need to know that we are all endowed with innate capacity which needs to be unfolded in our own ways.

Some of us have a keen sense of truth or justice or beauty or loyalty; some on the other hand, may be extremely intelligent but lazy, indifferent and play-loving.

While other may lie, hurt and remain selfish. As William Shakespeare also wrote in "Hamlet" – "What a piece of work is man, how noble is reason, how infinite in faculty, how like an angel and yet what a quintessence of dust". According to American author Brian Patrick Herbert- The educationist should nurture-

- Capacity-mind power to learn as a gift.
- Ability-sufficient power to learn as a skill.
- Willingness-will power to learn as a choice.

So it should be the task of education to help his students realize their admirable strength or their weakness (SWOT analysis) and then contribute to their growth and development on one hand, and eradication of demolish zeal on the other hand. So the motto of good education is to furnish a well-grounded personality (inner human) whereas mistaken it for beautifying our outer human which has nothing to do with innate personality. Education is a major avenue of upward social mobility. As we are living in a social dynamics, so newer challenges are evolved for the care and crown of the creature.

So we should turn to our marvellous heritage in which knowledge is structured in Consciousness engendering inner energy and harmony to fulfilments.

Such perception about "Education" is imbued with the whole word "Education" which is being illustrated alphabetically as follows-

E- stands for Etiquette

D- stands for Discipline

U- stands for Universal fraternity

C- stands for Creativity

A-Stands for Awareness

T- stands for transformation from beastly to human nature

I- stands for Integrity

O- stands for Optimism

N- stands for Nobility

So the alphabetical connotation implies to be adorned with unique personality of the individual-

सौभ्रांतं हि कुलीनता
Saubhrāntaṃ hi kulinatā;
Caritas Vera nobilitas-

So far as our classical "Education" is concerned it was under the aegis of religion in all countries. In Vedanta we find a glorious "Education" that can make a person better and nobler. It may turn the jungle (woods) of our mind into a beautiful garden of personality. Like-wise SWAMI VIVEKANAND said – "Education is discovering the divinity and glory already in a man". His philosophy of "Education" asserts to water more spiritual sprouts than mental exercise. Because when mind and heart collide, we ought to prefer our spiritual character to ignite inner spring of sensation where our mind cannot reach. A heartless fellow cannot gain the spirit of psalm for perfection. But the spirit of mankind is collectively let engaged in churning ocean-milk to get the cream (inner potency) and butter-milk for the heartless for logical propositions. SWAMI VIVEKANAND got the Cream to have annexed with world crown to achieve the highest equilibrium between the alien-force and world religion through physical and metaphysical science. Because both are complement to each other. He convinced that the education rooted in the tradition and moral conception of India was an essential gateway to real renaissance of the land in defiance of mighty savage of alien civilization.

We cannot ignore the fact that we have traces of 14 branches of science taught upto Gupta period in then universities. Such system of learning was trodden down by sinner sovereignties. Those 14 branches are-

Vedas-04
Vedanga-06
Purana-01
Mimamsa-01
Nyaya Darshan-01
Vyakaran
(Astadhyāyi of PANINI)-01
Total=14

Such classical "Education" emphasized on freedom from malpractices, jealousy, hatred, rivalry and disparity. It contributed to human values, character building of which the brain-bruised run of "Education" is bereft.

Here we cannot ignore the fact that in modern socio-dynamics we need to stimulate academic environment for promotion of techno-savvys in order to foster global competencies among students in billions for quest of excellence. Because the traditional system of "Education" does not cater to the social need of the economy in the field of agriculture, industry and Information Technology; and we may suffer interprenual problems which hamper curricular enrichment through design and planning for academic flexibility. Further courses or syllabi should keep with the emerging national and global interests & relevance to local needs.

So knowledge economy to enhance growth potential for environmental consciousness and innovation on digital and metaphysical nobs is needed barely. Since the dawn of digital learning Digishālas (Digital Pathshālās) should have social responsibility to collaborate vision and leadership for capacity building of the individuals in teach-learn researches. Digishalas should act as collaborateurs via IQAS (Internal Quality Assurance System), NIRF(National Institutional Ranking Framework), COE(Centre Of Excellence), NKN(National Knowledge Network), NMEICT (National Mission On Education Through Information And Communication Technology), UILC(University Industry Linkage Centre) & exchange of Innovatory knowledge through GIAN(Global Initiative Academic Network).

Digishālās should be treated as holistic educators to ensure life-skills and saviours. In order to run one's life on two wheels (physical & metaphysical), oriental studies should be a part of all curricula for all trades and disciplines to share global cooperation in multi-languages. Intermutual venture may enhance memory-power. Communicative Competence and aesthetic values to galvanize mankind with the cultivation of virtues, efficiency,excellence and other qualities.

But the modern sale and purchase of primary to higher education are gaining ground to hamper harmony and sympathy. The profit-and-loss trends of educational institutions are producing greedy citizens. Marketization of education dishonours family members, teachers, seniors, culture and scripture of the land. This is more or less what American professor Clark Kerr paraphrased as – "paradise lost" in education.

Thus we are left to lament for British Poet T. S. Eliot Om's mindset-

"Where is the wisdom we lost in knowledge?
Where is the knowledge we have lost in information?"

For the time being, the educational institutions are suggested to produce quantitative (No. of students classes, and mark-sheets and results) and qualitative (knowledge, skill, interests and buildings) stuff to serve and suit the society. Such productivity of educational economy with human capital (buildings, students, library, laboratory, academic know-how) be used to train a good personality forever. At the same time there is the need of change in online education- system to maintain input (cost) and output (production) balance to be affordable to all.

Now concluding the classical and modern views of offline education along with teaching norms, I want to focus on the feature and nature of Guru-jees or teachers to viable extent as follows-

In the word Guru-

The 1st "GU" means – Darkness

The 2nd "RU" means – dispelling or resisting

As अंधकार निरोधत्वात् गुरुरित्यभिधीयते

"Andhkāra Nirodhatwāt Gururityabhidhiyate".

In MATSYA Purans-

Guru is- आवाहनीय अग्नि (Avāhaniya Agni)

-Consecrated or oblated fire) which illuminates the pupil for righteous performance or perseverance. Again in (SHABDAKALPADRUMA) - (शब्दकल्पद्रुम a LEXICON OF Skt. Grammar) by king Radha Kant Deo Bahadur-

– गकारः सिद्धिदः प्रोक्तो रेफः पापस्य हारकः
ऊकारः शम्भुरित्युक्तः त्रितयात्मा गुरू स्मृतः।

- Gakāraḥ siddhidaḥ prokto rephaḥ pāpasya hārakaḥ
  Ukāraḥ shambhoo rityuktaḥ tritayātmaa guru smṛtaḥ.
- ग (G)- stands for lord Ganesh

- र (Ref)- stands for Darkness
- ऊ (Ookar)- stands for Lord Shiva

So Guru is the Confluence of tri-elements (Ganesh, Fire or Sun and Shiva)

Now the word "Teacher" consists of 06 qualities as-

(a) T- Tactfulness or trained in teaching methodology

(b) E- Enthusiasm

(c) A- Addressing power or attentiveness

(d) C- Capacity for leadership

(e) H- Honesty

(f) E- Emotional Stability

(g) R- Respectful or Reservedness

Further in modern age a teacher should have common merits mainly-

1. Personality prone ability- outer attraction, physical fitness, intellectual excellence, mental hygiene, moral conduct and social sense.
2. Academic ability- G.K. learning, thirst for knowledge, expressional skill.
3. Vocational ability- training before occupation, training during service, experience of teaching, faith for merits even after service.

Also Irish poet William Butler Yeats said-

"Education is not filling a pail but lightening of a fire."

Thus Guru opens a gateway to a lucrative career and works as an eye to flush out lassitude in life.

In olden days we were taught- गुरू शुश्रूषया विद्या

Guru suśrushayā Vidyā.

-Learning is obtained through devotion to the preceptor".

Again in अथर्ववेद (Atharvaveda) - आचार्य उपनयमानो ब्रहमचारिणं कृणुते गर्भमन्तः–11/3

Āchārya upnayamanō Bramhachārinam krnute GarbhaMantah.

A preceptor gives his pupil a new birth out of his knowledge-womb, as it were.

Here the word "Brahmachari" means one who vows to lead the life of celibacy – prone to knowledge as –

"नृतात्सत्यमुपैमि

Nṛtātsatyamupaimi"

The pupil may be turned from untruth to truth or unwiseness to wiseness.

Further the aim of a celibate is to develop his physical, mental and spiritual charity after sacred thread sacrament (ceremony). So he is called द्विज(Dvija) – twice-born (physical & spiritual) as conceived through the inner cavity of teacher's thought for 03 nights' upbringing. That is why formal or general education to obtain स्नातक (snatak)- ablutionary performance) or graduate degree is prescribed for 03 years to study vast syllabus. To be more clear as the mother through gestation brings up her child with chyme, So a teacher gets his pupil digested the essence of all disciplinary knowledge in due course. Further a teacher dispels 03- type of darkness (ignorance) of students' mind-

(a) Natural temper

(b) Spirit-force dormant in human body

(c) Uncaring the Supreme Soul

A teacher plays a vital role as life reformer to get his pupil relieved of all mundane pains to turn into purified personality towards perfection within life. This very notion is defined in योग दर्शन (Yog Darshan) of St. Patanjali) as 05-type of mundane pains needed to be cut off

अविद्यास्मितारागद्वेषाभिनिवेशाः कलेशाः–2/3

A-vidyā smitārāga dweshābhiniveshā kleshāḥ; /2/3

Nescience, egoism, passion, malignity, instinctive clinging to worldly life.- called pains

In this way, there was a filial affection between teacher and taught. But such conception was assailed under the colonial system of education by lord Macaulay. Subsequently we fail to create the feelings of love and affection for our teeming millions. So in order to save living beings from nuclear disaster we have to amend modes and curricula of the alien system of education which prepares students as disintegrate personality. So to cultivate our pristine conception we have to execute the command of The Vedas (Spectrum of wisdom) representing the summit of integral intelligence-

यस्तन्न वेद किमृचा करिष्यति

य इत्तद्विदुस्त इमे समासते–Rigved–1/164/39

Yastanna Veda kimṛcā karishyati

Yā Ittadviddusta ime samāsate.

"He whose cognition is not open to transcendental field what can the verses render for him. Those who realize this state of reality are dwelt in wholeness of life."

Such integrated approach to Education cultures the physiology of the individual void of stress, fear, weakness, helplessness and thereby ignoring the need for operational or panther drive. So the cogency or accuracy of educational system depends on the fostering nature of a teacher willing to decide which pieces of knowledge are relevant to modern livings. At the same time students should acquire with the findings of applied knowledge warranted in obedience, good conduct, noble mixing and etiquette. Such system must teach each new generation to observe how much existing knowledge can be used to develop new products, to observe new processes and production methods, and to improve the efficiency of organizations in business, public-private sector and social services.

In other words, education must help innovators to observe how to apply existing knowledge in positive manners. Such manners would help the innovators and inventors of future with techno-social knowledge to understand the world they live and work in and what they currently offer.

Under the context we should recall our seers' invocation-

धीमहि धियो यो नः प्रचोदयात्
ऋग्वेद - Rig Veda- 6/62/10

Dhimahi Dhiyo yo naḥ prachōdayāt.

"Knowledge & pursuit are invoked to the highest heritage of human beings".

In a nut shell, the purpose of "Education" is not cruelty and craving but love and devotion; only then we will be able to develop the freshness of feelings for Nature; the sensitiveness of soul to human need; we must foster the freedom of mind; humanity of the heart and the integrity of the individual. Further "Education" must foster inherent dignity of human society based on freedom, justice and peace for the world. But sorry to say, here, that we have been reluctant to cultivate the gems of wisdom reposed in our seers such as ADI SHANKAR ST. BHĀRADWAJ, St. KANĀD, St. CHARAK, St. YĀGYAVALKYA, St. DHANVANTARI, KUMĀRIL BHATT, JAIMINI, NĀGĀRJUNA, ĀRYABHATT, BHĀSKARĀCHARYA, ĀCHĀRYA KAPIL, VĀCASPATI MISHRA, JIMUTVĀHAN, VIGYĀNESWAR, ALBERUNI, DALTON, ALBERT EINSTEIN, RUSSEL BERTREND, ĀCHĀRYA MANU, PARĀSHAR MUNI, UDAYANĀ-CHĀRYA, CHĀNAKYA, GANGE-SHOPĀ

DHYĀYA, JAGADISH TARKĀLANKĀR, ĀCHĀRYA JAIMINI, VĀLMIKI RISHI, VEDAVYĀSA and etc.

So the utter concern for full problems warrants to seek guidance of the teachers who have fathomed the ocean of life. It is of utmost importance to have sublime teachers to teach about macro-micro truth deciphering or decoding the divine treasure within metaphysical sphere.

Lastly a teacher should not only transmit some external mass of factual knowledge but also emit fuel for spiritual sparking which might ignite positive aptitude and global conduction into students. So the leaner should have affinal mind in social sanctum –

मातृवत्परदारेषु परद्रव्येषु लोष्टवत्
आत्मवत्सर्वभूतेषु यः पश्यति सः पण्डितः।

Matṛvatpardareshu paradravyeshu lostvat
ātmavat sarvabhuteshu yah pashyati sah panditah !

"A learned man is one who sees about others' wives as own mothers, views others' possessions as clod and the whole substances of the world as mine or own".

1(C) - Human Chaos & Confusion

We boast much of the Age of Information Technology and Electronic devices for our easement. While the new generation or the youth pose a challenge to commit suicide due to keen contests or competitions. They prefer to live in solitude and make aerial dreams for encashment.

Industries of billians of dollars are being installed for a grand success in life. Still the new Era is full of frustration, insomnia and mental itching for marketing brain economics. All are betting life on risk-mode and waiting for hallucination.

Due to modern technology and bullet communication, our brains are gauging with many things. Facebooks and email requests expect quick reaction and response. Multi-tasks to increase production under overtime engagements emit stress hormones-Cortisol in a fight or flight situation; Andrenaline & cortisol warrant risk of depression. Such stressors increase anxiety, depression, digestive problems, heart problems, sleeping problems, mental problems and etc. So the bare need of the time is to craft our stress away. Remote – sensing devices and robot missiles are being launched to turn the world into paradise pose a threat to Biosphere including the inventors. Instead of peace and harmony we are confused with crimes, chaos, riots, riches, greed, terror and the like.

The chequered history shows that lack of understanding and tolerance on the part of different regions of the globe brought about ruin. The epoc-making act of merging about 600 princely estates into one roof of India by iron-man Sardar Patel is, today, being challenged by big giants- linguism, regionalism and communalism. Further the problems of internal ties which are tragedly reflected by conflicts with the Sikhas, The Tamils, the Alphas, the Naxalites, the Bodos and the Separatists pose the real challenge. Now the Govt. is confronting with mammoth task to tackle them. On the other hand human beings have been carnivores under the spell of continental dishes. Whereas we should have been herbivores to suit our bio- structure. But we are made to animate the morphia of life with beastial tastes. Such inhuman habits are thundering fierce bolts on human values of which the smug citizens are bereft.

They have forgotten their own codes of life and are hankering after alien bites. Such deviation from own code of life and culture started with the extinction of oriental safeguards. Post Maharsi JAIMINI, ruthless system of slaughter of beasts and birds for meal taste might cause catastrophe in term of epidemic havoc in the whole world. But if human being were taught the essence or value of The "MANUSHMRITI" we would not have been suffered clumsy calamities from time to time. The book on human codes has suggested reasons against dire consequences in chapter- 11/57-64/ & 11/153-160 as follows serially-

(a) Avoiding the Vedas or the scriptures

(b) False evidence

(c) Abduction or usurption of human race, horse, gold and the land

(d) Force-cross with virgins, teachers' wives, own sisters and wives of friends and sons
(e) Deserting innocent parents
(f) Charging excess interests
(g) Untimely sacraments
(h) Sale of ponds, orchards & female
(i) Bio-weapon operation
(j) Uprooting herbal areas
(k) Subjection or fascinating or enhancing for malevolence against the fair sax.
(l) Abetting for livelihood by the fair sax
(m) Consuming pastoral pig, donkey, crows and their ordure or dung.
(n) Consuming uncooked flesh, flesh of pig, camel, cock, cat, rat, dog, mongoose, leech, leathery night birds and etc.

These absurdities act upon human body to infect human vitals inviting cloudy catastrophe or calamities unexpectedly. So much so the infection may be transmitted through the shadow of epidemic organs. So to avert such hazard to humanity Acharya MANU has suggested to undergo severe penance in solitude or distant places for months together as sanitary measures.

Under the circumstances we should prefer consumable to non-consumable food-stuff. We see around that one who enjoys non-veg continental dishes in luxurious life might lose immune power to fight against anti-virus or anti-bodies chemicals and one who lives on veg-variety in active and industrious life does accumulate immune power to fight against anti-virus.

Further Acharya MANU makes us understand that one who kills innocent creature or animals for self-sweet taste, seldom, prosper in life and life beyond as one cares a fig for others' pains-

योऽहिंसकानि भूतानि हिनस्त्यात्म सुखेच्छया
सा जीवंश्चमृतश्चैव न क्वचित् सुखमेधते–5/45

Yohinsakāni Bhutani Hinastyātma Sūkhecchayā
Sa Jiwansca Mṛtascaiva Na Kwacit Sukhamedhate".

Further he suggests that animals or flying creatures are brought into existence for oblation to the fire in sacrificial rites. Such chopping-off system for sacrificial sake gets exempted from sins by the self-born God-Prajāpati-

यज्ञार्थं पशवः सृष्टाः स्वयमेव स्वयंभुवा
यज्ञेऽस्य भूत्यै सर्वस्य तस्माद्यज्ञे वधोऽवधः - Manu–5/39

Yagyarthan pashavah sṛshtāh swayameva swayambhuvā
Yagyasya bhutyai sarvasya tasmātyagye vadhovadhaḥ.

Although we, sometimes, celebrate sacrificial rites for centuries together. Whereas our ancestors were accustomed to celebrate 05-type of home yajnās daily at home or public yajnās at times to appease the Almighty. But now we have been exclusive to get killed animals or birds for sweet taste through markets profusely. Some of us claim to have got rid of sins for killing via Altar but sweet taste is intended innerly. Whereas no deity demands innocent flesh or blood for His/Her appeasement.

Besides, we find a vivid account of the natural state, utility, feature and worthiness of different types of animals and birds in oriental-literature which is needed to quote here-

(a) Firing animal- its energy is capable of averting pollution

(b) Smelling animal- It has special smell taken from the some Rasa by the God.

(c) Windy animal- Its presence averts pollution.

(d) The cow-emit O2 through their pores and healthy ghee is procured for sacrificial oblation to the Fire and human health.

(e) She-goat- its urine cures T.B.

(f) The hinning sound of horses cures cough and fever.

So the killer of animals and birds are like demons.

Thus the land, trees, animals, birds and human beings are complement to one another.

So they are, here, to help us and not hurt us. So we should have care and respect for the smaller creature too.

Achārya MANU is grave to inflict 08-stigma of ruthless killing as illustrated in chapter 05 in scattered ways.-

अनुमंता विशसिता निहंता क्रयविक्रयी
संस्कर्त्ता चोपहर्त्ता च खादकश्चेति घातकाः–5/51

Anumantā visasitā Nihantā Krayavikrayi
Sanskarttā copharattā cha khādkasceti Ghātakah.

1. One who orders for killing
2. One who carves for flesh
3. Killer of animals and the like

4. Buyer of flesh
5. Seller of flesh
6. One who cooks flesh
7. One who serves flesh
8. One who eats up flesh

Scientifically we do know that medical science prescribes one to treat blood infusion into human beings by testing even blood group of other ones. Still we are but intaking blood, marrow and flesh of any creature of odd blood group which might collide with our health and hygiene. As a result of which we are prone to bloody temper, bloody feud, bloody cruelty and betrayal to the extent of blood sucker. Thus we are confronting with human oppression at many dimensions in term of human fissures, riots, bloodshed, emotional starving, ismic fever, ethico-cultural crises and metaphysical disharmony to human avarice.

So someone has said to save even invertebrate insects also-

Step over ants
Put worms back in the grass
Release spider back
Into your garden
Open windows for bees
To fly home.

Because they are all little souls that deserve a life too.

We do know that human beings are the masterpiece of God's creation. Despite to have bestowed with blessed mind we are made to be destined to hank after felicity of mind and the spirit. scientists have dedicated their lives to have marvelous achievements for material well-being for the human race. In the Age of Electronics, well-furnished villas, fine fabrics, Ease-loving communication, star-food and merriment constitute together a royal life. But despite these enjoyments we have been all the more discontent. Because there is unhappy without riches and there is brain cudgel with riches. Further we should know that place and power do not give real happiness. We confess crime and cruelty done for accumulation of assets as excusable mistakes. And we weep for the crown of pompous prosperity by fate and chance. We ought to know that huge accumulation does discover vices and refine renunciation does discover virtues. That is why the New Testament coins "Do men gather grapes of thorns or fig of Thristles".

But our psychological chamber remains more active than our physiological chamber to tackle multi-task of hoarding endless assets. But according to Cognitive Miser Theory – Our brain extends the least amount of energy at a stroke which might have acquired more to solve multi-problems that encountering in our life around the clock. Such type of tug-of-war causes cerebral haemorrhage to the extent of deadly decay. That is why our Vedic canon warns us-

तेन त्यक्तेन भुंजीथा मा गृधःकस्य स्विद्धनम्–यजुर्वेद–40/1/

Ten Tyaktena Bhunjeethā Mā GridhahKasya swiddhanam – Yajurveda-40/1/

"Enjoy with the given quota of materials usually and not stoop to the greed of others' belongings or riches."

Further,We cannot get at satiety with endless riches. The more we have and the more we want to have riches. Vedopnishadic maxim (KATHOPNISHAD)-

न वित्तेन तर्पणीयो मनुष्यः

(a) "Na Vitten Tarpniyo Manusyah".

AN individual is not liabe to be satisfied with riches".

Again

अमृतानंदस्य नाशोऽस्ति वित्तेनेति

(b) Amrtānandasy Nasoti Vitteneti".

The perpetual felicity of life gets hampered by riches'.

कामिनीकनकेभ्योऽपि न सुखं शान्तचेतसाम्

(c) Kāmini kan-kebhyoapi na sukham shāntacetsām

Even the appeased mind is not pleased with fond lady and gold.

Because the equation of riches and bliss may be detrimental to one's life-span. Hence the necessity for human beings to ponder over this problem is general. So the quest for true happiness has been the instinct of mankind from time immemorial. Since yester times human beings have been, very often, asking the question as to the emancipation from the chain of discontentment or mortal coil. Such query was responded by Adi Shankar, Jesus Christ, Mohammad, Buddha, Guru Nanak, Confucius and the like who applied their cosmic-energy toward investing the subject – Universe-full of ever miseries. Further the metaphysical leaders of the world dedicated their intuition to the perception of the Self-culminating into eternal felicity. In their opinion, there are, at least, two reasons for human discontentment-

(a) Ahamtā (Egoism) – here Aham (I- Ahankār) (अहंकार) which is a mental manifestation of will power (इच्छाशक्ति-'I' Icchāshakti) being the nature of रागगुण Ragaguna (greedy trait). For example- 'I' hear, write, speak"- I am rich, I am a great scholar, I can support,

I can exploit it and etc. Thus a man execute all his whims of the mind with the help of 'I'. The entire thinking is encircled by 'I'. On the contrary we must know that "naught is mine". That is why Indian philosophers called it तादात्माध्यास - Tādātmādhyāsa (false identity). Due to this ego of 'I' our अहंकार- Ahankar (Egoism) gets strengthened day by day. This very 'ego' is the cause of miseries; it overpowers others; it wants to defeat, suppress, and exploit others. Therefore, there is a lurking danger of getting defeated in victory, of getting suppressed in oppression and of getting exploited in heroism. These dangers beget bestial life of avarice and arrogance.

(b) ममता- Mamata (Deep attachment or possessiveness) that is mineness or I-ness. For example – house is mine. He is my issues, the land is mine, this is my decision and so forth. Thus, we retain the impression of "mineness" to ascertain our relation with all assets. But our Indian philosophers called it संसर्गाध्यास - SANSARGĀDHYĀSA – (false co-existence). This false co-existence increases with our age-factor more deeply. Such conception of "false relation" causes innumerable miseries. The deeper the attachment the more intense becomes the discontentment.

Certainly the faculty of "mineness" is very a big "Illusion" or Nescience which reduces infinite power to finite one in mundane eddy. Such solicitous state of mind due to false identity and attachment becomes heavier with the movement of life towards the grave. The more we amass riches the more we suffer false attachment resulting pains and penitence. In order to erase such human concerns we do cling our mind to metaphysical observation and adeptation.

The Buddha philosophy also advocates such notion through its 12-successive spoke in the wheel of the world (the cycle of birth & death)-

1. Sorrows or miseries
2. The cause of miseries – rebirth
3. The cause of rebirth – the will to be born (भव - Bhava)
4. The cause of Bhava – Mental clinging (Upādan - उपादान)
5. The cause of Upādan – The craving (तृष्णा-Trshnā)
6. The cause of Trishnā – The sense experience (Vedanā - वेदना)
7. The cause of Vedanā – The sense of contact (Sparś a - स्पर्श)
8. The cause of Sparśa – Hexa sense organ (षडायतन- Sadayatan)–

9. The cause of Ṣadāyatan – The mind body organism (नामरूप-Nāmrup)
10. The cause of Nāmrup – The conscience or consciousness (Vigyāna-विज्ञान)
11. The cause of Vigyāna - The Impression (संस्कार-Sanskār)
12. The cause of Sanskār - The nescience or illusion (Avidyā -अविद्या)

Here the serial Nos. 1 to 2 stand for past life
the serial Nos. 3 to 10 stand for present life
the serial Nos. 11 to 12 stand for future life.

Such is the step-down sequency of causation under the cycle of Birth-Death.

In this way I have tried to treat human trials and tribulations, chaos and confusions with thematic approach to Orientology. So that we may enjoy life in mitigation and quiescence.

1(D) - Human rights & oriental sight

We must know that the objectives of the Human Rights Commission tally with those of oriental codifiers' mindset of yores.

Human rights are concerned with the dignity of the individual at the level of self-esteemed conception that secures, identifies and promotes human community.

It is a federal system between Judiciary and Human Rights Institutions which are vigilant to auto-develop the National protection system based on legislative Rules of Law.

The Commission undertakes punishable steps (verbal, bonds, censure, fine, capital transportation etc.) to suppress ill – hobbies – conducts – accidents.

As Universal Declaration of the Human Rights – since human rights cover people all over the world irrespective of social, cultural, racial, ethnic, creedal and communal differences. That's why the Charter of the United States was framed in 1945 and focused the principle of individual rights; its merit to affirm faith in fundamental human rights in worth and dignity of citizens, in equality of citizens of all Nations and to promote social progress and standard of life.

Further the United Nations has played an outstanding role in codifying human rights and the international Covenants on civil politics as well as economic, social and cultural rights embodied authoriatative definition of basic rights and fundamental freedom intending to serve all mankind.

In the other Era India was crowned as global Guru by virtue of holy life and culture. But the increase of devilish mind biased with metaphysical upsurge has been rampant every-where. We should know that peaceful and happy life is possible by holy livelihood only.

The prestigious and proper life of the place-time is supposed to be the main organ of the Code of conduct.

So the National Human Rights Commission was established in October 1993 to codify for the protection of human rights to curb riots, hurting and human hazard.

Let me deal as to how the aims and objectives of the Commission were enshrined in our seers of yores.

According to codifier Achārya Manu.-

Where the punishment is let loosed ill-practices crop up. So all should maintain mutual balance to enjoy good life against fear of punishment -

सर्वो दण्डजितो लोको दुर्लभो हि शुचिर्नरः।
दंडस्य हि भयात्सर्वं जगद्भोगाय कल्पते–7 / 22

Sarvo dandajito loko durlabho hi shuchirnarah thandasya hi
bhayātsarvam jagadbhogāya kalpate/ 7:22

Further the stronger exert hurts on the weaker in loose administration compared to fish – folk.

यदि न प्रणयेद्राजा दण्डं दण्ड्येष्वतन्द्रितः
शूले मत्स्यानिवा पक्ष्यन्दुर्बलान्बलवत्तराः–मनु॰ 7 / 20

Yadi na pranayedrājā dandam dandyeshvatandritah
shule matsyaniva paksyandurbalanbalvattarrah–MANU 7/20

Again slokas at S.N 11 to 13 in the 15th chapters of the Vanparva of the Mahabharat introduced Code of punishment.Wherein Arjuna speaks for yudhisthir that the punishment of cloudy and red colour (personal nomenclature) are vigilant to unhurt the public of the land.

Here the cloudy and colour red represent the fear of punishment and the pains of punishment respectively.

Again Manu suggests in Manusamrti

राजा निर्धूतदण्डास्तु कृत्वा पापानि मानवाः।
निर्मलाः स्वर्गमायांति संतः सुकृतिनो यथा–8/318

(Rājā nirdhootadandastu krtvā pāpāni manavāḥ/
nirmalāh swargamāyānti santah sukrtino yathā) -8/318

The govt. leaves behind the sinful citizens for enduring punishment and the sinless ones are destined to heaven as the pious sages do.

In this chain I am to define the oriental-based intuition and work culture of the Human Rights Commission. –

1(D)- i -Wine prohibition

Wine begets beastly mind to drink oneself. The body liquor damages neurological or circulatory system. I am to add that wine mongers justify themselves by giving example of soma Rasa. But in ancient times Soma Rasa beverage was used to relish the cooling reflection of the Moon or nectar taste as juice of knowledge. But in the Iron Age; Acharya Manu has prohibited artificial wine beverage- (गौडी पैष्टी च माध्वी च विज्ञेया त्रिविधा सुरा। यथैवैका तथा सर्वा न पातव्या द्विजोत्तमैः) –11/95

gaudi paisti cha Madhwi cha vigyeya trividha sura.
yathaiveka tatha sarva na paatavyaa dvijottamaih,

Again, Acharya Yāgyavalkya in his Yāgyavalkya-smrti' speaks of the anti – result of enjoying wine – beverage for the fair sex –

पतिलोकं न सा याति ब्राह्मणी या सुरा पिवेत्।
इहैव सा शुनी गृध्री सूकरी चोपजायते

Patilokam na sā yāti brahmani yā surā piveta
ihaiva sā śhuni grdhree sukari chopjāyte

The fair sex (brahmni - not brahman caste only) drinking wine – beverage are cursed to be bitch, vulture and sow.

Again St. Pārāshara in "PĀRĀSHAR SMRTI" speaks of atonement for wine – beverage

पतत्यर्द्धं शरीरस्य यस्य भार्या सुरां पिबेत्–10/27

– (patatyardham sarirasya Yasya bharjya suram piveta)-10/27

The wine- drunk lady morally falls off the half body of her husband.

In Valmiki Ramayana - the wine – beverage by Sugriva is prohibited by Tara, being the wife of Sugriva -

न धर्मार्थ सिध्यर्थं पानमेव प्रशस्यते
पानादर्थश्च कामश्च धर्मश्च परिहीयते–33/46

Na hi dharmārtha śidhyartham pānmeva prashasyte
pānādarthascha kāmasca dharmasca pariheeyate-33/46

In Yogavāsistha of st. Valmiki – the reluctance for instant enjoyment with wine as puberty has been expressed - because such transient puberty has temporal tastes for love dreams with painful ends in sudden repulsion or detoxification –

मधुरं स्वादु तिक्तं च दूषणं दोषभूषणम्
सुरा कल्लोल सदृशं यौवनं मे न रोचते–20/9

Madhuram swādu tiktam cha dushnam doshbhushnam
Surā kallola sadrsham youvanam me na rochate"

In "Apastambadharmasutra" the prohibition of wine-beverage is stated as -

सर्वं मद्यमपेयम्–1/5/17/21

Sarvam madyamapeyam-1/5/17/21

likewise the prohibition of wine beverage has been enacted in the Article – 47 of the Constitution of India.

1(D)-ii -The protection of women – woes and minor – rights

(a) Rapism – In Āpastambadharmasutra- in order to ban such contemptuous crime, much stress has been laid on the angle of vision and the nature of mentality -

बुद्धि पूर्वं तु दुष्टभावो दण्डयः–2/10/26/19

-Buddhipurvam tu Dustabhavo Dandayah 2/10/26/19

अबुद्धि पूर्वमलंकृतो युवा परदारां कुमारीं वा वाचा बाध्यः–2/10/26/18

Abuddhi purvamalankrto yuvā pardārām kumarim vā vachā
Bhādhyah-2/10/26/18

– the youth should be chastised to stop such unpleasant action, if done unknowingly. with other's lady or virgin

Manusmr.ti says - पुरुषानां कुलीनानां नारीणां च विशेषतः
मुख्यानां चैव रत्नानां हरणे वधमर्हति–8/323

Purusānām kuleenānām nareenām cha viśesatah
Mukuyānām çhaiva ratnānān harane vadhamarhati- 8/323

Specially in case of abduction of high – breed female figure and precious stones, capital punishment or slaying is liable to be imposed."

Now in the Kiskindhakand of the Valmiki Ramayana there had been no objection on unfraudulent looking at Laxman & Tārā-

तदागच्छ महाबाहो चारित्रं रक्षितं त्वया
अच्छलं मित्रभावेन सतां दारावलोकनम् – /33/61

Tadagachha mahabaho charitram rakshitam twaya
Acchhalam mitrabhavena satām dārāvalokanam.

In the 10th chapter of Parasharsmrti, there have been the provisions of many penal – torments like Chandrayana vrat (special penance or vow). Kṛchhra vrata (painful or miserable vow). Shikhamundan (head shaving), arthikadand (fine) and Prajapatya vrata (a vow to give away the whole assets before turning into ascetism or etc.).

"In Parasarasmrti" (पाराशरस्मृति)' there are the provisions of enduring 3 – Chandrayan and – 3 – Krichha vratas to the extent of penis-cutting against heinous crime committed with cognate sisters or daughters.

मातरं यदि गछेत्तु भगिनीं स्वसुतां तथा–10/10

Mātaram yadi gachhettu bhaginim swasutātām tathā /10/10

एतास्तु मोहितो गत्वा त्रीणि कृच्छ्राणि संचरेत्।
चद्रयानत्रयं कुर्याच्छिश्नच्छेदेन शुद्धयति–10/11

Etāstu mohito gatwātri¯ni krchani sancharet
chadrāyana trayam kurychiśnachhedena śudhyati-10/11

In "Manusmrti" – there is the provision the bio-section of one's nose-ears and exilement in a bid to inflict terror - inspiring corporal punishment by the king due to rape with other's wife-

परदाराभिमर्शेषु प्रवृत्तान्नृन्महीपतिः
उद्वेजनकरैर्दण्डैश्छिन्नयित्वा प्रवासयेत्–18/352

Paradārābhimarśesu pravrttānnrmahipatih
udhvejankareirdandai śchhinnayitwa pravāsayet /

Again in "MANUSMRTI' – there in the provision of penal -code of beating with waterlily against the crimes committed by women, child, insane senior citizen, the poor and the diseased."

स्त्रीबालोन्मत्तवृद्धानां दरिद्राणां च रोगिणाम्
शिफाविदलरज्ज्वाद्यैर्विदध्यान्नृपतिर्दमम्–9 / 230

Streebālonmattavrddhānām daridaānām cha roginām
siphavialrajiwādyairvidadhyānnrpatirdanam/9/230

Again in 'MANUSMRTI' - the fair sex are condemned or humiliated to have illicit connection for child-birth -

अपत्यलोभाद्या तु स्त्री भर्त्तारमति वर्त्तते
सेह निंदामवाप्नोति पतिलोकाच्च हीयते–5 / 161

Apatylobhādyātu stree bharttā ramati varttate
seha nindāmavāpnoti patilokāccha heeyate/5/161

So to avoid rapism, boys and girls must be taught to value and protect their chastity as the secret treasure and thereby save the unique gift of intimacy for conjugal life. They should be taught the importance of loyalty in marriage and avoid even the thought of adultery termed as the "fornification" by the Old Testament.

Both should assemble their family life – spokes around the hub of affinity. they should be vigilant on beautifying their dress and gait, lest they should be entrapped in awkward avalanche. Because to look for callous caressing is easier than to overlook as said by Shakespeare also – "beauty provoketh – thieves sooner than gold."

1(D)-iii -Prohibition of own embryo – abortion

In the Uttarkand of वाल्मीकि रामायण Vālmiki Rāmāyana – suicidal step by the pregnant lady has been prohibited in a dialogue between sitā & Laxman -

न खल्वद्यैव सौमित्रे जीवितं जाह्नवीजले
त्यजेयं राजवंशस्तु भर्त्तु मे परिहास्यते।

Na khalvadyeva soumitre jeevitam jāhnavijale
tyageyam rajavanśastu bharttu me parihaśyate|/ **

In PĀ-RĀSHARSMṚTI – there is the provision of atonement for artificial foetus – abortion by the doer or abeter for days proportional to months of gestation -

यदि गर्भो विपद्येत् स्रवते वौपियोषितः
यावन्मासास्थितो गर्भो दिनं तावत्तु सूतकम्–3 / 16

Yadi garvo vipadyet sravate va´piyositah
yavanmasasthito garvo dinam tavattu sutakam/3/16

This "PARAŚHARSMṚTI" provides different types of rigorous punishment for rape with relatives' falling under section 10 to 24 in the 10th chapter.

1(D)- iv-Prevention of dowry custom

There have seen tragic events due to dowry system in pre-post marriage life. But we ought to know that marriage in a ritual sacrifice in which each individual is dedicated to do good to the both family and the society.

It is ritual performance, human agreement and social institution in which a husband longs for tender feeling, friendship and zeal. While a wife longs for support, affection and compromise. conjugal life goes on soft penetrating and receptive mode. In Apasatambdharmasutra (आपसतम्बधर्मसुत्र) there in the provision of atonement to beg alms wrapped in the skin of the tailed ass in 07 houses for 06 months by husband to have breached conjugal life and by wife for 06 months with 12 – night Krichha penance for the same of breaching allegation –

दारव्यतिक्रमी खराजिनं बहिर्लोम परिधाय दारव्यतिक्रमिणे
भिक्षामिति सप्तागाराणि चरेत् सा वृतिः षण्मासान्दृ 1/10/28/19

Dāravyatikrami¯ kharājinam bahirlom paridhaya Dāravyatikramine
Bhikshāmiti saptāgarani charet |. Sā vritih sanmāsān.

And

स्त्रियास्तु भर्त्तृव्यतिक्रमे कृच्छ्रद्वादशरात्राभ्यासस्तावंतं कालम् – 1/10/28/20

Striyāstu bhartrvyatikrame krchhvadwādaśarātrā –
Bhyāsās tāvantam kālam.

1(D)-v-The ban on jail – misconduct or cruelty

The criminals under trial in the court are serious issues. The Science of Ethics says that criminals should be treated politely to solve the crux of crimes. But the cruel criminals should be threatened of dire consequences in times to come. Otherwise friendly treatment would fall one into a quagmire.

In view of u/s 12 (c) of the Human Rights Act 1993 to study the life status of the culprit in jail, The Chief Justice – cum-chairman of the Human Right Commission, while addressing the Chief Justices of High Courts of India through his circular dated 1/7/03 suggested to revamp the status of the criminals since 29.11.99

Because many culprits are not acquitted as they cannot afford to execute bail- bonds. They have to endure the pangs of jail towards the brink of death due to cruel – conduct of the Jail Administration as well.

Hon'ble A.S. Anand, ex- CJI in his circular dated 2.12.03 directed the Chief Ministers of the states and union territories not to snatch the lives of the culprits by Jail Administration.

It is a serious offence to murder the culprits in jail illegally. But it is not a crime to murder a culprit in combat as a self-security as interpreted u\s 46 of the Penal Code. At the same time there is the provision to treat the culprit lightly under capital punishment or transportation for life.

Hon'ble Supreme Court of India headed by Chief Justice R.M. lodha, in course of hearing public writ adjudged to acquit the enduring culprits who have spent the half of the maximum imprisonment without or with bail – bond u\s -436A of the IPC unless the prisoners are alleged for capital punishment.

Further the Central Gov. provided Rs.500 crores to rehabilitate Kashmiri pandits with essential amenities within their ancestral home – stead land.

On the recommendation of the Human Rights Commission the National Police Commission has given the following directions to reform the quality of policing system –

(a) Increase in human rights' alert

(b) Skill development in inquiry or investigation process

(c) Medical test at due intervals

(d) Impartial maintenance of documents

(e) Aid to physically disabled persons

Besides the Summit was convened by Human Rights Institutions of commonwealth & Asia pacific Regions with representatives of India, Nepal, Srilanka, Afghanistan, Figi, Iran, Korea, Mauritius, Malvi, Magnolia, New Zealand, Philippines, South Africa, Ireland, and Uganda on May – 26-30,2003 in new Delhi – wherein issues were discussed on confinement, prohibition of atrocities, environment presentation, emergency medical treatment, asylums, resorts and sanctuaries in the vein of our oriental enactment and succour.

Technical and economical help were voted for assistance or security of the Rights of the physically disabled persons.

In the 7th Convocation of the Central Human Right Commission, the issue to implement of the Rights for the physically disabled persons was raised in collaboration with the Asia- pacific High Commissions and U.S. Forum. Such assistance had been voted already by oriental-pioneers also. For the time being the focus – point network has been installed for them.

1(D)- vi - Emergency medical service (E.M.S)

Trauma centres have been provided on recommendation of the Central Human Rights Commission corresponding to oriental Rules "जीवानामार्त्त नाशनम् - jivānām ārta nāshnam"- relieving of acute sufferings of the living beings.

Further it has been provided under Article – 21 enroute to Article 39(c),41 and 43 of the Constitution of India to entertain health and treatment service as the fundamental rights. Still there has been epidemic eruption in injuries, pains and mortal-rate due to urbanisation, fast-life Style, growing life needs, industrialization, traffic load, automated machine, terrorism, social – high-handedness. So more reforms and innovations in E M S are needed. Thus it may be said that the work-culture of the Human Rights Commission is more or less, based on oriento statutory suggestions and codes which warrant viable changes on global sphere.

1(E)-Life state & oriental light

The modern man has lost sanity of life in the turmoil of modern Science. Rightly a poet has said –

What is this life, if full of care,
We have no time to stand and stare,

The world is full of evil and darkness. The thought & culture of The Asia became retrograde and morbid under alien domination.

We do not live the life of the present rather mindful of the Past needs and the future plan. So we do miss the sweetness of the present life passing in melancholy.

We do know that future is as hollow as fear of dire consequences Further –

"we look before and after
And pine for what is not
with some pain is fraught"

Being absorbed in passing trivialities we hanker after the standard of living which decreases the standard of life. We have fallen prey to trials and tortures at different levels such as-

(a) **At the individual level**– we behold a tragedy in creating psychic disorder, addiction to drugs, hard drinking leading to high suicidal and Homicidal rapes.

(b) **At the domestic level**– break down in family harmony causing devorces, orphans, wife-killing and the like.

(c) **At the city level–** violent escalade of offences is often observed.

Industrial relations are severed by tensions. Charges and counter–charges culminate into stale-mate in production. There are brutal attacks on politics. Learned professionals in law and medicine have disrupted Ethics. Public figures have bidden farewell to morality. Crimes inside and outside prisons and public stations are rocketing to such an extent that we are not free to move. Children are in peril of being kidnapped. Cities are houses of terrors; newspapers are morning announcement of character killing, murder, rape or burglary, riot and exaggeration of negativities, stress and distrust. To me the reason of all hums and suffocations lies in the loss of sense of values of which the present education is bereft. Such loss of sense of values may be summed up in 03 dimensions –

(a) Where in the life we have lost in living

(b) Where in the wisdom we have lost in knowledge

(c) Where in the knowledge we have lost in information.

On the other hand, we live in the Age where we have conquered the highest mountain, Moon planet, Plane or etc. Undoubtedly we are the storms at sea and the dawn on the mountain and the twilight on the Metro – town. But we have yet to master ourselves.

We have hi-tech buildings but shorter temper, more assets but lesser pleasure, and fuller mind but more vacuum lives.

So it is futile to try for sophisticated life where we are brethren labours in the cataclysm of life. So the bare need of the hour is to cultivate moral courage and strength for the well – being of others. Artists, scientists, engineers, technicians and merchants are moving by cars or rails or subways within the soil surface and by aerial planes for success in life. But in all these movements the real purpose is to earn assets for comfortable life. We wander for material glamours but not interested in transcendental knowledge. But material knowledge does not know as how to convert negativity of life into positive philosophy. Sublime thoughts transcend all that lighten you down. As a result of which we suffer with blazing fire of anxiety and invest more and more material mirth to face with 03 pains –

(a) Pains pertaining to the body and mind

(b) Pains pertaining to the troubles imposed by the society, community, national and the living entities.

(c) Pains inflicted upon by natural calamities earthquake, famine drought, floods and epidemics.

On the other hand we have no time to dive deep into the precious knowledge reposed in our classical disciplines. Working or superficial knowledge of a particular topic tends to entangle us in the morass of Nescience languishing under greed. grudge and disharmony due to Illusionary Energy as follows–

(a) Desire for high regions

(b) Desire for vast material assets

(c) Desire for royal issues and so on & so forth. That is why king भर्तृहरि (Bhartṛhari) in वाक्यपदीय (vākyapadiya) speaks of the underlying truth to have experienced towards the twilight of life -

भोगा न भुक्ता वयमेवभुक्तास्तपो न तप्तं वयमेव तप्ता:
कालो न यातो वयमेव यातास्तृष्णा न जीर्णा वयमेव जीर्णा: ।

Bhogā na bhūktā vayamevabhūktā tapo na taptam vaymeva taptah
kālo na yāto vayameva yātāstrisnā na jirnā vayameva jirnāh.

"We did not consume fruition rather we have been consumed by pains; we did not burn painful austerity, rather we have been burnt; the Time is not gone but we are gone. The greed has not been decayed or tattered rather our life- age has been tattered. To be more clear, we have not enjoyed wordly pleasures, rather our anxiety for enjoyment has consumed us, we have not practised devotional austerities rather ill-fated pains, material pains and metaphysical pains went on afflicting us for life. We did not pass over The Ravaged Time through enjoyments rather the Ravaged Time drove us to the last decay persisting greed and avarice. In this way the whole activities are targeted towards the goal of merriments profusely and there by diving deep into the abyss of darkness under the spell of Nescience. So hankering after apartments, Villas, summer – boat houses, lands and shoreless wealth gets culminated into a mirage like phantasmagoria or illusionary dreams which arrest the progress towards self – realization. So the fanciful or impulsive conception of life ignores the real peace of mind or receives mortal coil. Because the purpose of life is not sense – gratification but self- realization in peerless cosmic consciousness. Here sense– gratification leads one to accept next life as a confinement or jail. On the other hand the daily grinding of life has been so tough that human beings are succumbed to mental pressure for quick success culminating into haemorrhage and infractions. Their efforts for voluptuous life roll down in moral and cultural crunch.

Here the irony lies that while we are young, We pass our days in striving and keeping up social expectations. But we are so busy in chasing life's big pleasurs in dancing in a park with all kids and waiting for the sunrise, most of us fail to discern life till the twilight of life or death bed with a hope to play precious role within. lastly we die in bereavement void of leisure on chronological mirage. In between risks of survival we seek medical help to propagate our lives but we fail to pick up real pleasure.

Because life in too short and true happiness is rare. Mind that since adolescence we should be aware to judge the rest span of life. Because the night is brief. So the life is what is left for our lovely time to pass as busy bees stop and smell the roses (fragrance of life). They sip or coopt life's sweet moments in clustered cooperation. Mind that pleasure is not a place to reach but a state to create. The fulfilled pleasure of life comes when we utilize our higher human talents that differ from other lives purposely. The purpose of life is a life of purpose viz-to recognize oneself being the true – self of Nature. To get more from life you need to be more in life. We should start living and walking through life instead of complaining and growling. Life is to create creative way for life. The youth should come forword to tear darkness of mind and be inspired to work for higher goal of life with right person to bring out the best version of you. Such all round integral attitude to life can be developed only when the youth realize the divine potentiality in life with an unprejudiced mind.

That is why our great philosophers tried for maximum use of life-span with the spirit of the Ages. To their perception Swami Vivekānanda was faced with grave challenges in his short-span of life engrossed with multi diseases but meagre resources. But his metaphysical as well as theosophical resources received by his Gurus surpassed all obstacles to modify socio – economic culture of the Nation. Further he inspired the youth to cultivate spiritual integration to universal brotherhood for thousands of years to come.

At the same time he gave a clarion call to mankind to unite and preached Vedo' -panishadic canons to enrich human minds.

Such oriental mission in life would invite virtues of real happiness and true beauty of excellence.

Here is apt to mention German philosopher,- Max Muller's views on Vedantic synthesis – "when read Vedanta books, Upnishads have the solace of my life, My happiest hours are those and they will be the solace of my death, These books are to me like the light of morning, like the pure air of mountains"

In his famous Cambridge University lecture in 1882, Max Muller went to the extent of telling – if we were to look over the whole world to find out the country most richly endowed with all wealth and beauty that Nature can bestow in some parts as paradise on the earth. I should point to India."

So life is not a mere intellectual or critical but sturdy.

A person who in grounded in divine life would transcend sufferings in a flight to an aerial region of buoyancy where passionate clouds of sorrow cannot darken the light of life. Thus the life in geared to a sort of splendid torch which I have got to hold up for the moment to let switch on brightly as possible before handling it over to future progeny. So that we may die happily in the fulness of life.

Because life is best when we live for others' and life is worst when we live for ourselves. Here mind that we are born to empower our inner potentiality and should have trust within the vast self of sanctity. Someone says that life is not measured by the number of breaths that you take but by the moment that takes away our breaths.

Lastly the Idealistic Theory of life is not to gather huge materials rather avail immaterials and moral values. The tragedy of life is not death but what we let not die negativities inside us. We suffer agony in our capacity of becoming and unknown to what we have become in fact. Because there in difference between simply existing and truly living. To be more clear, there is a difference between simply surviving and really thriving. The reason being that we have lost inside of human gifts that lie within ourselves. Our inner chamber is a bouquet of fresh flowers to get more from life according to our karmic balance-sheets.

That in why Sri MADBHAAGVĀ-TAPURĀṆA affirms that life in not meant for so-called economic development or material advancement. It is not a mere involvement in hedonic philosophy of drinking and dancing which play havoc in the society. Because the rational animal enjoying palatable dishes without spiritual values are not good for the society. Since the great purpose of life is the self realization which can satisfy our bare needs of life under Vedantic culture. Barbara Tuchman (American historian & winner of Pulitzer award) was asked to point out the bare need for the coming generation, where he told- "personal – responsibility to look after."

Generally it in easier to avail surface glee in errors than diving deep for pearls in life as English poet. John Dryden says-

"errors like straw upon surface flow,
he that would search for pearls must dive below."

But the living entity full of false pride, ignores Super Being and consider himself to be the performer of Actions and enjoyer of all. So such mistaken perception punishes the living entity by forcing him to transmigrate from one body to the next under the spell of Illusionary Energy as the गीता (the Geeta) says –

प्रकृतेः क्रियमाणानि गुणैः कर्माणि सर्वशः
अहंकारविमूढात्मा कर्त्ताहमिति मन्यते /3/27

Prakrteh kriyamānāni gunaih karmāni sarvaśah
Ahankāravimudhātmā kartāhmati manyate.

Further the Geeta advises the individual to invoke the Supreme Being as the cause of all living organism for the best success in life –

यतः प्रवृत्तिर्भूतानां येन सर्वमिदं ततम्
स्वकर्मणा तमभ्यर्च्य सिद्धिं विंदति मानव. – /18/46

Yatah pravrttirbhūtānām yena sarvamidam tatam
Swakarmanā tamabhyarcya sidhim vindati manavah.

But alas to mention here that we, Indians, feel inferiority complex to follow the commond of our pristine and privileged wisdom. Whereas we ought to know-that without the knowledge of the Self, human life is confused in pseudo – serenity. Whereas our great human endowment is liable to revamp and remean difficult circumstances in a more enlightened and empowering way. Such divine gift makes us human which animals cannot do. So we should accept complete care around us and resolve to change us before seeking to change others. So it is not what we have in life, it is who we have in life that matters.Great English Romantic poet **P.B. Shelley says**

"One sweetest things are those that tell us the saddest thoughts" This is the trusty device of a person of strong character. Blaming of circumstances in the way of life is nothing more than excusing ourselves. Because life's greatest setbacks always reveal that of the biggest blessings. So in stead of sailing through life as a passenger, we should be the Captain of the ship of life to navigate with the direction rather reacting the changing tides. American philosopher William James wordifies – "humankind's common Instinct for reality has always held the world to be essentially a theatre for heroism. Further to get more from life you need to be more in life; Do not be orthodox but be un-orthodox. Because being different from all, the right vision is a wise way to live in for others". In this way an individual can attain the highest immaterial wisdom of life by devoting to the Supreme Being and sacrificing for the sake of the Supreme Being who is all pervading and by whose control every living entity receives the real comforts on his global propensity.

Here I am to clarify against calumny or backbite conception in human - folk being untouched with Oriental scriptures like the Shree Madbhagavata Purana, the Geeta and the like, lest we should fall in ascetism or nunnery to avoid worldly pleasure. But such pseudo – Conception runs to mystify the mass as an intrigue by the least mind of the society. On the contrary these holy books focus on the pioneering life-management for the youth. That is why the Shree Madbhagavatapurana's discourses are systematized between young king Parikshit and 16-year old Shukdeo congregated by almost 84 thousands of general public.

Lastly there are 07 Mantras of life for true success; mind to quest for true tranquility and ...

1. Our physical body contains nectar and poison So life is a song to sing and a tragedy to face it.
2. No comforts for confusion. It is a struggle to accept it.
3. Satiety in our mind and not in the heaven.
4. No pains for being anxious but deal with patience. Life is an adventure, dare it.
5. Expectation on the earth seldom fulfils like ocean (fathomless).
6. Our genuine or sincere thirst gets queenched as water on fire. Life is too precious, do not destroy it.
7. No eyes like self- consciousness.

In Indian perspective, we are born to repay 5 – type of debts by sacrificial favour such as –

1. Divine debt
2. Ascetic debt
3. Parental debt
4. Guest debt
5. Creatural debt.

But sorry to say that we have been infatuated to our own nuclear nexus. So at every step of life, we should try to execute social and national sacrifices towords the Catholic track of global sanctity and satisfaction to heave a blissful life for ever. Mind that egoic achieverments are not the true end of life.

To me –

dawn of success not the end of life
Dusk of destiny not the end of life
Once well done not the end of life
Once goal- gain not the end of life.

Chapter - 2

Oriental Brains & Creedal Culture

2(A) - Oriental mindoscope and modern science.

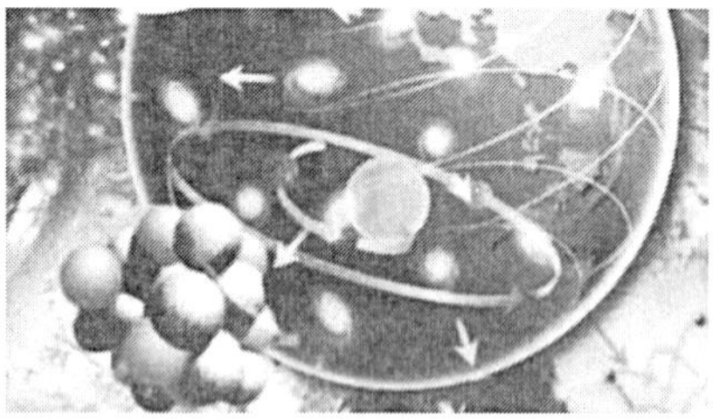

After centuries of extensive researches, modern science has come to the conclusion which intuitive seers of yores already recorded more than thousands of years ago. What our oriental minds said about the nature of the Ultimate Reality seems to be coincided with the mind of modern scientists regarding the baffling nature of the Matter. But our techno – oriental theories were smeared by the malice design of the alien powers who misconceptualised pristine knowledge to be the primal discoveries of alien brains.

Material Science interprets that all material body is one. The cause of smell being animate atom inserts into our body and our body also emits that smell which in not felt deeply for want of weak sense – organ. Further Material science vouchsafes the law of Congruity in which the effect of the action of our body falls on its parts spontaneously.

If we push a leg of the table, all legs are let pushed at a time. This occurs owing to the fact that all legs are rigidly fixed with one another. A clump of forest-trees defies the wind. While a tree standing alone is blown down. Such mutual procedure advocates congruity.

Modern Physics has discovered one of the 4 basic forces of Nature which structures the Cosmos; the other 03 forces are weak – interactions which play an important role in the Energy production in the Sun. The strong interaction binds the nuclei of the atoms together and gravitation is responsible for sustaining planets and stars on cosmic level; and as such the whole material power is the reflection of "self – consciousness" which may be divided into 04 parts –

(a) Electro – magnetic force
(b) Weak – nuclear force
(c) Strong force
(d) Gravitational force.

A Canadian psychiatrist Richard Maurice Bucke (1837 – 1902) in his "cosmic consciousness" has divided the same into 04 cerebral parts viz –

(a) Perpetual mind
(b) Receptual mind
(c) Conceptual mind
(d) Cosmic mind or consciousness

Here conceptual mind is inherent in insects; perpetual mind prevails in developed beings; cosmic consciousness of the highest rank makes us feel non-dual. At this very stage we are apt to perceive the Self in all and all in the Self. Thus when cosmic consciousness is satisfied that you are really a great channel we would realize the nature of God: we would see god everywhere in everything and at least we would be able to love all living organism in the light that the entire creation is the manifestation of God as the conception of Pantheism. Consequently our love to God would be love to humanity and the world. Because the world is cosmos and not confusion.

I am to add that the material scientists carry on researches in laboratories to detach flowers into pieces but immaterial scientists turn them into flowers by virtue of their philosophical spirit in a unified life. The metaphysical scientists invented and discovered all that are imbued with the mystery of the Divine Self and penned in esteemed mythology.

Our acquisitive seers were well-versed to accomplish 8 - Super natural power or Faculty (animā, Mahimā, laghimā, prāpti, prakamyā, ashitā, vashitā kāmvasayita) to correlate themselves with optical organs of the Sun to attain atomic view for divine meditation & intuition. Now let me discuss and define the Divine Theory of Cosmic Creation in a nut shell –

1. The Origino – Cosmic goddess reigns the fabulous Island amidst ocean of nectar and such Island is superior to Himalayan region of lord Shiva & Kuber; the heaven of lord Vishnu and Cow – heaven. All Brahmandas dwell under the umbrella of this fabulous Island surrounded with nectar – oceans, honeyed ponds,

ornamental gardens & Jewel gardens, wheels and airports. The Origino – Cosmic goddess has 32 dynamic Commanders where each commander/Commandress is capable of destroying one lac brahmandas with Her 218700 war – chariots, many elephants, 656100 horses and 1093500 foot – soldiers.

Firstly the Cosmos was created by the Supreme Spiritesso – Spirit in co – graces –

1. Prakrit on left side of the Cosmic Consciousness with negative charge to analyse as –
   (a) Pra – stands for prakrishta (superior or excellent virtuous trait)
   (b) Kr̥, - stands for sr.s.ti (creation – semi – virtuous trait)
   (c) Ti, stands for tri – traited formless – (the principal prakriti or non – virtuous trait)

As the true spiritual knowledge about the Brahmā (supreme spirit), The Supreme Forcess, being initiatrix or Creatrix created the whole moveable and immovable world –

as depicted in Shreemad-Devi-Bhagwat – purāṇa –

मन्माया शक्तिसंक्लृप्तं जगत्सर्वं चराचरम्
साऽपि मत्तः पृथङ्माया नास्त्येव परमार्थतः–7 / 33 / 1

Manmāyā shaktisamklr̥aptam jagata sarvaṃ charācharaṃ
Sā′pi mattaḥ pr̥thammāyā nāstyeva parmārthataḥ – 7/33/1/

This Cosmic Goddess, being of primal nature and personified as the Brahm, is illumined in the heart – cave of the Brahmā called – cavern mover (Guha char).

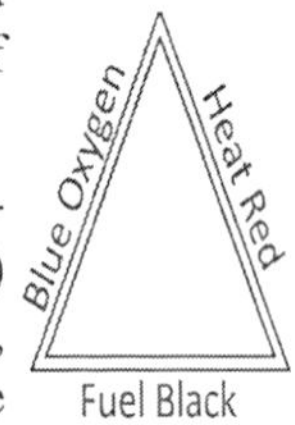

This Gender queer or Agender or the Singular Condensed-Character is Bhuvaneshwari (lord of the vast multiverse) being dynamic in feminine and static in masculine Form, or the Supreme Energy beyond the multiverse has all the properties of the Absolute Spirit as ever blowing in the Fire Triangle.

With broad composition of

(a) 01 (solitary existent void of Illusion)

(b) 02 (dual with Illusion)

Total 03 (tri – Vedic)

Here the 03 deities (creator, conductor and destroyer) appeared as Her partial manifestation to govern the world under agender or transgender (supreme forcess) jurisdiction. Such Grand Unification Theory (GUT) is responsible for Cosmic Creation. The Super – She has 1000 heads, 1000 eyes and 18 hands, 1000 feet with optical lustre of crores of the Suns pervading the Heaven, the Earth and the Space; and Her organs caused the existence of all jivas, 14 planets, celestial bodies or Nature's phenomena which are not going to be mentioned in details for fear of being corpulent of the topic. Yet out of 14 planets –

1. Upper planets from the earth one above the other successively –
   1. Bhūloka – terrestrial planet
   2. Bhūvarloka – ethereal planet
   3. Swarloka – heavenly planet (Space)
   4. Maharlok – the infinite planet (between heaven and janloka)
   5. Janarlok – the heaven of deified mortals
   6. Japarloka – ascetic planet for self-Conscious excellence
   7. Satya Lok – the Supreme world.
2. The rest 07 lower planets below the earth downward successively.
   1. Atal – planet of bottomless
   2. Vital – the planet of privation
   3. Sūtal – the planet of bottom shelter
   4. Rasātal – the planet of hell
   5. Talātal – the planet of bottomabottom
   6. Mahātal – bottom & infinitum
   7. Patāl – the planet of serpent demon
3. 05 elements
4. Eternal Time
5. Fruititive Activities
6. 03 modes of Material nature (sat, raj, tam)
7. The celestial Ganges are the universes in which infinite egg-shaped planets or the universes are pervading.
8. Each twinkling star is the real Sun to monitor its own planet.

   The stars seen closely have elliptical motion at a distance of billions of miles among one another.
9. Somewhere we perceive queer Creation
10. Movements of creature in oblique vulvas
11. Inundation of the entire universe
12. Planet void of creature.

Now Shree Mad-bhāgavata purāna – affirms –

यन्मायाशक्ति संक्लृप्तं जगत्सर्वं चराचरम्
तां चितं भुवनाधीशां स्मारमः करुणार्णवाम्–4/19/11

Yanmāyāśakti sanklrptam jagatsarvam charācharam
Tām chitam bhūvanādhiśam smaramah karūnārnavām. – 4/19/11

We recall the grandeur of Oceanico – Vast – Chief Commander of multiverse and Mass of cognitive radiation attributed to primordial Cosmic Energy who created the moveable and immovable multiverse. Such Cosmic Energy is accountable for creation with conscription of the Brahmā standing for dynamic force for work as The law of Thermo-dynamics implies. In short, the Formless, Genderless and Tranquil Supreme Being, being the source of Electric light manifests into PURUṢA (Illuminator) and the PRAKṚTI (Illuminated world) for creativity. The Supreme Being as Non – Trinitarian remains constant before Time & Space i-e- the multiverse.

Again the Super-She or the Supreme Being has 03 graces –

1. PARAM – the Supreme and the most distinguish Spirit as in Visnuyā-mal Tāntra –

मातास्त्वत्परमं रूपं तन्नजानाति कश्चन्

Mātāstwatparaman rupam tannajānāti kaschan.

The property or the feature or the character of the Supreme – She transcends the ken of knowledge.

2. Corpus – structural figure of Brahman whose organs are described in myths, hymnology and the Tantrology.

3. Sukshama (subtle) – manifested in the Tantra – base as.

अमूर्तौ चिस्थिरो न स्यात् ततो मूर्तिं विचिन्तयेत्

Amurtau chisthiro na syāt tato mūrtim vichintayet.

Further the Super She has 02 – type of status

(a) An Abode of elegance and complete tranquility where God Vishnu Himself worships His spouse.

(b) Complete fierceful and wrathful figuress (She-figure) whose one sound of defiance or uproar turns the Whole – demo – Army into ashes in a moment.

According to Her state – character - Her colour changes due to Varied performances-

(a) White colour – emancipator

(b) Red colour – administress

(c) Saffron colour – bestower of riches and opulences.

(d) Rose colour – fondness and affection with elegant decoration.

(e) Black colour – indulging in cosmic holocaust,

Here one may confuse with the tern "cosmic holocaust" as to be the supreme dissolution of the Cosmos. But one should treat it in 04 – type of dissolution –

(a) Regular dissolution – regular decaying of the jivas

(b) Occasional dissolution of the cosmos on completion of one day of the Brahmā or average 1080000 years of mortals. Where-in there has been the great annihilation of the creation.

(c) Natural – mahāyuga or 432 millions of years of mortal's completion in which the life – time of the Brahmā dissolves with Itself.

(d) The Supreme dissolution – the jivas get merged into the Supreme Being.

The Super – She manifested 03 para – forcess (feminine force) as Brahmani (goddess Saraswati), Vaishnavi (goddess Laxmi) and Rudrani (goddess Parvti) with Brahmā, Vishnu, & Mahesh respectively to come or control the cycle of the cosmos as in Shri-mad-Bhagavat purana – 3/6/p – 223 (1st volume).

The Vedanta, also, agrees with such doctrine as the universe in 03 specimens is the entertaining endeavour of the Supreme – Goddess. Where Her manifestation or advent is that of the tri-universe and Her Cosmic Disappearance is that of the vast tri-universe as in the Shri-Mad-bhagavata purana

शक्ति जातं हि संसारं तस्मिन् सति जगत्त्रयम्
तस्मिन् क्षीणे जगत् क्षीणं तच्चिकित्स्यं प्रयत्नतः।

Shakti jātam hi sansāram tasmin sati jagatrayam
Tasmin kshine jagatam ksheenam tacchikitasya prayatnah

The Prakriti or Illusionary She – Potency is called – Conjuror of eventful conjunction simultaneously.

2. Puruṣa (The Supreme Being). The Supreme Being was manifested as the primal 1st jiva of positive charge to permeate into 05 - Element, 05 Matter – measure, the Brahma, the Nescience and mind – coopting The Time – power simulataneously in the event of the failure of the Great Substantive Power for Cosmic Creation; and these group of Elements activated the unseen jivas who brought forth – The Vast - Being with this secondary incarnation. Meaning thereby that the assimilation and dissimilation of these

potential substances are the resultant of the Vast – Being in which all universes are existing as the Geeta – says by Arjuna –

पश्यामि देवांस्तव देव देहे सर्वास्तथा भूतविशेषसङ्घान्।
ब्रह्माणमीशं कमलासनस्थमृषींश्च सर्वानुरगांश्च दिव्यान्–11 / 15

Pashyāmi devāmstava dev dehe sarvāstatha bhuttavishishasangān
Brahmānmisham kamalāsanasthmrasheensh ac sarvānuragānsh ca divyān

Arjuna sees all gods, all elements, all groups, Brahmā on lotus seat, lord Shiva, all Rishis and divine serpent, root base of all plants – all phenomena of the Nature.

The Vast – Being passed over 1000 light – year in the egg – shaped shrine beneath water accompanying all jivas.

Here He inauguratd 14 wings and 12 – type of worldly affairs –

14 givas – 01- the mind- heart with 10 sense – organs
10 – life - wind or energy, serpent, tortoise etc.
03 – sufferings (corporal, calamital, physical)
Total = 14

12 wordy affairs –

(a) Brahmā
(b) Nescience (illusion)
(c) Class of the created beings
(d) Knowledge and works of sense – organs
(e) Sense – controlling deities
(f) Ignorance
(g) Botany
(h) Herbal medicine
(i) Creepers
(j) Twaksār
(k) Viradha (general shrub- plant which grow after being cut for shoots)
(l) A tree of paradise

It is worthy of note here that the Vast Being is different from the Cosmic Being (Brahmā). But we read in the 10th hymns of the 10th Mandal of the Rigveda & the Yajurveda (31.5) as –

TATO Virādajāyat (ततो विराडजायत्) i-e the Virat Purusha was born. Here the meaning of the word VIRAT –

यो विविध नाम चराचरं जगत् राजयति – प्रकाशयति स विराट्।

"yo vividha nām carācharam jagat rājavati – prakāshayati sa virat,

The "Virat" figure in one who illumines or enlightens the universe in many ways. So I mean the term "virat" stands for Cosmic Being as the Brahmā – consists of the Vast Being + embodied spirit or conscious ness + Nescience or the embodied spirit ionised with Nescience which does create, sustain and dissolve the universe.

According to great Rishi Valmiki in Yogavāsistha (योगवासिष्ठ)- the Absolute Brahmā as स्वप्रकाशत्वम् (swaprakāśatwaṃ) or auto – light as tunned in the Old Testament also – is none of lustre, darkness, shape, visible, vision, mass physical object, manifest, unmanifest, Timeless, Timeful, vacuum of sight, infinite, undecaying or imperishable, auspicious, primal - middle - last, void of causes and innocent - 9/51/

Further in योगवासिष्ठ (Yogavāsistha) of great sage Valmiki -

इत्थमनन्ता ब्रहमकोट्योऽस्मिन् ब्रहमाण्डेऽन्येषुच
समतीताभविष्यन्तीतिसन्तिचेतराऽनन्ता यासां संख्याऽपि न विद्यते–116/16

Ithamananantā Brahmā kotyosmin Brahmāndednyesucha
samteetābhavisyanteeti santi cetarananta yāsam sankhyāpi na vidyate.

"crores of universes have been speculated in each atomic structure of the universe also: that is why we hearsay infinite universes (Ananta Brahmāndas) were passed over, are passing on and to be passed into other universes countless or number less - i - e. ∞ (Infinity)

Let me unfold the manifestation of the Supreme Being as the Primal jiva with positive charge (+) to permeate into 23 Matters viz -

(a) 01 (primal giva or soul (total material energy) - state in which Puruṣa is bounded to Prakṛti and the fusion led to the emergence of Consciousness (MAHAT tattwa - Buddhi).

(b) 05 elements (earth, water, fire, air and ether).

(c) 05 matter property (smell, taste, effective image, tangibility & sound).

(d) 10 (sense of organs) – 05 sense of perception (ear, skin, eyes, tongue, and nose) 05 sense of Action (voice, hands, feet, the organ of generation and the anus)

(e) 01 – the mind – is the incorporeal organ of the Self in 03 facets – consciousness sub consciousness and unconsciousness. It includes Intelligence and Spirit to decide and declare consciousness respectively. As the Moon was enlivened forth with the Mind of the Gigantic Embodiment of the lord on the serpent couch in the milky ocean, the divinity of the oriental mindoscope visualised the herbal hub of chandraloks (moon world) as a tribute to Space science in shree-mad-bhagavata purana –

सोमं मनो यस्य समामनन्ति
दिवौकसां यो बलमन्धायुः
ईशो नगानां प्रजनः प्रजानां
प्रसीदतां नः स महाविभूतिः–8/5/4

Soman mano yasya samāmananti
Divoukasām yo balmandhāyuḥ
Isho nagānām prajanaḥ prajānām
Praseedatām naḥ sah mahavibhūtih,

Tenor – soma (the Moon) is the source of food grains, strength and longevity for all celestial beings: the vital force of all shrubby trees; the source of breeding of all living entities and opulence. Also we see around that the moonshine is the vital source for all greeny vegetation.

(f) - 01 (egoism or spiritual ignorance falling prey to anguish,apprehension, anger, avarice, ardent desire, delusion (infatuation), delight and life – death cycle)

Total – 23

(g) – 01 coopting the "Time – Power" being the Supreme Being by Itself simultaneously in the event of the failure of the Great substantive power for Cosmic Creation, and assented to the Timeless Prowess to assimilate and dissimilate with 23 potential substances which activated the unseen jivas and the resultant of which is the Vast – Being in which all universes are existing as shree-mad-Bhagavat purana vindicates –

Grand-total- 24

काल संज्ञां तदा देवीं बिभ्रच्छक्तिमुरुक्रमः
त्रयोविंशति तत्त्वानां गणं युगपदाविशत्–3/6/2/

Kāla sangyām tadā devim bibhrachhktimuru-kramah
Trayovinśāti and tattwānām ganam yugapadaviśat

प्रबुद्धकर्मा दैवेन त्रयोविंशतिको गणः।
प्रेरितोऽजनयत्स्वाभिर्मात्राभिरधिपुरूषाम्–3/6/4/

Prabuddhakarmā Daiven Tryovinshatiko Ganaḥ
preritojanyatsvābhirmātrābhiradhipuruṣāṃ

"Here the undecayed Time and The Supreme Being are the same and Eternal by Itself: but The Creator or Initiator of others along with Infinite or unending Being by Itself are to end others.

Further it is worthy to locate the significance of number – 24 in the following aspects also –

1. Gayatri mantra – 24 alphabets
2. Rishis – 24 (Vasishta, viswāmitra, Kapila, yājnavalkya, Bharādwāj, Vedavyas, Gautam, Durvasā, Kaushika, vatsa, nārad, Kashyap, lomash, shaunaka, shukrāchāya, kanva, Pārāshar, attri, vāmdev, Agastya, jamadagni, manduka, pulastya, mudgala)
3. Deities – 24 (Agni, Prajāpati, Moon, Ishān, the fifth, Sun, Brhaspati, Mitravaruna, bhag, Ishwar, Ganesh, Twāstra, pausna, Indrāgni, Air, vāmdev, Maitravarun, Vishwedev, Mātrik, Vishnu, Vasudevan, Rudra, Kuber, Ashwini Kumar)
4. Female Force – (goddess – 24 (Vamdevi, Priya, Satya, Viswa, Bhadravi-lasini, Pravati, Jayā, shāntā, Kanta, Durgā, Saraswati, Vidrumā, Vishleshā, Viswayoni, vashā, Padmālyā, Parā, Shobhā, Bhadrā, Durpadā, Vyapini, Vimalā, Tamōpharni, Sukshmā)
5. Image or natural figure – 24 (champa, linseed flower, coral crystal or quartz, lotus-flower, rising sun – conch – shell, jasmine, petals of red lotus, ruby, indigo – gem, moon stone, saffron, collyrium, red sandal, vaidurya, honey, milk like, turmeric, surya – kant – gem, tail of parrot, Ketaki, Malika & kaner flower)
6. Posture & poses 24 – well - faced or easily faced, casket, elongated, or stretched, ample, bi-faced, tri-faced, quad- faced, penta- faced hexa-faced, below faced, above faced, joint palms of hands as cavity full of water for libation, cart, restraint locks, knotty, front – faced, pendulous or dilatory, pugilism or fisticuffs, fishery, tortoise, hoggish, lion- treading upon, great horse – stepped.

   While narrating the cosmogony I should allude to Nāsadiya Sukta of the Rigved – (10/129)

नासदासीन्नो सदासीत्तदानीं नासीद्राजो नो व्योमा परो यत्
किमावरीवः कुह कस्य शर्मन्नभः किमासीद्गहनं गभीरम्–01

Nāsadāsinno sadāseettadānim nāsidrajo no vyomā paro yat.
Kimavarivah kuh kasya sarmannabhah kimāsidgahanam gabhiram.

1. Prior to the origin of the cosmos,
there was neither nullity nor entity,
none of the paradise, mortal land, abyss,

or space land was existed and nothing beyond.
Where was the concealing or covering element?
In which custody the world was kept?
Or who was the Creator of the universe?
What was the plunging object
to fathom the deep sigh as cipher –

2. न मृत्युरासीदमृतं न तर्हि न रा=या अह्न आसीत्प्रकेतः
आनीदवातं स्वधया तदेकं तस्माद्धान्यन्न परः किञ्चनास।

Na Mrtyurāsidmrtam Na Tarhi Na Rātryā Ahna Ā sitpraketan
Ānidvātam swadhayā tadekam tasmāddhānyanna parah kinchanasā.

In the state of the devastation of the world
there was neither the noose of the death in mortals,
nor the immortality being the essence of death,
neither the Sense nor cognizance of day & night,
there was the true existence of the Supreme Spirit,
charged with pranic energy but cipher of actions,
and condensed with the Creative Potency in integrity,
nothing beyond the passive Brahmā with vulva of Nature –

तम आसीत्तमसा गूढमग्रे प्रकेतं सलिलं सवाऽइदम्
तुच्छ्येनाभ्वपिहितं यदासीत्तपसस्तन्महिनाजाय तैकम्

Tam Āsittamsā gudhmarge praketam salilam sarvāedam
Tuchhayenābhvapihitam yadāsittapasastanmahi-nājāya taikam.

3. In the state of annihilation of the world
The universe was enveloped in gloom,
and existed in the root cause of,
blackish ignorance viewed as oceanic deluge,
then was the league of cause & effect efficiency
the universe was invariably concomitant,
and wrapped in negative ignorance of fallen foot.
So the universe was created with volition,
& venture of the Brahmā,
procreator under the dual working of the
cause & effect efficiency.

कामस्तदग्रे समवर्तताधि मनसो रेतः प्रथमं तदसीत्
सतो बन्धुमसति निरविन्दन्हृदि प्रतीष्या कवयो मनीषा।

4. Kāmastadagre samvartatādhi manaso retah prathaman tadasit
Sato bandhumasati nirvindanhrdi pratisyā kavayo manisā.
At the time of the creation of the universe the force
of passion for creation causing the primal seed,
in the cognitive Instrument of the Supreme Spirit,
the revolving foreseer (sages) sought the cause of material,
the world's stall or knot with this true state,
of knowledge in unique negation & absence.

तिरश्चिनो विततो रश्मिरेशामधः स्विदासीदुपरि स्विदासीत्
रेतोधा आसन्महिमान आसन्त्स्वधा अवस्तात्प्रयतिः परस्तात्।

5. Tiraśchino vitato rashmiresamadhah swidāsidūpari swidāsit
Retodhā āsanmahimān āsantswadhā avastātprayatih parastāt.
In earlier mantras, there was the concomitance,
like sun rays in Nescience, choice vow at will,
and cosmic seed – Cause.
Whether he was in oblique or crooked,
or middle or the last devotion - - - - ,
omnipresent in balanced extistence,
this way there was the living entity sustaining,
seed – effect of some objects in the created world,
And some objects were of the Nature's Great,
Ethereal and etc objects,
Worldly illusions as an object of martial,
enjoyments or possessions were of lower level,
and the enjoying objects were full of excellence.

6. को अद्धा वेद क इह प्रवोचत्कुत आजाता कुत इयं विसृष्टिः
अर्वाग्देवा अस्य विसर्जनेनाथा को वेदयत आबभूव।

Ko addhā veda ka ih pravocatkuta ājātā kuta eyam visrstih
Arvāgdeva asya visarjanenatha ko vedayata ābabhūva.
Who knows The Truth regarding the dawn of the universe,
and who can divulge the displaying of the world's creation,
as to which material and instrumental causes,
occured in the Creation of the multiverse.
The deities did come into being after the dawn,
of the multiverse and they fail to state,
about their prior performance.
So who knows the cause of creation of the whole world?

7. इयं विसृष्टिर्यत आबभूव यदि वा दधे यदि वा न
यो अस्याध्यक्षः परमे व्योमन्त्सो अंग वेद यदि वा न वेद।

Iyam visrstiryata ababhūva yadi vā dadhe yadi vā na
Yo asyādhyakshah parme vyomantso anga veda yadi vā na veda.

The creation of the multiverse with material and
instrumental causes is known to the sustainer,
not other than the Supreme Spirit who is reposed,
or celebrated in the light of Bliss,
O'dear listers! |the blissful Supreme Spirit in
ecstasy knows the very clue and non-others.

Thus the Nasadiya Sukta concludes that the Cosmogony is based on speculative philosophy wherein the Sole Brahmā is Constant through Ages in infinite character to create existent and non – existent universe corresponding to life – death cycle.

Afterwards I should narrate the portent creation of moveable and immovable plants done in scalariform conjugation as follows. –

1. Large forest trees bearing fruits apparently without any blossoms – Pipal (Ficus religiosa) Gular (Ficus racemosa). Vargad (Ficus benghalensis) etc.
2. Periodical and deciduous plants. Paddy, wheat, nut etc.
3. Creeping plants – Brahmi (Bacopa Monnieri) Giloya (Tinospora cordifolia)
4. Tropical grass – free with hard bark and its stem as stick – bamboo etc.
5. Spreading creeper which grows after being cut – water melon, rose etc.
6. Palm or long vertical trees which bear cluster of blossoms to be turned into fruits – mango, black berry etc.

Again

1. Animal and birds – horizontal alimentary canal with oblique shape.
2. Human beings which have vertical alimentary canal.

After endorsing major responsibility for cosmic creatin to Divine Trinity, the Brahmā entered into the sheath – petals of lotus prevading the whole universe created tri-word (heaven, earth & lower region) which might be extended to 14 or more worlds in colossal circumference as The Shreemad Bhagwat purān – expouses 24 Evolvents also –

01 (the Great Intelligence (PRAKṚTI) – 01)

Subtle objects – 05

Egoism – 01

Quantum of the Nature – 01

Senses – 10

The mind – 01

Gross element – 05

Total – 24 – Evolvents constituted the case of primordial Egg out of which the multiverse is in about 600 crores km in circumference having successive 07 layers. Wherein the supreme Abode of the Supreme Spirit, being the cause of all chief causes is reposed in Atomic quantum –

तदाहुरक्षरं ब्रह्म सर्वकारणकारकम्
विष्णोर्धाम परं साक्षात्पुरुषस्य महात्मनः–3/11/41/19 (Shree Madbhagvat)

Tadāhuraksarm brahm sarvakārnakārākām
Vishanordhamparm saksātpurushasya mahātmanah

Now I turn to trace out the life and contribution of our Oriento – metaphysical scientists, philosophers, torchbearers, thinkers, polyhistors and others at par in different fields. Where they enlightened their mindoscope for global benefit and benevolence. Undoubtedly philosophy in deemed to be the mother of Science. It relates to Physics, Mathematics, Ethics, Psychology, Sociology, law and Politics having, 03 offshoots – Ethics, Epistemology, & Metaphysics.

1. Sage laureate KAṆĀD – of Mithila (300 B.C) – he lived on cereal – particles by collecting at night but geared his life on meditation at day time to devulge the mystery of the Cosmos. His nature resembles owl. So the God preached him in owl's Cognitio. He was a micro – metaphysicist and expounder or pioneer of the Vaiśeṣic philosophy which conceived the special Matters in the form of determinants or discriminants among constant Matters of The Naiyayikas' proposition. Wherein the Time, The Space, the Self and the Mind as the subtlest undivisable atomic component of 05 Matters like Water, Air, Earth, Fire and Ether are purported.

   These atomic Components must have their inherent properties in micro-macro states due to attraction & repulsion. The creation of the multiverse is done with Atoms. Although he has deciphered 10 Matters including the Self & Super-Self having 94 properties.

   He proclaimed The Theory of the Atom on the basis of Atman and Salvation. Because in Metaphysics the Soul or the Self is the ultimate Indestructible, Indivisible, Eternal and Microcosmic phenomenon. The Micro cosmic phenomena are created and accomplished. Likewise Atom, being further indestructible and etenal, is the ultimate state of the manifest universe which tends to ocular state due to further atomic assimilation. So his metaphysical flair triggered the minds of the material scientists to develop proficiencies in useful experiments further viz –

Electron (-) – electrical energy

Proton (+) – into neutral position.

According to his Atomic Theory, atom-particles of the universe remain vibrating & tremulous in motion in which diameter of the each of them is 10 – millionth point of 01 inch as conjectured with divine metaphysical Spectometer. Such point is the centre point on which the life – essence of the Atom is centred: and human body is the abridgement of Applied Atoms revolving round the centre. In every Atom there are worlds within worlds.

According to oriental Philosopher M.M. jagdish TARKALANKAR Bhattacharya in "TARKĀMṚTAM" (NYAYAVAISEṢIC)

जालान्तरस्थ सूर्यांशौ यत् सूक्ष्मं दृश्यते रजः
भागस्तस्य च् षष्ठो यः परमाणुः स उच्यते।

Jālāntarasya suryānśou yat sukshamam drishyte rajah.
Bhāgastasya c sastho yah parmānuh sa ucyate.

"Atom is the ultimate particle and inferable only as the 6th part of the air particle seen in the rays of the Sun,

Again

जालांन्तरगते रश्मौ यत् सूक्ष्मं दृश्यते रजः
तस्य त्रिंशत्तमो भागः परमाणु स उच्यते।

Jālāntargete raśmou yat sukshaman drisyate rajah
Tasya trinsattamo bhagah parmanu sa uchyate.

The 30th parts of the air – particle seen coming in the rays of the sun in called atom.

In the VĀyupurāna –

परमाणुः सुसूक्ष्मस्तु बावग्राह्यो न चक्षुषा
यदभेद्ययतमं लोके विज्ञेयं परमाणु तत्–39/117

PARMĀNUH sūsūkshmastū bāvagrahyo na cakshusā
Yadbhedyatamam loke vijneyam parmānu tat. – 39/117

"The smallest particle which is undiscernible and indestructible or impenetrable is called Atom. It is neither generated nor destroyed in chemical reaction. It has special kind of dimension called anu (atom-small). Such vaiśesic (वैशेषिक) school of Atomiśm is known for its insights in Nature. Further it is a form of atomism in Natural philosophy. It postulates that all objects in the physical universe are reducible to Atom and one's experiences are derived from the interplay of the substance (function of atoms, their number and spatial arrangements), quality, activity, commonness, particularity, and inherence. Everything is composed of atoms and properties are emerged from aggregate of atoms. But the aggregation and nature of these atoms are predetermined by Cosmic forces.

Further Maharshi Kan.ād says that the all that is knowable is based on energy and motion in orbital state. His ascribing centrality to Physics in the understating of the universe, also, follows from his variant principles. For example – he says that the Atom must be spherical since it should be the same in all dimensions. He asserts that all substances are composed of atoms – two of which have mass and 02 are massless.

This Vaiśeṣic Philosophy is of altruistic pluralism dealt with inner & outer world. Its ideas are known for the contribution to "Inductive inference" and often coupled with "Inductive logic" of the sister school of Hinduism called the NYĀ YA Darshan. According to M.M. Jagadish Tarkalānkār (Bhattācharya) in TARKAMṚTAM (Nyaya Vaisesic philosophy), The 04 Matters (Earth, Water, Fire & Air). are of 02 types

1. Constant (atomic cause)
2. Inconstant (effect) in solid, liquid, vapour, gas & vacuum (Ether) states.

Our body is made up of 04 atoms (the earth, water, fire and air), the 5th is ether (undestructible). All substances are made up of these particles. So the NYĀYA & Vaiśhesic Philosophy interpret how the earth or the substance is created with the coalition of the Atoms.

(a) Lord Maheshwar (Shiva) wishes to vibrate air atoms with His mystic forces. Due to this vibrating action which creates "dyad, triad" adjoining to create 01 - त्रषरेणु (Trasrenu – modern – 06 atoms or 03 Anu (atom) and in one day-night- 2624400000 Anu); – fourfold conjoins to create – quadriad. In this way a huge air is created.

(b) The mutual assimilation or combination of water with such air created – water dyad, water triad and etc. to huge water accumulation.

(c) Dyad earth, triad earth creates huge sea – water.

(d) So lastly a great glare is created with huge water. This is the theory of Atomism of the Vaiśeṣic Philosophy.

According to Physical Science the substance may be equivalent to Basic Matter in which the mass of the Self and the Mind is included. Here the 04 Basic Matters are direct causes of the universe.

The Plasma (Akāsh), The Direction, The Time, The Self and The Mind are to be experienced through organs of perception (skin, tongue, eye, ear and nose) in which the Self is the looker on or sight seer. These Basic Matters are combined with Length Vector & Time.

I find the definition of such Basic Matter in the intended chapter of "NYAYAKANDALI" a Commentary by SHREEDHARĀCHĀRYA, (oriental Mathematician –cum-philosopher) -sub- paraphaser of "Praśastapād-Bhāsya" (a commentary on KANAD'S Vaisesic as follower of Kanad school of philosophy) proclaiming Quadratic equation formula by Prasasta Devacharya on Vaisesic Sutra school of Philosophy pioneered by Micro-Physicist Rishi KAN.AD under 06 facets-

1. Dravya (substance) – the basic physical quality)-with-property

   (a) T-hosa (solid – the - earth)

   (b) Ap (अप् - liquid)

   (c) Tej (energy)

   (d) Vayu (Air)

   (e) Ākāś (the plasma)

   (f) Dik (length vector)

   (g) Kal (Time)

   (h) Atma (organism)

   (i) Man (मन) – mind/attention – atomic

2. Guṇa (property) it is not the free – cause of combination and division but of .27 characters –

   1. Rupa (colour)
   2. Rasa (taste)
   3. Gandha (smell)
   4. Sparśa (temptation tangible)
   5. Sankhyā (number)
   6. Parimani kai (unit)
   7. Pṛthakatwa (separateness)

8. Samyoga (conjunction)
9. Vibhaga (disjunction)
10. Paratwa (priority)
11. Aparatwa (posteriority, smallness)
12. Gurutwa (gravity)
13. Drawatwa (cohesion)
14. Shehatwa (adhesion)
15. Sabdavrdhi (wave aspect)
16. Buddhi (cognition)
17. Sukha (pleasure)
18. Dukkha (pains)
19. Icchhā (desire)
20. Dwes.a (aversion or grudge)
21. Prayatwa (volition)
22. Dharm (cosmic orders)
23. Adharma (cosmic degeneracy or enthropy)
24. Samskāra (sacred force)
25. Yāntric (mechanical or mechanics)
26. Sthitisthāpaka (elastic)
27. Vegātmaka (emotional)

3. Karma – (motion) – depends on basic physical mass but deprived of property and free for combination & division – is of 05 characters
   1. Utpretsan (motion against gravity)
   2. Avakshepana (motion along gravity)
   3. Ākunchan (motion causing sheer stress)
   4. Prasārana (motion causing tensile stress)
   5. Gaman (linear motion)
4. Sāmānya (set) – the cause of solitary symbol is of 03 characters –
   (a) Parsāmānya (universal set)
   (b) Parāpar sāmānya (sub - set)
   (c) Aparsāmānya (elemental)
5. Viśeṣa (part-lessness) – the cause of the perception of the prime varieties. is of 02 characters –
   (a) Parmanu (quantum or finite)
   (b) Vibhu (continuum, infinite)

6. Samvāya (concomitance) – disjoint union of existence between location – locked i.e. basis & based relationship or mutual – dependent relationship (adhārādheya bhāva sambandha)

So Physicist cum – Philosopher KANĀ D'S Micro – Marco status of the Atom is based on metaphysical truth which is an abstract Science loaded with philosophical and ethical overtones. Whereas the laws of Physics are not an eternal truth: but it in a claim to be tested and probed into. Such physical laws wait for the challenge of experimental data. However both types of scientists have divinity to discover laws and their theories in almost quasi – speculations. According to Vaisesic philosophy the substance or the Matter (dravya) is the substratum of property and action –

क्रिया गुणवत् समवायि–कारणमिति द्रव्यलक्ष्णम्

Kriyā gunvat samvāyi karanmiti dravyalaxanam

Here the samvāyikaran – the thread of the cloth.

The substance(Dravya) has 02 parts.

1. Existent – having 06 features –
   (a) Substance
   (b) Property
   (c) Action
   (d) Generality
   (e) Particularity
   (f) Inherence

This existent substance is of 09 kinds – water, ether, fire, air, space, earth, Time, Self and the Mind.

Whereas 05 physical substances have their own 05 properties

Substance – **property**

1. Water — taste, through urine, semen, tissue blood and the like.
2. Earth — smell through skin, bones, vessels, pored- hair and flesh.
3. Fire — colour, (visible object) through hunger, thirst, lustre, idleness, sleepiness etc.
4. Air — touch through shrinking, expanding, running, surpassing and trial.
5. Ether — verbal connectivity (Sabda) – bothering, loneliness.

The Ether, being void of Atoms, may be inferred with properties. Now the ocular Actions are prone to division towards subtler mode culminating into indivisible and further part-less – Atom i.e. imperishable and constant.

The mind – being part-less and indivisible – is eternal.

His Vaiśeṣic Philosophy is called Aulukya Philosophy where God gave instructions on the properties of the Substances and etc. in owl's cog-nitio as told earlier. His philosophy has some effect on CHARAK SAMHITĀ.

2. non – existent – under the Vaises.ic Philosophy the 7th substance (non – existent) denoting the absence of something being the cause of something else at a particular time and space i.e. the cause of the Brahmā is the negation of the universe.

It is of 02 main kinds –

(i) sansargābhāva (non – existent of co – relation) – the negation of fire in water or the negation of smell into air.

This sansargabhava has, furthers, 03 – sub – kinds –

(a) Prāg bhāva (pre – negation) – a pitcher or water jar has negation before it was made.

(b) Pradhwansābhāva - (negation due to destruction) a pitcher once made is destroyed (negation)

(c) Atyantābhāva - (absolute negation- Never in the past, present- and future - sky-flower.

(ii) Anyanyābhāva – (negation of co-existent) – the detachment of 02 Substances – viz-a horse is not a cow – the negation identity.

Also the MAHĀYĀN BUDDHISTIC philosophy of Nagarjuna agrees to the absolute negation (Nihilism) or affirmation of the Positive Reality as non-dual Consciousness (Adwa-yam) based on conditional existence. Because the nature of the Primal Matter depends on the other One.

In negation we feel the glimpses of "No Mind" state in which all emotions and speculations achieve the state of "Pure Consciousness" or Perfection. So negation or nothingness is the state of full satisfaction which one feels in the exercise of metaphysical formula. His physico-Metaphysical mindset may be concluded-The Atom is the Truth. & The Truth is the Atom.

2. Sage laureate Achārya Kapila – he, being micro - metaphysicist and pioneer of the Sānkhya Philosophy on Cosmology vouchsafed the idea of electro – division of the Atom further through his electro – intelligence. To him the Atom has circumference and diameter and reaches the status of odd or even equinimity – is called the Ultimate cause of the Nature as akin to its further division into electron, proton & neutron.

This Sankhya Philosophy is based on pietism (satkāryavāda) i.e. work is not done without cause. Cause in the essence of the effect of the work having 02 parts.

(a) Parināmvāda (effectiveness) – causes transformation into effect actually as oil from sesamum, curd from milk.

(b) Vivartavād (Illusory Appearance). Here the transformation is unreal based of fallacy of reasoning as a serpent in a rope.

Further this philosophy ascertains also that the universe is comprised of 02 independent entities –

1. Puruṣa (Consciousness or Transcendental self, Absolute, imperceptible, passive enjoyer, atomic electron)
2. Prakṛti (unconscious Primal Matter - an object of enjoyment – atomic proton). Further its Theory of knowledge – Nature acknowledges 03 modes of proof as the reliable source of knowledge out of 06 ones.

   (a) Perception

   (b) Verbal testimony or credible words,

   (c) Inference

Here the Inference is explored by hypothesis, reason and illustration to conclude the knowledge of the Nature

Again the universe was created by Purus+Prakriti entities infused with varied combination of 23 objects out of which 16 unnatural objects are effects and not causes.

05 – organs of perception

05 – organs of action – positive properties

05 – Gross Elements (- negative property)

01 – the mind – positive property

Total – 16 (effect)

+ And 07 (natural objects are cause + effect)

	1a	– the primal principal of intellect
	1b	– egoism (an attribute of Nature)
	05	– subtle elements – negative property
23=	16+7	(cause + effect)
+2	+ 1	– (Puruṣa – neither Nature nor A-Nature)
	+ 1	– (Prakriti)
Grand Total= 25 –	9(7+1+1)	

Further the Puruṣa (consciousness) is compared with the Light that enlightens the material form with verbal – haecceity assumed by the mind. So the Intelligence after having cognitive structure out of the mind and the lustre out of the Pure Consciousness beget complex memory that appears to be conscious. Since the mind is an evolutive or evolutional to the Matter, mental events are granted causal energy to initiate physical motion. As the Sānkhya system rolls around the interaction of the Puruṣa + Prakriti, the Prakriti remains concealed as long as the tri- property is in statical equilibrium. But when Prakriti merges with the Puruṣa this equilibrium is confused. Such disequilibrium of tri- Guns stirs the Theory of Evolution that causes the Manifestation of the Universe from the unmanifested Prakriti on the attraction and repulsion of the magnetic phenomena. When one of the 03 constituents properties (Sat, Raj, Tam) of the Nature presides over the 02 inferior ones a variance occurs. If there is no variance there would be no resultant between the emotion (ional force) of the Mind and the Affinity in order of priorities. We know that our body is the collection of potentialities which get activated in other potentialities. The body has many potentialities in our daily life. So Emotion in terms of love, Jealousy happiness, fear and etc. is present in emotional form as Material. Always such emotions do not remain exposed unless discrepancies occur. Such emotions are exposed or created within the physical body and not from outer perception of the Universe. The feeling or love is a self – creation for one entity and the feeling of happiness for the other one lies in the same occurrence. The feeling of varied emotions warrants at random due to piston-like compression in the abstract organs of the phenomena.

However conscious experience consists of 03 objects –

(a) Specific relation

(b) Cognition

(c) Specific emotion.

If these 03 constituents are left alone there is no conscious exercise i.e. the creation of the world. Because the soul or the transcendental Self remains in deep slumber. Whereas in the dissolution of the world, the 03 eternal ingredients have separate identities which can be integrated or disintegrated to put forth multiverse.

Further the Prakriti is the primal principle of the universal constituent of 03 inevitable features. Whereas some Evolutions can cause the existence of further phenomena as Evolvents – viz. Intelligence, while created by Itself out of Prakriti causes the Evolution of egoism (self-consciousness) and is, therefore, Evolvent. Here the 05 elements are the essential cause of all living entities – that can be called Evolvents: because the living entities are not separated from 05 elements in essence.

There 05 subtle Elements are themselves Evolvents and the creation of the 05 Gross Elements (ether air, water, fire, earth) is the cause of Action that evolves. Here 23 Evolvents of Nature are tabled as follows –

Primal matter	Prakriti/Puruṣa	Root Evolvent
Internal	Intelligence or mahat, egoism, mind	Evolvent
External Agent	05 sense organs 05- action organs	Evolutional
Subtle Elements	Sound, smell, form, flavor, touch	Evolvent
Gross Element	Ether, Earth, Fire, water, Air	Evolvent

Characteristic Properties of the Elements

Distinctive properties	Earth	Ether	Water	Fire	Air
Nature	weighty	vacuum	cool	heat	unsettled
property or merit	Compactness	pervasiveness	liquidness	warm	Motion
Colour	brownish	Bluish	whitish	reddish	greyish
Shape	oval	spherical	crescent	Triangle	round changing
disc-wheel	Mulādhar	Vishuddhi	swādhisthān	Manipur	Anahat
Mantra	Tam (तं)	Ham (हं)	Bam (बं)	Ram (रं)	Yam (यं)
Subtle Elements	Smell	sound	taste	seen (form)	touch

On the other hand the Matter, being the substratum of variance has radical diversion in cyclical nature. Further the Matter, being the cause of these variances, is restraint to preference and not restraint on Nature.

It is of 02 types

1. **Guṇa** – responsible for enjoyments and sufferings on the habits of our past lives
2. **Action** – which is united with the positive trait of the Self "I". Due to actions, we come in contact with different things including human affinity. Here the both are produced by priority. If the priority is changed the Guna + karma are changed also.

To me the Puraṣa and Matter (prakriti) are analogical with some differences – the Purusha has 03 ingredients such as – Sat, Chit & Anand. Whereas the Matter has 03 sat, Raj & Tam in terms of relation, cognition & emotion. Here only the difference is that the Puruṣa (the Self) has the potential of self – relation, self – cognition and self – enjoyment which the Matter does not have. Still both are similar because the both have variance among the 03 components (dormant or active) in Superioro – inferior or vice-versa or pell-mell structure cyclically. As a result of which the dynamic equilibrium redesigns world's Creation. So all physical events are deemed to be the revelation of the Metamorphosis of the Prakriti from which all physical entities are derived. Each living being is the fusion of Puruṣa + Prakriti when the Puruṣa is freed from Its Material Body.

Now a tabular form is given to have vivid glimpse of the physical events of 25 characters –

1. Puruṣa (Consciousness)
2. Prakriti (Primal Matter)
3. The distinctive Intellect
4. Egoism

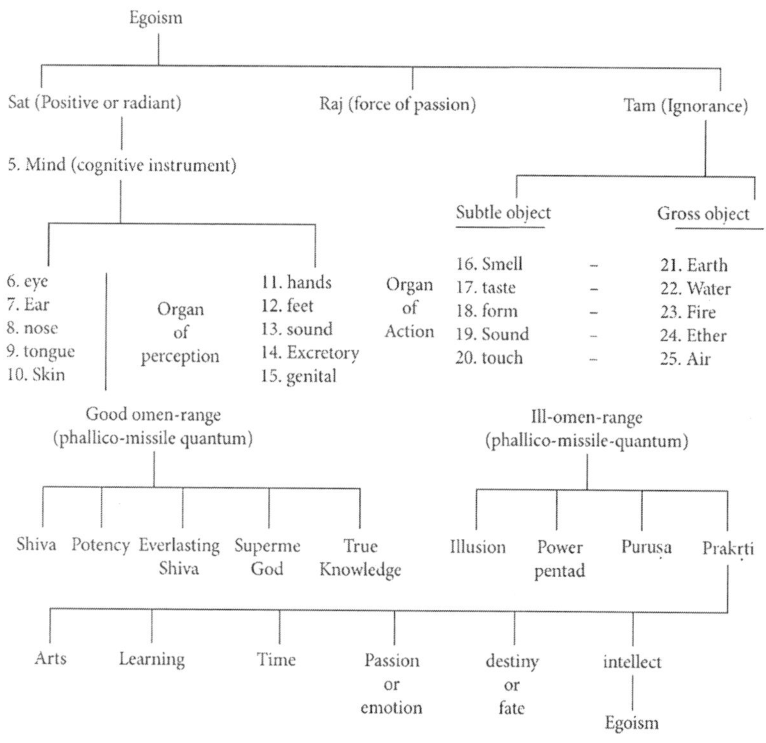

To Sum up the outline of the Science of Nature, let me deal its vision –

(a) There are 03 properties of Matter.

(b) All 03 properties of the Matter are probables which assimilate or dissimilate to create Conscious experience.

(c) The assimilation or dissimilation warrants variance and contrariety but the priority is applied to resolve it.

(d) This conflictive proposition through priority begets moral consequence. So be careful of prioritizing or preferring habits to have good or ill-omened changes. So the specific Theory of "The Science of Nature" has been illustrated here.

Here it is in the fitness of thing to deal the Quantum Theory of Acharya KAPIL being the pioneer of the olden atheist – theistic Hindu philosophy or the Father of Cosmology.

To be more clear, Quantum must be the minute iota of a pear having all the 05 properties (taste, touch, smell etc). But you pass it through dimension of one of those properties to be exposed by chance . The pear in the quantum conception is the assimilation of sense – data (smell … etc). In cutting the pear into pieces (independent substances) apart, they would not miss the impression being quanta of sense data. On measuring each of the quantum of the properties one perceives the same essence in each particle without overlapping across management. Now a question crops up that which piece of pear begets which property? Such is the outcome of the mind's fluttering at a given moment. But the new conception of Atomism asserts that the pear object is mentally perceived and the 05 properties are measured by 05 different senses in collation of the mind and the senses. Wherein the mind perceives the pear and the senses perceive the properties of the pear. Because the quanta of atomic theory are the property units. So the Sāmkhya Philosophy is the atomic unit of sensations as cut-pieces of a pear imbibing all 05- property and not void of smell-unit or the like out of the rest 04-property of sensations (taste, sight, touch & sound)

Here Sāmkhya philosophy relates to the properties of the Matters (smell, taste, sight, sound & touch) ascribed to 05 Elements (earth, water, fire, air, & ether). Further atoms of 05 elements are the units of electric charge (coulomb-c) in 01 Ampere. So we may assume unit of senses as the atomic property. These atomic properties can be identified simultaneously due to their varied measuring senso- instruments. Here simultaneity may occur quantum probabilities due to the harum-scarum of the Mind as in real life. There are substances parallel to other objects with a slight variation but with specific combination of the properties of the senses into a single piece of object. Here the mind does not have counter parts to perceive individual sensation in the whole observation. It is none of the sensation of taste, touch, smell, sound, light in the observation of the pear. Hence the truth is conceptual and observations are perceptual. Here the quantum object, property unit and value of the same property may be true from different perspectives as in leaf, branch and twins in a pear tree.

A close observation unveils that there are infinite numbers of property in addition to 05 properties as alluded to above. Such as colour may be classified into dye, saturation and brightness: dye may be classified into shades like, blue, green, and red, and each of them may be classified further. Thus a successive mixing of 03 modes of infinite properties in Matters is activated. In this way the same thing is a property and a value of some properties. Further the same thing is a substance, a property and a value in different view points concluding a quantum object. So when you measure a property we would measure an atomic particle.

In Samkhya's quantum theory of Acharya KAPIL, there are 02 kinds of entities

(1) Matter

(2) Soul (non-material)

Besides, there are many deeper layer of Matters between physical properties (senses, intellect, Mind, egoism etc) and the Self. In gross & subtle Matters, it is difficult to lessen subtle matters from the gross ones which may cause quantum problems. Because the world is full of nihilistic spiritualism based of detective explanation of quanta phenomena.

Samkhya's philosophy, further, assumes material objects as VĀK (sound) which is the expression of the Mind (Mental state). So if you measure the physical property of a sound- such as frequency, amplitude, wave length etc, We cannot be satisfied with these properties alone. For example – a high amplitude sound intends loudness VS softness. A high frequency sound intends high note VS lower note. You cannot avoid these physical properties i.e. amplitude and frequency rather observe the frequency of the sound; the volume of the sound may determine the wrath and rejoicing of an individual; high note sound may denote pleasure at other time. Thus there are 02 types of the property of the sound –

(a) Quantitative value (pitch)

(b) Qualitative value (frequency)

Here if you measure the quantitative value of the amplitude only, we are not sure to assess the wrath or happiness of the person from the perceiver's view points. In a given moment if one is angry silently the volume of the sound would be rough and low. If one is happy and surprised, voice would be cheered with loud tone. Here our senses measure the pitch tone of feelings or emotions. It, also depends on the introversion or extroversion of the state of the observer.

But as the Science deals physical property only. So it cannot forecast human observation and may be probabilistic claims of being happy, angry or sad and etc. Whereas Science should have an exact and precise predictions on cause-effect relationship.

But The Sāmkhya system has the privilege of presumption to detach Matter from the mind for determination of the prediction which is unsuitable to material or modern Science.

The Sāmkhya espouses that the living entity burst into being by the auto – combination of the physico- chemical combination of the quanta under specific spirituality to attain Moksha (salvation) . In order to recognize the Spirit or the Self, you should attend to 03 aspects of the self "I" Identical –

(a) Relation – I am a son or father or citizen, daughter and etc.

(b) Material and causal relation – I am tiny, tall, intelligent, white intellect, mind or the body as an identity.

(c) Identical emotions – I am happy, enjoying, liking, feeling-emotions are identified.

These 03 modes in the soul (Self) are further, called – Sat Chit & Anand having material counterpart in relation, intelligence and emotions to correlate Matters and The Self.

(a) SAT- refers to existence arising out of consciousness. – I am a daughter – one relationship one bears to other. Such identical relationship is applied to Matters which have different or independent identities radically.

(b) Chit – refers to cognition and Action. So when you are aware of the external objects through consciousness. We observe some sensations taste, touch smell, sound and sight. After that you have a conceptual knowledge of the external object- bike, T.V. etc in the observer's knowledge. Here the material universe has 05 subtle objects and my senses are objectified in Matter. My senses interact with the objective representation of 05 subtle properties and exhibit what you call – scruple of conscience. Likewise the physical world is created through Actions and you can observe how it was created.

    Here the 2nd point is the law of the Karma (Action). God's substance or object to enforce the consequence of Karma should be philanthropic or generous. But the common philanthropic motto of the God should not have created the world full of pains, struggles and sufferings. His innate freedom may be devoid of wish or desire resulting no Action. But according to Samkhya system of philosophy the wish is an attribute to Prakriti and not Puruṣa.

(c) Anand–refers to feelings and emotions at the observation of external objects in terms of happiness or hatred or neutrality. Our emotions & feelings go on changing with the mentality of knowledge or Action as the circumstances warrant. These sensations are derived from inner globe of the body as potentials. Such feelings lying in still are excited into expression at random. So, today, the Quantum Theory of Achārya Kapil (physicist) is relevant due to specific modes of spiritual hypothesis as alluded to above.

(3) **Aryabhatta-I** (Pataliputra-Bihar-499AD) As an oriental Astrophysicist, he gave the knowledge of Zero (Sunyavāda), Algebra, decimal-system and explained clearly the day-movement-rate of the Earth. He invented "Zero" on the philosophy of the infinite proposition or property about The Absolute Brahmā (Being) without being altered, modified & deviated from natural state viz-Constant. His concept of computing 'Zero' in persuance of its place value system as its potential value(i, xx, cc, m or k $\bar{x}$, $\bar{c}$, $\bar{m}$ and so on) from right towards left proved a great good to the world.

"Ankānāṃ Vāmāgatiḥ"

Due to the philosophy of the infinite proposition of the Absolute Brahmā (being) without being altered, modified, deviated or reacted out of the raptured or reposed state resulting constant as-

$0 + 0 = 0$

$0 - 0 = 0$

$0 \times 0 = 0$

$0 \div 0 = 0$

Further he invented Mathematical concept of PI (approx.) in the Vedic period on the basis of mythological dicta and data -

Out of 33 categories of the Hindus-gods, There are 12 Sun- gods who were entrusted to control solar system of the multiverse-

(1) Now 12 - Adityas (sons of Aditi + Rishi kashyap)

No:10 - Here one (01) is the beginning or the Saguna Brahmā (Shaped Being) or monism and Zero (0) is Nirguna Brahmā (Shapless Being) or Nihilism, neither negative or positive pervading the multiverse and both-digits (10) represent completion of cosmo-cyclic system as whole.

$10^3 = (10 \times 10 \times 10)$ = here 03 times represent tri- sound of cosmic syllables - (A+U+M) resounding the multiverse. Further number- 1000- Being one of the 12- Sun-gods embodied as the vast figure of Lord Vishnu having one thousand heads, eyes and etc pervading the whole multiverse.

(1) Equation = $12 \times 10 \times 1000 = 120000$ (distance around the global creation)

Now 04 - parts, padas, steps or feet of the stars (lunar constellation) in ellipticals motion due to Earth's rotation.

And again- 1000- signified as above col. – 1

(2) Equation = $4 \times 1000 = 4000$

Now adjoin equation - 1 & 2

Or - 120000 + 4000 = 124000. col. – 2

3) Now for Equation for perimeter of universal circle $\Big\} = \dfrac{124000}{2} = 62000$ (the philosophy of division to balance between 02 odd celestial bodies as the sun & the moon, Day & Night, life & Death, Light & Dark and etc.) – 3

(4) Equation of diameter on dividing by 03 (Trinity divine or Tri-world or TRIJYA or TRIJIVAS or sine in a triangle- vulva of the Cosmos) + power of 10 (perfect digit) to Saguna Brahma-01 in = 3.1 decimal figure = $\dfrac{62000}{3.1} = 20000$ col – 4

(5) Now $10^2 = 100$ = Signified as above- perfect + 4 = signified as above in Equation/Column-01 earlier.

Total = 104×8 – (Signifies =

(a) Symmetrical balance of the Cosmos in physical, mental and spiritual being

(b) infinity symbolised horizontally-∞

(c) 08- Vasu - as

05- Gross Elements

01- The un

01 - The Moon

01- The Star

Total = 8×104

=832 col – 5

(6) Now add Equation No- 3 + 5 column

Or - 62000

+ 832

= 62832 col – 6

Now Equation $\frac{\text{Column-6}}{\text{Column-4}}$

Or $\frac{62832}{20000}$ 3.1416

π That is PI-value3.1416 (decimal)

π Or PI-value3.1428 (fraction)

(4) **Aryabhatta-II** (950-1150) He penned Mahasiddhant (astronomical Compendium) based on Vedic axioms which improved upon The Rules of Mathematics propounded by Aryabhatta-I. He explored the Theory of Geometry and Indeterminate Equation. Further he explained the causes of solar & lunar eclipses and the like.

(5) **Vārāhmihir-** (505 CE-587 CE) As astrophysicist and poly-mathematician he invented Space Theory in which human solar circuit is controlled with the Law of The Mobile-elliptical circuit of the planets around the centre of their masses under mutual interaction on the focal point in The Solar System. He edited the oriental palm version of Suryasiddhanta. So he interpreted the movement of all 14 planets of the vast universe having innumerable natural phenomena in orbital circuit without collision. Further he wrote Br.hadasmhita and discovered the version of Pascal's triangle to calculate binomial coefficient theorem.

In the absence of Anemometer he visualized the solar system with his mindscope to measure the wind speed of the Space-Sun as experienced and assessed in human body.

Because our body is a small universe in which 07 organs of the body (head, mouth, eyes, life-energy, middle portion of the body, urine region & anus) are compared to 7 organs of the Cosmos (Heaven, Abyss or Netherworld, glow of Agni below the summit of Meru fabulous mountain- Air, sky, water, & Earth) around which all planets are said to be revolved like the realm of the Sun. We may locate geometrical concept of multi-petalled lotus series with the part & parcel of the body from crown to toe in which the Omniverse is embodied. His masterpiece –PANCASIDDHA-NTIKA'- gives summary account of 05 most – astronomical works in use. He dealt Astronomy, Botany, Physical Geography, Natural History in Bṛhatasamhita. He was a geologist to find out fire, water and etc beneath the Earth.

Further he made us known- The diameter of The Sun- 13 lacs 90 thousand km (approx.) and 109 times greater than The Earth. It is the vast storage of Hydrogen & Helium. The Sun generates Energy in its Centre with atomic dissolutions. But a small unit of energy passes on The Earth.

Its high gravitational power deserves to attract The Earth and other planets rotating in different orbits. The photo-energy released through The Sun undergoes photosynthesis with bio-chemical reactions which are the life-base on The Earth. Further it affects the climate and atmosphere on The Earth. As The Earth and other planets rotate around The Sun, so The Sun rotates around The Centre of the milky Ganges in which 22 to 25 crores of years taken to complete the round called NIHĀRIKĀ year.

(6) **Brahmagupta** (628BC)- In between Mathematicians Aryabhatta I & Aryabhatta II, he penned Brahmasphutasiddhānta on Mathematical contents, square root, linear and quadratic equation. He wrote Kuttakaganita on Algebra. He discovered the law of Gravitation many Centuries before Newton.

(7) **Bhaskaracharya-I** (7th century) – He was the first to write number and decimal system with a circle for the zero. He further commented on Astrology Aryabhata's work as Mahābhāskariya and Laghubhaskariya.

(8) **Bhaskayācārya-II** (12th century) – He was a great Mathematician and Astrologer until modern time. He wrote- Siddhāntśiromani- consists of two Mathematical and two Astrological parts, he further interpreted the coined global view of The Earth's Gravitational Theory and introduced Algebra, Calculus, and Trigonometry. Further he wrote Lilāvati(named after his daughter) on computing numbers as multiplications, square professional for common understanding to ease geometrical solution, He discovered Gravitational force, 500 years before Sir Newton. His masterpiece Siddhāntasiromani is divided into lilavati, Beejgamit, Ganitadhyāya and Golādhyāya. His mathematical geometry is based on - 9A facets -

1. Actuation
2. Adaptation
3. Authentication

4. Amelioration
5. Assumption
6. Assimilation
7. Analysis
8. Answer
9. Application

(9) **Bhāradwāj** - He invented the Theory of Aeronautics, in his book " Yantra Sarvaswa". He has elucidated the manufacturing skill of ships and aeroplanes as referred to in our ancient Indian scripture. French traveller - WALTER has mentioned the piloting of hundreds of Indian ships in his book "Le Hindu"

(10) **St. august** - He invented Electricity in August samhita"

(11) **St. Charaka** - A court physician of Kushan king " kanishka" His works are available on medicine and surgery. Details are mentioned in Āyurveda topic ahead.

(12) **Nagarjuna** - renowned Chemist in Buddha era, His works are mostly preserved in China and Tibet. About chemistry he said "As long as the science of chemistry prevails, let not - hunger, pain and poverty can torment man.

(13) **St. Garga** - (son of Bhāradwaj) - an Architect, Agro scientist and Physician available in "Garga Samhita",

(14) **Nārad** - he enumerated Astrology and Arithmetic as cited in "Chhāndogyopnisad"

(15) **Aswini kumar** - Beautician and herbo - plastic surgeon to have rejuvenated Chyavan Rishi, he was a bio-technologist to implant iron - leg into lame viswapalā (wife of vandan Rishi) as mentioned in the rigveda.

भुवं वन्दनमश्यदादुदूपभुर्यवं सद्यो विश्वपलामेतवेकश्थः–9/39/8

(16) **St. Patanjali** - Alchemist, Planto - medicamentologist, Phytologist as available in Agnipuran, Brhadsamhita.

(17) **Kautilya** - Plantalogist, scientist of Polity

(18) **Vatsyāyan** - his work on erotic aphorism and applied Botany. He wrote Kāmsutra on human sexuality or sexology to attain spirituality beyond slave to one's passion. It is worthy of note here that the Science of Botany was connected with religious life of the ancient Hindu to perform ritual scarifices having accurate knowledge of morphology and physiology of the plant - kingdom in agricultural India.

(19) **King Bhoja** - horsologist

(20) **Jaydutta** horse - physician or veterinarian
Nakur as quoted by paraphraser
Deepankar Mallinath in "Hayalilavati"

(21) **Palikapoya** Elephantologists
Brhaspati
Nilkantha
Hemadri

(22) **Sahdeo** (pandavas) - Gavāyurveda (cow-physician)

(23) **Hansdeo** - expert in beast - birth science or ornithologist

(24) **Atharvaveda** we find zoological indices to the care
Manusmrti and crown of the creature enumerating
Arthasastra 84 lacs in all as oviparous, sweaton,
Garudapuran sprouted and viviparous beings.

Here animals like horses, elephants, were used in war chariots and race sports : besides camels were used to carry on burdens cows were useful for life-care.That is why we find their illustrations in Aswāyurveda Gavāyurveda, Gajāyerved in Charaka samhita; elephantś treatment centers were in North East India and horseś treatment centers were in North-West India.

(25) **Viṣnudharmottarpurana** - We find illustrative texture of tombs, towers, pillars, and temples

Now Ayurveda (lexicon of life - care) is the byproduct of the Rigveda in formulas which are dealt elaborately in Atharvaveda. According to Ayurveda - samhita, hierarchical transmission of such healing Science was delivered downwards (successively)-

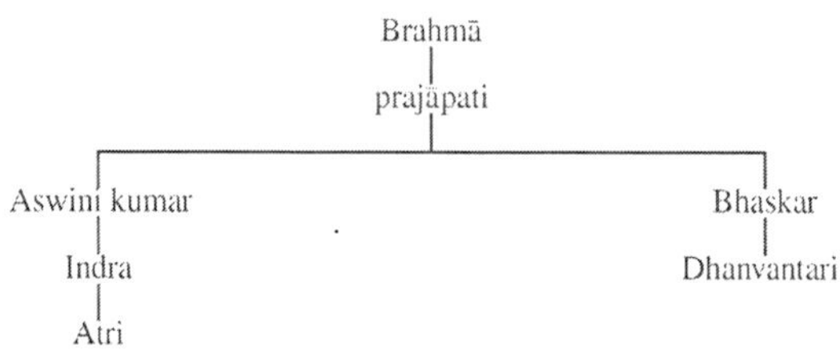

This healing science has 03 schools-

1. Bhāskar school
2. Atrey school
3. Dhanwantari school

In Ayurveda Samhita we have -

1. Charaka samhitā } Complete
2. Sushruta samhitā }
3. Bhela samhitā } Incomplete
4. Kasyap samhitā }

Here in Charak Samhitā we have branches of

(a) pharmacology

(b) surgery

(c) E.N.T

(d) Psychotherapy and witch - craft - subdivided into

  (a) Tantric cult

  (b) Brahminic cult

  (c) Magic

  (d) Alchemy

  (e) Sorcery.

(e) Paediatrics

(f) Toxicology--99-types of healing medicines against poison (toxin) are illustrated in the Rigveda - 01/8/191/13

(g) Citology

(h) Life - care

Besides the Rigveda deals with Hydro-therapy, Solar therapy Meditative therapy and Radio therapy through sacred fire worship and etc.

Thus in days of yores our ascetic brains were aware of the Applied Science in Ayurveda in pathognomonic fields - Medicine, Surgery, E.N.T.Paediatrics, Psychology Rejuvẹnology, Chemical science, Toxicology Embryology Veterinary science, Plantology, Ornithology and etc.

Now I mention prominent oriental legends in General Science.

1. PĀṆINI - (OF TAKSHASHILA) - legend lingua-scientist par excellence who expounded micro- structure of verbal testimony linked with Semantics. He classified lectio - difficilior and lectio simplicior interpolation with lipographical system in octavo - chapter.

2. Jaimini (Nepal). A great Mimansist being the pupil of Vedavyasa and precursor of PURVA - Mimansā (Karma Mimansā) and Uttar Mimansā (Wisdom) with 02 categories of Science for intuitive perception and its proper use through empirical knowledge-

(a) mundane elevation (physics, chemistry, zoology, geography, geology and political science)

(b) vision of the Supreme being.

(c) It has 02 schools promulgated by Kumaril Bhatta & Prabhakar Mishra.

3. ACHARYA GAUTAM of Mithila - He flourished in Treta Era. His masterpiece - NYĀYASUTRA "OF NYĀ-YOLOGY - narrates about salvation

तदत्यन्तविमोक्षोऽपवर्गः–1/1/22

Tadatyantavimokshopvargah,

The ultimate liberation from worldly locks is - Absolution & Ultimate Beatitude. It in worthy of note that Nyāya Darshan is a judgement & rules through experiment of the principles with testimonies or proofs as Acharya Vatsyayan says -

प्रमाणैरर्थपरीक्षणं न्यायः–1/1/22

pramanaerartha parikshanam nyayah:

It paves way to salvation also.

4. Achārya Kumāril Bhatta of Mithila - he was the great champion of Purva Mimansa school of Hindu philosophy; he was credited with logical formulation of the Mimansā belief that the Vedas have auto-origin. He came from Mithila (north India) and persecuted the Buddhists and Jains in the south. His philosophy consists of 03 sections -

(1) Investigation for the knowledge of the Supreme Spirits.

(2) Philosophy to know the true nature of the Brahmā.

(3) Investigation to purify customary observances. His pupils are Prabhakar, Parthsarthi, Mandan Mishra, Bhavabhuti and etc. His daughter - Bharati (spouse of mandan mishra). His contemporary - Adi Shankracharya, His pioneer paraphases on Shānkarbhasya are

1. Slokavārtika

2. Tantravārtika

3. Tuptikā

His philosophy is in 03 facets

(i) Wisdom - investigation after investigation

(ii) True nature investigation

(iii) Customary investigation, His aim of philosophy - investigation & determination to ascertain one's religion, rites or proper Court of conduct -

अथातो धर्म जिज्ञासा

Athāto Dharma Jigyasā.

His code of action or duty is of 04 kinds.

1. up-casting or up throwing
2. collecting, curving and contraction
3. extension or spreading abroad, diffusion
4. Motion or Movement

In addition to 04 true - testimonial instruments of knowledge or the sacred authority of the Naiyayikas Mimanskas or Vedantins add 02 more -

(a) Inferential presumption from circumstances as

पीनो देवदत्तो दिवा न भुंक्ते

Pino deodutto diva na bhunkte-

Here apparent inconsistentcy in fatness and not eating by day time ie. that is eating by night - called-

कौमुक्तिकन्याय

(kaumuktikanyaya)

(b) Non -perception or non recognition

His views on the universe - true real as Matter's - not prone to new reaction and new dissolution but prone to auto - creation and dissolution as opposed to Advait Vedant.

5. Udayanācharya – Mithila (984A.D) – A great logician expounded in "Atmatavaviveka" – The significanc of the proclamation of Br.hadranyakopnishad. He has averred in expressive verbis that the teaching of the Upnishad is to realise the Self for salvation from weltschmerz (weltschmerz). Such practice of the Upnishedic reflections heals conceptual sickness being the cause of untrue entrapping.

असतो मा सद्गमय

Asto mā sadgamaya

तमसो मा ज्योतिर्गमय

Tamso mā jyotirgamya

मृत्योर्माऽमृतं गमय।

MṚtyormāmṛtam gamaya

This immediate realisation of the Self involves 03 Successive Steps-

(a) Sravana (conceptual thought)- The analysis of the nature of the concept of the Self.

(b) Manana (ratiocination) - hypothesis of the feasibilty of the Self

(c) NIDIDHYĀSAN (cognitive meditation). for the realisation of the Self. So when all these 03 steps concentrate on focal felicity ie. the Self-it is directly revealed as an ex consequenti. His masterpiece - Nyāya Kusumanjali & Tataparya-suddhi, a sub - treatise (tataparyatika), He refuted the Theory of atheistic Buddhism.

6. MANDAN Mishra of Mithila - a Great Mimansak & Vedantin (8th contury) and his latter name - sureshwarāchārya.

His diademo - excellent masterpiece on Advait Vedanta -

1. Brahmsiddhi

2. Vidhiviveka

he says in Brahmsiddhi about salvation -

अविद्यास्तमयो मोक्षः सा संसार उदाहृता
विद्यैव चाद्वया शान्ता तदस्तमय उच्यते–3/106

Avidyāstamayo mokshah sā sansar udāhrta
vidaivā cādwayā śāntā tadastamaya ucyate.

"Salvation is the absence of the Nescience or wordly affairs or Non dual tranquil Intellignce or the negation of Nescience. It coincides the Canon of the Absolution of the Self from metempsychosis as depicted in Bṛhdaranyakopnishad (4/4/7)

Here" Geeta Sruti" of Yāgyavalkya says-

यदा सर्वे प्रमुच्यन्ते कामा येऽस्य हृदिश्रिताः
अथ मर्त्योऽमृतो भवत्यत्र समश्नुते–2/49

"yadā sarve pramucyante kāmā yeasasya hrdisritā
Atha marttyo-amrato bhavatyatra samaśnute.

When all instincts of worldly passions get extint, the living beings become immortal or are liable to be merged into the Supreme Spirit. So we may not deny such life emancipation.

In Mimansaka's views the sense organs are responsible to the recognition of an object knowledge, the signifying authenticity in the object - is called signifying power (Arthakriyakāritwa) - viz when our eyes reflect on water-jar, wherein water in the jar acknowledges the signifying power to quench our thirst.

7. Vācaspati Mishra of mithila (9th country) being pupil of trilocan and hexa- philosopher wrote,
   (a) Tattvasamiksha tātparya (paraphrase) on - Brahmsiddhi"
   (b) Nyāyavārtika tatparya (paraphrase) on Nyāyasutra of St. Gautam
   (c) Bhāmti (Sub-paraphrase) on Brahmsutra Shānkarbhasya.

It in worthly of note here that six - orthodox schools of philosophy were proclaimed to understand the Vedas with pioneers or precursors as follows-

1. Purva Mimānsā - Maharsi Jaimini
2. Vedānt (uttar Mimānsā) - Maharsi Vādarayan
3. Vaiśeṣic philosophy - "Kanāda
4. Sānkhya philosophy - "Kapil
5. Nyāya philosophy - "Gautam
6. Yoga philosophy - "Pātanjali

   In addition to these above, Brahman Granths and Upnisads were added to the purpose. He gave lesson to the society to discern good or evil deeds to avail the grace of the Supreme Being. So the practice of good thoughts and tranquility in the society is mandatory. Further he proposed to invoke the Supreme Being to erase one's woes on uprooting earnest passion and hates.

   His Bhāmati narrative gives the lesson of dedication, affection and tolerance to have partaken in conjugal life as a challenge which immortalized fortunate Bhamati under justice.

8. Gangesopadhyāya of mithila (14th country) - extraordinary New-logician and Torch-bearer of Nāvyanyāya Philosophy captioned Tattvacintāmani" a jewel of thought on the nature of the substance. It in a commentary on "Nyāya sutra" of Gautama decoding valid cognition-

प्रत्यक्षानुमानोपमान शब्दाः प्रमाणयति

"pratyakshānumānopmān sabdāḥ pramānayati"

- consists of 04 sections of Epistemology-

(i) Pratyaksh khand (Perception)

(ii) Anūmān khand (Inference)

(iii) Upmān khand (Analogy)

(iv) Shabdo khand (Verbal testimony)

Now Pratyaksha - means

य इन्द्रियार्थसन्निकर्षजन्य ज्ञानं प्रत्यक्षम्

Indriyārthasannikarsa jānya gyanam pratyaksham.

इन्द्रियार्थसन्निकर्षोत्पन्नं ज्ञानमव्यपदेश्यमव्यभिचारि व्यवसायात्मकं प्रत्यक्षम्।

indriyarthasannikarsotpanna gyanmavypdeśyamavya -bhichari vyavāsāyatmakam pratyaksham.

So the perception(pratyaksham) due to sense - contact - consists of,

1. Sense of action
2. sense of knowledge
3. the mind (introvert & extrovert).

   Further the perception is of 02 types -

   (a) Ordinary perception by external senses viz-

   ophthalmic perception

   Auditory perception

   olfactory perception

   taste perception (flavour)

   (b) Contactual perception - - - - - -

   such philosophical propositions dealt, hitherto, may foil the fallacy of reasoning or researches, and help to infer true consequence on gradual experiences and experiments.

9. Kālidāsa - A poet laureate of Aesthetics was well - versed in Geography, Meteorology & Nephrology and Chemistry. Further he studied the effect of changes in aquatic kingdom, territorial kingdom and atmospheric kingdom. That is why he succeeded to portray metaphorical feature of the Himalayas, rivers mountain, confluence, earthquake, eclipses. tides and air - trip piloting in his epoke- making works on Nature, social phenomena and mineral ores. Here random illustrations of Nature's phenomena are being pointed out in brief-

   (1) knowledge of cloud components -

   धूमज्योतिः सलिलमरुतां सन्निपातः क्व मेघः।

   Dhumajyoti salilmaruam sannipataḥ kva meghaḥ

(a) Meghadutam -

1. Ramgiri mountain

2. Gandhamādan mountain-16/46

3. Vaidurya mountain - 16

(b) Raghuvanśam -

kaustubha jem - 17/29

Diamond - 3/17

pukharaj (saffire) - 18/32

aerial navigation from Ayodhya to mithila / 11/33-34

Troposphere -13/2

Malayachal mountain - 4/46

Trikuta mountain - 4/49

Solar rotation - 4/66

River's velocity - 10/69

Saraswati river - 13/9

Shal wood - 1/38

lunar eclipse -14/40

from ocean to pond portrayal - 1/2, 2/3, 3/28, 4/32, 13/13/07seas - 1/30, 2/3

Atmosphere - 13/20, 10/40

(c) Kumār Sambhavam -

Maināc mountain - 1/20

solar rotation to north - south poles in seasonal changes - 3/25

Iron - 12/39, gold - 8/81

Tides due to moon's affinity - 17/4

Troposphere - 17/4

(d) Ṛtusanhāra - Rivers - - - 2/7

(e) Abhijnānasākuntalarn - Rivers - 3/11

Troposphace - 7 the act

Megha components - 5.

10. Occult- philosopher Madan Mohan Uphadhaya of Mithila (Mangrauni) in the 17th country. He was an ardent devotee of Kāmākhyā Devi at Ramgiri mountain in Guwahati (Assam), His miraculous character bears testimony to his life - wonders and marvels in Tantrology.

(a) wonders - he alone used to take off aerial trip to worship goddess Kamakhya Devi daily from his native village - Mangrauni (Madhubani - Bihar) to Guwahati by virtue of marvallous Tantro - yogic skill called Animā (atomic nature of the Super human power) & Laghimā (successive lightness & levity at will). After bathing daily he used to leave blown his put out dhoti (traditional lower apparel - 15' × 4') in the sky with uttering sacred formula (mantra) and avail it to put on next day.

In one Navratra festival he accompanied his young son to worship Kāmkhyā Devi where his son was getting pulled under the enchanting spell of yogini (female magician) even with the Idol Herself. In utter helplessness his father (M.M. Upadhyaya) advised his son to catch hold of his father's feet. Then goddess Kamakhya graced him to dig a pond at his native village and she would come out in Yantra (triangular image) to install in the temple called Budhi Māya Durga Asthan for Her worship. Further he with his family members was forbidden by lordess Kamakhya to come here (Guwahati) for Her worship and Her Command is still persisting.

(b) One day he (M.M.Upadhyaya) was sitting in the court of Bhour - estate (Madhubani, Bihar, India) on the 15th day of the half - dark part of the lunar month. But M.M. Upadhyaya declared in the court as Purnima (full moon day). Later on he beseeched his tutelary goddess Kāmakhyā to convert Amavasyā into Purnimā (full moon night) to prove the apex of his miraculous power - to save his prestige. So She enlightened the sky with Her Bangle blown to have a view of full moon night.

In the 1st part of the 20th country 11 - phallus of lord Rudras (Shiva) were installed in the premises with sacrificial rite presided by celebrated Tantric Late pashupati Thakur of Barha (Bhanipatti - madhubani, Bihar). Such in the majesty of the mystico- luminary land of Mithila.

Thus our oriental philosophers,scientists, thinkers, torch-bears, or precursors succeeded to radiate thier brain - dynamos to explore the universe and Nature's phenomena for centuries. Further they were engaged to decipher the branches of (1) the vedas (vast quantun of wisdom) and (2)vedangas which may be classified as follows -

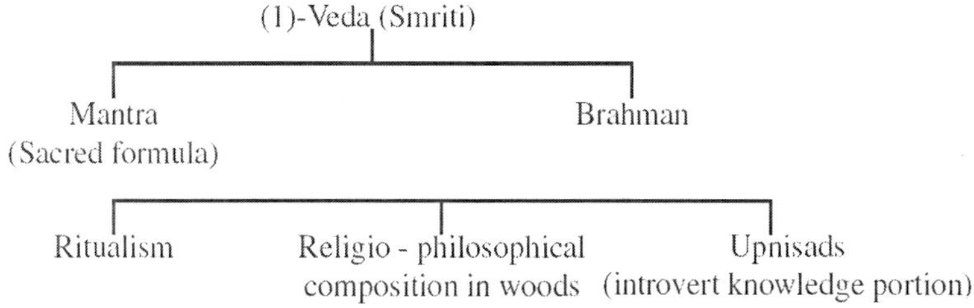

Here let me decipher the derivation of the term "Upnishad" and its main kinds - it has 02 prefices -

1. "Up" (2) "Ni" added with "quip" suffix from the root "ṣad" - having varied meanings,

   (a) obstruction

   (b) momentum of wisdom

   (c) concluding or ending state.

Further a learning which abandons material & wordy affairs from all mischieves and unfastens the fencing chain of Nescience of a causative worlds to attain the recognizance of the Brahman - is called Upnisad. It is the last portion of the Vedic literature to attain salvation-being the Ultimate Aim of life. The main Upnisads are -

A. Iśa-vāsyopanisad - the last 40th chapter of Madhyandin Samhita (compendium) of The Shukla Yajurved.

B. Kathopniṣad - the kath - branch of the Krishna Yajurveda.

C. Mundkopnishad - the product of saunoka Samhita narrating the origin of the Upnishad and Brahmā reflection.

D. Mandukopnishad - A pocket book on the Atharva Veda.

E. Taittiriyopnishad - the last portion of Taittiriya branch of the Krishna - Yajurveda.

F. Chhāndogyopnishad - Brahman book on Kauthum Samhita of the Sāmveda.

2. Vedāngā (Ancillary science) - 06

   (a) Euphonic science or orthoepy - it teaches syllable, sound, foot or unit of measure, utterance as -

वर्णस्वराद्युच्चारणप्रकारो येन शिक्ष्यते उपदिश्यते सा शिक्षा

varnasvarādyuccaranprakāro yen śiksyate - updiśyate sā śiksā.

   (b) Rules for ceremonial or sacrificial rites (grammatical treatise for phonetic charges to accents) - Atharveda, Vajasheyi, Taittiriya, Sāmtantra and the Rigveda.

(c) Grammatical analysis - hiatus for perfect pronunciation between words or foots.

(d) Glossarial interpretation of obscure Vedic foots by Yāskāchārya before PĀNINI. His technical treatise on Etymology and Typology, lexical category and the semantics of Vedo - sanskriti words are key to explain and interpret with brief annotations. His masterpiece "Nirukta" - is looked upon as the oldest available authoritative treatise concerning derivation of certain Vedic words grouped into thematic categories. He further divided Vedic deities in 04 dimensions mainly-

(i) - Terrestrial (the fire)

(ii) - Intermediate region between heaven & earth (Air),

(iii) - Heavenly or Intermediate world

(iv) - Prosody metrical science in the Vedas, Celestial science.

- As a concluding touch, The Indian philosophy proclaimed the path of final Beautitude to librate the Self or the Soul from metempsychosis. So the liberal state of the Soul in static equalibrium transcends all 03 types of pains and fetters of phenomenal creation.

ORIENTAL LEGENDS

(1) Achārya Kanāda, precursor of Vaiśeṣic Philosophy and Atomism termed its state as -

दुःखातीत–Dukhātita (free from pains)

(2) Achārya Akṣapāda Gautam, author of Nyāya sutra" says -

दुःखजन्म प्रवृत्तिदोषमिथ्याज्ञानानामुत्तरोत्तरापायेद–नन्तरापायादपवर्गः–1/1/2

Dukhjanmapravrttidosa mithya gyanaNAmuttarottarapayeda nantarapaya dapvargah.

Further salvation or liberation of the Self is derived with the Substantive knowledge of 16 substances such as -

1. प्रमाण - pramāna (testimony or authority)
2. प्रमेय - prameya (theorem)
3. संशय - sanśaya (doubt)
4. प्रयोजन - prayojan (motive)
5. दृषटान्त - dṛstānt - (illustration)
6. सिद्धान्त - siddhānta (true logical conclusion or proved fact)

7. अवयव - avayava (components of syllogism)
8. तर्क - Tarka (hypothetical reasoning)
9. निर्णय - nirnaya (settlement)
10. वाद - vāda (discussion)
11. जल्प - jalpa (wrangling)
12. वितण्डा - vitandā (cavilling)
13. हेत्वाभास - hetwābhasa (fallacy of reasoning)
14. छल - chhala (quibbling)
15. जाति - jati (sophisticated refutation)
16. निग्रहस्थान - nigrahsthān (chastisement),

3. Mahars.i Jaimini - precursor of Purva Mimamsa
4. Udaynacharyā - precursor of Nyāya Kusamanjali defended such conception also.
5. Achārya Kpil - precursor of Sānkhya-darshan termed its state as - अत्यन्ताभाव - Atyantābhāva (absolute non - existent or non - entity) - such axiom is elucidated successively in "Brahmasutra" of Vādarāyan vyas - wherein the logical causes of existence are prioritised from cereal to super consciousness via gross to micro-judgement (seen to unseen).
6. Vedanta philosophy (ब्रहमसूत्र शांकरभाष्य) Brahmasutra Shānkarabhasya termed its state - negation of desire or ब्रह्मलीन (identified with the Supreme Spirit as ब्रह्म समश्नुते ब्रह्मैव भवत्यर्थः - Brahmā samasnute brahmaiva bhava tyarthah - 4/4/07

   (Brhdaranyakopnishad) such free state of the Self is called extra - state i-e beyond the spell of 05 sheaths (personal fetters & tethers) -

   (a) the cereal

   (b) the prana - energy

   (c) the mind

   (d) the wisdom

   (e) the eternal bliss.

   wherein each in encompassed in inner ones as follows -

   (a) corpus body - cerealness (Annarasamaya). Because this body has 05-maladies -

      1. the state of pleasure and pain

      2. producing growth

3. consequences
4. decaying
5. perishable.

(b) micro - subtle body - energy or inner soul (प्राणमय अन्तरात्मा)
prānmaya antarātmā
Mindful - (मनोमयान्तरात्मा)
manomayantarātmā
wisdom - (विज्ञानमयान्तरात्मा)
vigyānmayantarātmā

This body dwells in 17 mechanical arts -

(a) 5 senses of wisdom
(b) 5 senses of action
(c) 5 life - energy
(d) 1 mind
(e) 1 cognition
Total – 17

(c) causal body – Eternal bliss (आनन्दमयान्तरात्मा) - Ānandmayantaratma This body -

(a) un-utterable or indescribable
(b) eternal
(c) nescient or Illusive
(d) causal formula
(e) like virtuous wit and free from impediments or contemplation or abstract Meditation (samādhi).

So Ultimate - eternal bliss is the highest goal of human beings. The Jain Philosophy termed it निर्वाण (nirvān) - final liberation from the Matters or reunion with the Supreme. The Buddh philosophy termed it Supreme bliss or highest felicity"

Vedavyās, Shankarāchāry, Lord Mahāvir, Sri Narāyan Guru, Ramanujācharya. Manu, Mohammad, Chaitanya Mahāprabhu, Aurbindo Ghose, Gurunānak, Kwazāmohiuddhin Chisti, Aurbindo ghose, Kutub Shah, Nadu, Kabir and the likes are mentioned ahead under relevant context. Now thanks to our foreign scholars and philosophers like Russel, Burn off, Rothe, Maxmuller. Grossman, Pissel, Grifith, loomfield, Willian James, Oldenberg, Wilson and the like who translated Vedic mythology, Hindu literafure and lexicons as magnum bonum to the world Besides -

1. Alberuni - his books on History, Science and Astronomy in the court of Md. Gazani.

2. Einstein Albert - German -Swiss famous scientist known for the Theory of Relativity.
3. Russel Bertrand - an Enghish Philosopher and Mathematician. his works "Marriage & Moral" The problem of Philosophy & Human Knowledge.
4. Dalton - U.K. Physicit and Meteorologist - the Atomic law of chemical combination - analyser of the Atomic Theory.
5. Homer - famous Greek - epic poet" the author of "the classics" Eliad & Odyssey"

Modern science - hitherto, has provided ample benefit to our life's easements undoubtedly; and we do hope to avail more to ease our material lives with pomp and prominence. But at the same time emotional hazard in metallic world and behaviorable crunche - are prone to pychoanalysis and psychiatry,

2(B) –Oriental views on social segments'

Today fraternity is being severed by ethnic segmentations. we are confronted with class and sub - class divisions in the society for selfish causes. We despise and grudge against one another. The political stalwarts manipulate particular sections of the society for thier own ends with lovely temptation; whereas our great seers have integrated the main 04 - class - system on equal and indispensable importance among varied conceptions. We ought to perceive the Chief Commander as Primogenitor of the infinite Universe in the grace of Gigantic Being (Viswakarmā or Brahmā) on consultation with 07 Rishis - Marich, Atri, Angira, Pulastya, Pulah, Kratu & Vasistha as the Yajurveda states -

विश्वकर्मा विमनाऽऽद्विहाया धाता विधाता परमोत सन्दृक।
तेषामिषृानि समिषा मदंति यत्रा सप्तऋषीन् पर एकमाहुः–17/26

viśhwakarmā vimanāādwihāyā dhātā vidhāta parmot sandṛki,
tesamistāni samisā madanti yatrā saptaṛsin par ekmāhuh.

Besides Hindu, this 07 number is auspicious in multi - religions also such as

07 Rishis (Christian)
07 " (Quran)
07 " (Buddhism)
07 " Jainism and etc.

This Colossal Being was manifested by reflection for energetic diffusion to generate the creature and celestial bodies pervading the infinite Globe with His thousands of heads, eyes and feet. Practically the infinite

Space was manifested by his navel, the heaven by His head and terrestrial earth by His feet to locate tri - universe, wherein the Moon by His mind, the Sun by His eyes, the life - wind by the Vedas (incorporeal) and the Fire by His mouth were observed. later on His mouth, arms, thighs and feet where conceived with - 04 - class - system such as Brāhman (knowledge oriented) Kshatriya (defence oriented) Vaishyas (business oriented) and Shudra (personnel oriented) respectively to adorn the vast embodiment of the Gigantic Being as the Rigveda states-

ब्राह्माणेऽस्य मुखमासीद् बाहू राजन्यः कृतः
ऊरु तदस्य यद्वैश्यः पदभ्याग्वं शूद्रोऽजायत–10/90/13

brahmanoasya mukhamasid Bahurajanyah Krtah
urutadasya yadvaisyah pavabhayagwn Sudro-ajayat

Here the Brahman existed in His month, The Kshatriyas (princely class) were made with his arms, the Vaisyas (business class) from His thighs and the Shudras were brought forth with His feet. Here we cannot ignore any component of the whole embodiment in view of physiological importance for work - up. So these 04 organs or tools or agents have equa - composite importance for social life. I cannot ignore any one of the 04 - agent, to drive - wheel chariot of human life fruitfully. Such Vedic class - system was outlined on cooperative or composite pattern. But some of us undermined to have inferior complexity regarding "Shudras" being born out of feet of the Vast Body. But the feet of the Body should be regarded as the base or foundation of the great Embodiment. In order to fulfil the gradual demand of the society, the 1st 03 class were assembled in chronogical system and the last class Shudras was brought forth for the well-management of the society. In days of yores the land was exercising Vedic Enterprises or Brahmic Rituals. Later on those Brahmins were made Kshatriya due to have been indulged in passionate pursuits; Vaishayas were made due to have been indulged in passionate and odd pursuits and the Shudras (personnel - staff) were made due to have been indulged in awkward activities.

Acharya Manu (canonist) has quoted the feasibility of reciprocal conversion of class system -

शूद्रो ब्राहमणतामेति ब्राहमणश्चैति शूद्रताम्।
क्षत्रियाज्जातमेवन्तु विद्याद्वैश्यात्तथैव च–10/65

Shudro brāhmantameti brāhmanscaiti shudratām
kshatriyajātamevantu vidhyād vaishyāttathaib cha /

The Shudras adapted Brahmanism and the Brahamanas adapted Shudrism. The same view should be annexed with Kshatriya - born and shudra born-fellows on skill and merit.

It in worthwhile to note here that orthodox views on the 4 - class system with much wrath at the use of the term - feet interpose social stigmas and bites to the extent of conflicts and riots. But it is the outcome of our Superficial interpretion of the Rigvedic purport. whereas I come across further vedic statement as -

पदभ्यां भूमिर्दिशः–10/90/15

padabhyan bhumisdishah : Yagurveda.

The land - manifestation of His feet is an object of respect and esteem as the mother -

माता भूमिः पुत्रोऽहं–पृथिव्याः–12/01/12

Atharveda - 12/01/12

The land being the mother and I being Her son"

That is why we touch reverently His lotus feet and none of His body organs or limbs.

Again Shreemadbhāgvat Purāna says -

पदभ्यां भगवतो यज्ञे शुश्रूषा धर्म सिद्धये
तस्यां जातः पुरा शूद्रो यद्वृत्या तुष्यते हरिः–3/6/33

The radical conception of all religions as - servitude is manifested by the feet of the Supreme Being. Such authoritative yeomen servie was bestowed to Shudras for His delight due to their righteousness. Their duty or work is for self prowess different from the rest 03-class.

Further Shree-madbhāgvat Purāna says -

ब्राह्मणी सर्वकार्येषु जयार्थे नृपवंशजा
लाभार्थे वैश्यवंशोत्था मता वा शूद्रवंशजः।–3/27/5

-"Brahmani sarvakaryesu, Jayārthe nrpvansajā-
Lābhārthe vaisyevan-shottha Mata va Shudravanshjaḥ".

The maiden of the Shudras should be adored for propagation or genesis with the least of class discrimination. Here I want to clarify also that the term "service" is misunderstood as related to lower class. But service to mankind is the command of the Supreme Being prone to global welfare, mercy, kindness and ocean of compassion. Besides Service grants peace, power, self-pleasure, obeisance, munificence, sacrifice, proficiency, tolerrance, fearlessness, surrender & simplicity. In this way we should not underrate or misjudge hierarchical segment or scalene class-system as a whole. Because each class - had its own importance in the past viz.

1. The Brahmans with their intelligence were employed to teach and train the society in proper way.
2. the kshatriyas with their arms and strength were employed to secure the society in the event of danger.
3. the Vaishyas with their stout thighs to travel were employed to supply the essential commodities to the society by moving from place to place.
4. The Shudras were whole - heartedly employed to sustain and serve the society.

Such integrated approach to 4 - class system helps us to establish fraternity and amity. It would help to maintain coalescence between haves and have - nots. Thus we are not detached but attached to the existing society. God created the people to rule over the land in perfect harmony at His will.

All the Shudras were allowed to study the Vedas as "Apastambaddharma Sutra" states-

अन्तर्धिनो वा शूद्रः

Anthandhino vā shudrah:

That, in Gurukul, the students of the shudra - class were allowed to beg alms to maintain their studies for the Vedas with no discrimination. Such Vedic learning was seconded in, "Brihada Gautam Smriti" also -

ब्राह्मणः क्षत्रियो वैश्यः शूद्रो वा चरित व्रतः
गायत्रीं मम वा देवी सावित्रीं व जपेत् ततः?–Chapter-16

Brahman kshatriyo vaisyah shudro va carita vratah
gayatrim mam va devi savitrin va japet tatah.

In order to pose a placid platform for collective pervasion we should honour the merit or quality or feature or mobility or activity of an individual not by birth merely -

जन्मना जायते शूद्रः कर्मणा जायते ब्राहमणः

janmanā jāyate shudrah karmanā jāyate Brāhmanah.

The upper class be granted grandeur by virtue of noble conduct and not by birth only. Again lord krishna says in the Geeta.

चातुर्वर्ण्यं मया सृष्टं गुणकर्म विभागशः–ध4ध13

- caturvanyam maya srstan gunakarma vibhagashah.

The 4 - class system should be ordained by virtue or in order of good - conduct. Again -

गुणाः सर्वत्र पूज्यन्ते पितृवंशो निरर्थकः
वासुदेवं नमस्यन्ति वसुदेव न मानवाः।
"Gunāh sarvatra pujyante pitrivansho Nirarthakah/vāsudeom namasyanti vasudena manvāh:"

Merits are honoured every where and not one's own clan or dynasty: People honour lord Krishna and seldom His father Vasudeo.According to" Brhadaranyak-opnishad & Chhandogyop-nishad all 04 - class of the society are deemed to be equal in Brahmalok (Brahmā world). So even the out - caste have the authority to avail the remnant of the sacrificial rites. Such class - system come into existence on professional basis for public propagation in early Vedic period. The profession was not genealogical which we see in the periodical interval of Time. So our early Vedic period was untouched with such division of class - system. the Rigveda advocates respective professional skills among the members of the same family for riches or livelihood-

कारूरहं ततोभिषगुपल प्रक्षिणी नना
नानाधियो वसूयवोऽनु गा इव तस्थिमेंद्रायेन्दो परिस्रव–9/112/3

karuraham tatobhisagupal prakshini nanā
nānādhiyo vasuyavonu ga eva tasthimendrayendo parisvava.

"I have skill in handicraft, I may be a doctor to apply my mind where I wish, I may be a designer of the temple architecture. In this way my professional skills are present in my mind - set as per sense organs command high or low selection.

So O the enlightened one! my selection to lead profession for life be ushered for high dominion. Because the surly and sinful Brahmins were despised as the vilest in the Shanti Parva of the Mahabharat. Here we see that the same member of the family imbibes varied skills.

The connotion of the above skt.verse - I am a poet, my father is a doctor and my mother grinds cereals. Here all members having varied skills constitute the same family. So it had been unusual to pick, choose and categorise the group on the basis of professional skill with the gradual growth - of population. so it was but irksome task to change and discriminate professions and was left on genealogy in exclusion and aversion. Now I mean that the hierarchical class - system is needed to be reshuffled on merit and nature of varied professions.

In the line of Adi shankaracharya, swāmi Rāmānand gave a clarion call against inhuman or inharmonic system of social connections. He strived against ritualistic discriminations for centuries together and invited the downtroddon to exercise holy recitation for super - perfection or beautitude.

Now to a great deal, we ought to invalidate hereditary hedges and build up the equal footed society irrespective of class, creed, caste, and gender.

Although the mind in haunted with our social tendency to prefer commercial superfluity to super excellence in superscilious style. The conception of super and inferior personality is assessed by the post and property of a person irrespective of his positive or negative thoughts. But meseems that a person with high rank in administration, education, management, technology and leadership may be expert in his field. A person with high package & perks may be billionaire: but a person with altruistic or self-denying dispositions based on Ethics is overlooked in our society. Such tendency in needed to be condemned to care for consonance and clarity. we have come to the universe to reap the fruits of our own deeds and should succour one another for sincere serenity of life. Here it is worthy of note that sage Shalwin, his wife (itara) and his son (Aiterey) of service caste togetherly decided to elevate reward for endeavour compared to the caste. In due course Aiterey underwent ritualistic discourses and learnt The techniques of Vedic hymns. later on his masterspiece "Aiterey Brahman" was applauded by all in Vedic - hymno - semantics competion. At last the priestly class paid him most respect to his magnum opus in the field of Vedic learning. that in why some poet says -

Honour and shame from no condition rise,
Act well your part,
there all the honour rise"

Again in the 4th century B. C. Skt. dramatist BHĀSA celebrated espousal between Brahmin Chārudutta and courtesan Vasantsena by virtue of her noble behavior or conduct as a challenging measure to the society.

Our history is replete with the accounts of reward for monumental performances by historio-mythological geniuses as follows -

(a) Veda vyāsa became respectable for his neat works.

(b) Kings of Maurya dynasty became like kshatriyas.

(c) Kings of Gupta dynasty became like kshatriyas.

(d) Dharmrāj Vidur who surperseded the characters of Bhishma, Dronacharya and etc for his brilliance, protection of religious verge or boundaries, dauntless statemanship and monumental works on Ethics. So the caste system may be revised for sociolistic pattern of the society which would give solace to the mass.

2(C) – Cult-religion & Global-fusion

Dharma deals the philosophy of life in a practical way. It was emerged to erase wide pains and problem in life. It is a way of life based on specific spiritual outlooks with regard to the world and life as a whole. It means preservation of human life and spiritual values essentially. It is customary laws on Ethics. It should boost up bosom benevolence and not beset the billions from the back-door.

Sheemadhbhāgvat Purāna unveils

धर्मः स्तनादितरः पृष्ठतोऽभूत–8 / 5 / 40

Dharmah stanāditarah prsthatÓbhuta.

The doctrine of religion begot from His bosom and irreligion from His back-side. It does teach morality and non-violence.

But the dogmatic significance of the term "Dharma" deciphered by the sectarians or the impostors of various schools causes exploitations over the weekers or innocent sections of the society. These fanatics got the better of the intellectual backwardness of the society to the extent of theocratic change and such practice is, still, in vogue. Whereas Shree Chandrashekharānda Saraswati Swami (68th Jagad Guru of kanchikamkoti peetha) preaches- "all religions declare that there is only one God. That one God will surely accept worship through any religion".

Hence there is no need for anyone to leave one's religion and get converted into other. But even Gandhians, unlike Mahatma Gandhi's gospels, are conducting corrupt and furious experiments with the Truth. Consequently civil and cold wars seems to be in a continuing process. The whole system is derailed and runs away from the law abiding consciousness of the society. We ought to avert such narrow approach to cult which elevates the lives of lacs of the innocent poor or the helpless tempted to caste-crunches. We should condemn communal disharmony to the extent of crusade which exploits religious feeling into practical bellicosity.

According to Gandhi jee – Apostle of Sarvodaya religion- "Believe in ordered moral government of the universe". He had faith in inter-religious unity surpassed from individual to the universal level. He was a deeply religious person wedded to the concept of communal harmony. In this way the heart of the society should nurture its inner integrity and outer sobriety through collective rules of Conduct.

Dharma observes the arcana of Nature slightly different from physical science. But So called superintendents of religious enterprises have got us confused with Science and Religion. Whereas Physics, Chemistry, Botany, Zoology, Psychology came into study for Bio-welfare.

Now I try to classify the both on reciprocal effect or dependence as follows-

Science	*Religion*
1. Science is tested to have immediate benefit to mankind.	Religion is tested to have unseen or future benefit to mankind.
2. Science is for material mirth & happiness within the world.	It is for material & immaterial mirth within the world and zenith of happiness beyond the world.
3. It aims at research, observation, Experiments, operation and sensory pleasure.	It aims at revelation, version of high soul, divine vision, super physical and mystical experience and extrasensory pleasure.
4. It is to observe aimed action & reaction, uses of effects and properties in static change, transformation in Nature based on the Theory of Matter and Energy.	It is to observe fit action or unfit reaction to enhance character and moral values, human qualities, perception based on Code of Conduct.
5. The renunciation of patience,	The renunciation of impatience or unpleasure.
6. "The philosophy of Science is limited to one's life-end only.	The philosophy of Religion is extendable to life beyond as well.
7. It is the chemistry of carnal/sensual craze.	It is the chemistry of spiritual filial craze.
8. It is an experimented Truth.	It is an experienced Truth.

India, being the sacred land of the Vedic Philosophy and rites annexes characteristic feature on religion. Here let me cite oriental views on religion- the term 'Dharma' is derived from the root "धृञ्" धारणे (म + करणे) मन् (sufix) that which sustains the people or is adopted by the poius soul. धरति लोकान ध्रियते पुण्यात्मभिः इति वा धर्मः–

1. Acharya Manu -

आचारो हि परमो धर्मः

Āchāro Hi Parmo dharmah.

The nobal conduct is the prime of religion.

Again -

धर्म जिज्ञासमानां प्रमाणं परम श्रुति। श्रुतिस्तु वेदो विज्ञेयः

Dharma jijnasamānām pramānam parām sruti/Srutistu Vedo Vijneyah.

"Dharma is the utmost testimony of the Vedic inquisitiveness."

2. Acharya Medhātithi, commentator on "Manusmriti" flourished in the 17th of the 3rd Yuga of the universe as contemporary of Veda Vyas deciphers

धर्म शब्दः कर्तव्यता वचनः

Dharma Sabdah Karttavyatā vacanah.

The term "Dharma" is duty commandment.

3. Maharshi Jaimini- states is "Mimānsā sutra"

अथातो धर्म जिज्ञासा–1

Athāto dharma jigyasā-1

चोदना लक्षणोऽर्थो धर्मः

Chodanā laxnortho Dharmah.

Actions prone to inspiration of the Vedas called Dharma and Actions against the command of the Vedas are Adharma (irreligion).

4. Acharya Kanāda-

यतोऽभ्युदयनिःश्रेयससिद्धि स धर्मः

Yatóbhyudayanishresayasiddhi sa Dharmah.

That which warrants public upheaval and beatitude with physical (abhyudaya) & metaphysical (Niḥshreyasa) visions-Dharma-

5. Acharya Vashistha-

श्रुति स्मृति विहितो धर्मः

Sruti smṛiti vihito Dharmah.

Dharma is the command of the Sruti (perception) Smriti (Inference). Since Vedic Era all social activities are linked with religion from birth to death of human beings based on good social network, good character and good nature.

6. Nighantukar Yāska (glossarian of Vedic word in Nirukta)-
   - धरति लोकान् इति धर्मः
   - Dharati lokān iti dharmah.

   Dharma is sustaining the subject (people)

   Again-

   धरति लोकां वा धरति लोकोऽनेन वा धरति
   विश्वं वा ध्रियते जनैरपि धर्मः।

   'Dharati lokān vā dhartilokanena vā dharati
   viswam vā dhriyate janairupi Dharmah.'

   Sustaining the subject or the subject is sustained or sustaining the universe or the universe is sustained by the public – Dharma.

7. According to Padmapurān (srstikhand) as Ethics of Reciprocity –

   श्रूयतां धर्म सर्वस्वं श्रूत्वाचाप्यवधार्यताम्
   आत्मनः प्रतिकूलानि परेषां न समाचरेत्–19/357

   Sruyatām Dharma sarvaswam srutwocāpyvadhāryatān,
   Ātmanah pratikulāmi Na paresam na samacaret.–19/357

   Dharma, in toto, be heard and on hearing it be sustained. Actions which are harsh to oneself should not be dealt with others. The behaviour which one feels hostile to oneself should not be imposed on others.

8. Lexicographer (Kośakār) states synonymous words of Dharma- (Holiness, happiness, righteousness, meritorious action, judgement, positive behaviour, good contact, good comparison, solemn sacrifice, non-violence, sacred doctrine, charity and the like.

9. Maharshi Valmiki says-

   धारणाद्धर्ममित्याहुर्धर्मेन विधृता प्रजाः
   धर्मादर्थ प्रभवति धर्मात्प्रभवते सुखम्।
   धर्मेन लभते सर्वं धर्मसारभिदं जगत्।

   Dharma causes riches, felicity, receives all belongings. Dharma is the quintessence of the universe"

   धारणाद्धर्ममत्याहुः धर्मो धारयति प्रजाः

10. Mahabhārat (Karnaparva)-

    Dhāranāddharmamityahuh dharmo Dhāryati prajāh.

    Sustenance is the cause of Dharma which warrants the subject to be existed in their own state.

or

यस्याधारण संयुक्तः स धर्म इति निश्चयः–69 / 58

Which rears up & holds up the society in unified-mode- Dharma

Because Dharma provides all welfare and upheaval of mankind to foster or sustain the mass. Dharma which does not oppose or tease others is the real Religion

11. Swami Dayanand in Rigvedabhāśyabhūmikā (Vedokta Dharma) speaks –

येन च निःश्रेयसं पारमार्थिकं मोक्षसुखं च, स एव धर्मो विज्ञेयः।

Yena cha nihsreyasam
pārmarthikam moksha sukham cha sa eva dharmo vigyetah. (P-299-400)

That which causes perfection, happiness and emancipation – is the only religion. Hitherto I have explored the etymlogical derivation of the term "Dharma" from the root - धृ+(मृ+करणे) dhr or ध्रियतेऽनेन इतिधर्मः m- karane or driyatenen iti dharmah-is to sustain, unite, shape the society or the universe in integrity beyond caste, dynasty, clan, land & the like.

12. Sufi cult- Indo-Islamic culture created an atmosphere in which liberal sentiments and views could grow and narrowness in Dharma was shunned up.
13. Bhakti cult (true devotion) God is one- one must avoid image worship, caste discrimination and class- hatred. It preaches universal brotherhood and emphasizes equality of all men. The teachings of Kabir, Guru Nanak, Ravidas helped or help to reform Indian society.

It is worthy of note that Achārya Manu's masterpiece "Manusmriti" is the confluence of Jurisprudence, Sociology and Political Science.

Besides it deals Military Science and War strategy as well. He is said to be the 1st codifier and his "Manusmriti" is treated as "Law book" as envisaged in Encyclopedia by alien publishers. So he has furnished 10 features of Dharma in Manusmriti-

A. धृतिः क्षमा दमोऽस्तेयं शौचमिन्द्रियनिग्रहः
धीर्विद्या सत्यमक्रोधो दशकं धर्म लक्षणम्–6 / 92

- Dhritih Kshamā damoastéyam shauchmindriyanigrahah,
Dhirvidyā satyam A krodho dashakam dharmlakshanam. /6/92 as the following

1. Patience in weal & woe or self-command.

2. Bestowal of pardon.
3. Subjugation or unexcitedness.
4. Theftlessness.
5. Practice of sincere union with Supreme or Pure Almighty.
6. Sense-Control in lovely or ugly scene.
7. Scriptural intelligence or understanding & carefulness in life.
8. Metaphysical knowledge of theism.
9. Virtuous assertion.
10. Absence of wrath in wrathful incidence. Because wrath begets violence.

B. Again "Padmapurana" advocated 10 features of Dharma.

– ब्रह्मचर्येन सत्येन तपसा च प्रवर्त्तते
दानेन नियमेनापि क्षमा शौचेन वल्लभ। अहिंसया सुशांत्या च अस्तेयनापि वर्त्तते एतैर्दशभिरगैस्तु धर्ममेव सुसूचयेत्।

1. Brahmcharya- Chastity in studentship.
2. Satya- True assertion.
3. Tap- Penance or religions austerities.
4. Dān- Munificence.
5. Niyam- Lawful conduct.
6. Kshamā- Bestowal of pardon.
7. Shauch- Purification of oneself through sanitation.
8. Ahimsā- non-violence
9. Shānti- Cessation of hostility or absence of passion.
10. Asteya- Theftlessness.

C. Sage Yāgyavalkya has furnished the same sort of feature of Dharma in "Yāgyavalkya Smriti".

- अहिंसा सत्यमस्तेयं शौचमिन्द्रियनिग्रहः
दानं दमो दया शान्तिः सर्वेषां धर्मसाधनम्–1/22

- Ahimsā Satyamasteyam shauchmindraiyan Nigrahah
Daram damo dayā shantih sarvesam dharm Sadhanam.

Here Yagyavalkya speaks of true or spiritual indulgence in activities like good conduct, Self-command, non-violence, munificence and scriptural studies – being the features of the primal Dharma,

Now Shree Maddevi-bhāgwat explains – as following–

शौचं तपस्तितिक्षां च मौनं स्वाध्यायमार्जनम्
ब्रह्मचर्यमहिंसां च समत्वं द्वन्द्वसंज्ञयोः–11/3/24

1. Saucham – pertains to both inner & outer sanctity, and free from the taints of egoism.
2. Japa (auserity) – despite irrational impulses of the mind, one should remain fixed while performing procedural duty in life to the extent of the control of anger and wanton sex-urges. One can dedicate one's professional duties to the Supreme God.
3. Titikshā – (Vindictiveness) tolerance to forgive mental revenge which taints spiritual upsurge.
4. Mauna – Tranquility to discuss the real aspect of human life to revert to the supreme God.
5. Swādhyāy – Vedic studies should be performed to receive spiritual wisdom.
6. Ārjana (Rectitude of Conduct) – Uprightness or open heartedness & sincerity to deal with others in a plain way (celibacy).
7. Brahmcharya – In order to procreate pious progeny one should neither desert housewife nor follow Vedic constraints for her till the tenure of celibacy.
8. Ahimsā – Non-violence against violent laws of Nature.
9. Samatwamdwandsangayoh – Unflinching state of mind in dual manifestation.

Now let me correlate and compare the canvass among 09 principal dharmas of the world for assessment as follows –

1. Hindu- temple – The Vedas, the Ramayana, the Mahabharat
2. Islam-Mosque – Its founder – Mhd. Prophet- it relates to submission, surrender to the will of Allah. It teaches Absolute Monism. Its primary goal to enjoy eternal life both physical and metaphysical in heaven with Allah. It affirms that the soul or the self of an individual is immortal embodied once on earth. It enters into heaven or hell upon death according to one's conduct or faith on the earth Spreading in the Middle East, Indonesia, Pakistan, Bangladesh, Africa, China and eastern Europe.
3. Sikhism – Gurunānak- (Punjab, India) It has 02 cults – (I) Mandāri (II) Nirankāri

   It follows the path of Japa (Muttering) and hymns-Satnām There is no deity/image worship.

   Adigrantha- Scripture and sole repository of the spiritual authority.

   Salvation- means release into God's love through muttering and hymns.

4. Jainism-Temple – It has 02 sects – (I) Digamber (Sky-clad)

   (II) Swetamber (White robbed)-

   spreading in Central & south India especially in Mumbai. Its supreme ideal – Ahimsa

   Objective – Soul itself is pure consciousneous, Blissful and omniscient.

   Bhagwan Mahāvir, a great spiritual hero, preached the philosophy of world religion by virtue of his Syadāvada (collective religion) Theory which respects all religions under socialistic pattern of the society. His Theory of bondage and libration is very useful to integrate human beings of the world. In his views bondage- means free from anger, haughtiness, pride, greed and infatuation.

   and liberation may be achieved through –

   (I) Right Path

   (II) Right Knowledge

   (III) Right Conduct . . .

5. Buddhism- Bodhavihar

   Scripture –Tripitaka, Jātākmālā

6. Christianism-Church –

   Founder- Jesus of Nazaretha

   Scripture –The Bible, the Old & New Testament

   It has 04 mains sects –

   (I) Roman

   (II) Catholic

   (III) Eastern Orthodox

   (IV) The Protestants

   His salvation comes only through faith in Jesus Christ.

   Good Christians live a life of virtue and obedience to God out of gratitude to Him.

   Further human beings attain salvation through the Rule of God as found in the holy Bible and His grace.

7. Zoroastriansim – Fire Temple (Mumbai, India, Iran)

   Founder – Spenta Zarathustra

   Scripture – Zend Avesta (Parsi)

   Its Followers are called – Persian

   Here man's life is a moral struggle for Knowledge and Enlightenment.

Salvation – is found in obedience to the will of Ahura Mazdā as revealed and taught by His prophet – Zoroaster.

Its followers value the ethical life most highly.

8. Confucianism – China, Japan, Burma, Thailand

Its followers teach the importance of harmony in the family, law and order in the state and peace in the kingdom. Its purpose is to create a true nobility through proper education and inculcation of all the virtues. Because Caritas Vera Nobilitas.

9. Judianism – Synagogue (Temple) – Egypt, Canada, Israel

Founder – Ibrahim

Scripture –The Torah (15 + 5 books of the Old Testament) Jews (followers) are divided into 03 sects with regional and ethnic divisions as –

(I) Orthodox

(II) Conservative

(III) Reforms

Here the highest Morality is possible through obedience to the Torah which pleased God. One must follow justice, charity, ethics and honesty being true to be the one with the Supreme Being.

Thus we have seen more or less similar conception or interpretation of all religions or cults in which moral standard and practices as – the ultimate aim to be inculcated. So it is needed to introspect and evaluate our rich ancient heritage critically and conform the Constitutional values today.

Now I try to find out the derivation of divine "words" with sanskrit roots—

(I) (A) Allah (अल्लाह) - अल्‌लटाप्‌ is expression or conception of the mother potency.

(B) लाति – गृणाति ज्ञानम्–divine wisdom averting Nescience

(C) अल्ला – Ātmā ishwar sarvavyāpishakti–the universal potency of The Self

(II) EESA (ईशा–ईशति–शासति–रक्षति इति ईशशासाकः) –

- The Incarnate Messenger and Boss as well to rule and rescue all beings.

(III) गोड (God) - गुप रक्षणे guprakshane-'D'(Suffix)= god where 'go' stands for Atma-(Light)

(IV) राम (Ram God) – रमु कान्तौ–अण्‌ (Suffix) =RAM He who illumines all with His divine light.

(V) कृष्ण (Krishna God) - कर्षति पापान् दुःखान् (karsati pāpān dukhān) कृष्ण

He who tills or uproots pains and sins of all.

Thus the intention of all global religions is circumlocutive to infer the same essence through varied connotations as the Rigveda states –

एकं सत् विप्राः बहुधा वदन्ति
अग्निं यमं मातरिश्वानमाहुः–01/164/46

Ekam Sat Viprāh Bahudha Vadanti,
agriim yamam mātriswānmahuh–01/164/46

- The truth is one which connotes as the Fire, the Yam and the Air as stated by the learned or the wise.

(a) Again the Geeta says-

यथा नदीनां बहवोऽम्बुवेगाः समुद्रमेवाभिमुखा द्रवन्ति–11/28

Yathā Nadinām Bahavo Ambuvegāh Samudramevābhi Mukhā Dravanti. –11/28

Water of rivers takes course to its consequential journey towards the ocean (essence), so the consequential essence of all religions of the world give the same fragrance.

आकाशात्पतितं तोयं यथा गच्छति सागरम्

(Akāshātpatitam toyam yatha gacchati sāgaram)

(b) These schools of cult like rains from the sky going back to the ocean. "Mundak opnishad" says –

यथा नद्याः स्यन्दमानाः समुद्रेऽस्तं गच्छन्ति नाम रूपे विहाय बहमै वेदं सर्वम्–3/2/8

Yatha Nadyāh syandmānāh samudreastam gacchanti nām rupe vihay brahmai vedam sarvam./3/2/8

Someone says –

"that my inward proclaim thou,
all instructing one I know through thee.
And if I utter Allah's hundred names.
A name, will, each one echoes,
be meant for thee."

(C) Muslim sait Rumi says- 'All the real aspects of religion, cult are mountain paths leading to the same summit, they all are shelter under the same roof but not the roof of the universe which is blue but to the roof higher than the universe."

(d) Muslimst Ali Emrān says-

कुन्तुम् खै–र उम्मतिन् उखरिजत् लिन्नासि त अमरू–न
विल्म अ् रूफि व तन्हौ–न अनिल्मुन्करि व तुअमिन् न बिल्लाहि

Kuntum khair ummatin ukharijat linnasi ta-amaru –na.
Bilm-a-Rufi va tanhou-na anil munkari vttu-amin-na.
Billāhi- The Quran – 4/3/110

One who advises good deals and forbids bad ones and has faith in the Almighty, excels of all cults".

There is much crisis in Hindu Dharma itself.

(d) But Kashmiri poet Gandharvarāja Pushpadantāchārya tried to cast off sectarian courses of Dharma "at will or interest leading to the ocean as in Mahimna stotram?-.

त्रयी सांख्यं योगः पशुपतिमतं वैष्णवमिति
प्रभिन्ने प्रस्थाने परमिदमदः पथ्यमिति च
रुचीनां वैचित्र्याद्दजकुटिल नाना पथजुषां–
नृणामेको गम्यस्त्वमसि पयसामर्णव इव–7

Trayi sānkhyan yogah pashupatimatan Vaisavmiti
Prabhinne prasthane parimidmadah pathynamiti ca
Rucheenām vai-citryādrikutila nānāpathjusām
Nr.nāmeko Gamyastwamasi payasāmarnav iva."

This Vesrse covers 18 branches of learning elucidating as-

1. Vedas – 04 (Rig, Yaju, Sām & Atharv Veda)
2. Vedang – 06 (Sikshā, Kalpa, Vyākaran, Nirukta, Chhanda & Jyotish)
3. Upāng – 04
   (A) purāna
   (B) Nyāya (including vaiseṣic)
   (C) Mimansā (Vedanta)
   (D) Dharmashāstra- Ramayan, Mahabhart, Sānkhya, Patanjali, Pasupata & Vaisnava.
4. Upveda – 04 (Āyurveda- including kāmśāstra of Rig-Veda, Dhanurveda- archery of Yajur-Veda, Gandharveda music of Sāmveda. Arthsastra- Economics of Atharva Veda)

   Total – 18 vidyās

   (a) Here Sānkhya Philosophy of Achārya Kapil (05 chapters) त्रिविध दुःखात्यन्त निवृत्ति पुरुषार्थः) – Trividha dukhātyanta nivvtipurus.ārtha
   (b) Yoga Philosophy of Patanjali – 04 feet-

I. Chittavrittinirodhah

II. 8 yam to Samādhi

III. Yogavibhutayah

IV. Kaivalyam

(c) Pashupati philosophy – to liberate from beastly fetters – 05 chapters viz –

I. Jivah (living being)

II. Kāran (God Pashupati)

III. Yoga Pashupatan – Observance of the mind

IV. Bhasmanāvidhi – Sacred bathing

V. Dukhānta sanyoga – Salvation oriented

(d) Vaisnava philosophy of Narad – 05 night

Such theistic philosophy is displayed discouraging 06 of Atheistic Philosophy as –

(e) (1) Shūnyāveda Prasthān – Madhyamic (one of schools of Buddhism)

(2) Kshanikvigyāngya Mātrāvāda – one of the 4 schools of Buddhism.

(3) Jnānākārānumeya Kshanika Bahyārth Vāda - one of the 04 schools of Buddhism (Sautrantkas)

(4) Saugatnām prasthān – One of the schools of Buddhism.

(5) Dehatmavāda prasthān – One of the 04 schools of uddhisam.

(6) Dehatirikta dehāparināmvāda- II chapter of Digamber school.

(f) Brahman texts –

I. Shruti – lengthy illustrations of legends or stories or revelation like hymns themselves of 03 types –

i. Commandment

ii. Explanatory statement coupled with illustrations.

iii. Both extra-ordinary with auspicious marks.

(g) Oriental Jurispdudence – 04

i. Shabdabhāvan – Bhātta

ii. Niyogvidhi – Prabhakart etc.

iii. Istasādhanāvidhi – Logicians

iv. Sarvovidhi- Social Scientists

(h) Sikshā of PĀNINI

(i) Vyākaran – Knowledge of complete formation of Vedic words

(j) Nirukta – Etymological interpretation or glossarial interpretation of obscure vedic words – 14 groups

(k) Purānās – 18 – Brahmā, Padma, Vaisnava, Shiva, Bhagvata, Nardiya, Markandeya, Agni, Bhavisya, Brahmavaivarta, linga, Varah, Skanda, Vaman, Kurma, Matsya, Garuda, Brahmand.

(l) Mimansa – 02 –

(I) Action

(II) Wisdom

(m) Dharmasastra – 22 – Manu, Yāgyavalya, Visnu, Yama, Angirā, Vasistha, Daksha, Shātāpt, Samvarta, Pārāshar, Gautam, Sankha, Likhit, Harita, Apasthamb, Ushana, Vyās, Kātyāyan, Bṛahaspati, Deval, Nārad and Paithnisā.

(n) 64- skill-Arts or crafts in human career –

(1) Music

(2) Instrumental Music

(3) Dance

(4) Drama

(5) Painting-writing

(6) Special hemming

(7) Emotional offering of meal or flower

(8) Flower picking

(9) Coloring of teeth and garments

(10) Jewel decoration

(11) Bed arrangements

(12) Water based musical instruments

(13) Water stroke instrument

(14) Knowledge of wonderful vision

(15) Ability of garlanding

(16) Head-garland fixing

(17) Actor-costuming in green room

(18) Ear ornaments of flower

(19) Use of perfume

(20) Use of general ornaments

(21) Jugglery

(22) Use of brushing
(23) Readiness of activity
(24) Activity of herbal picture
(25) Distillation of beverage essence
(26) A particular gesture or gesticulation
(27) Cord-pastime
(28) Playing on lute or tiny drum
(29) Conundrum of 16 beads of embracing
(30) Stress-speaking
(31) Book-reading
(32) Narrating or playing of comedic composition
(33) Fulfilling of poetic riddles
(34) Alternating silken cloth-feathered with arrows
(35) A pin upon which cotton is firstly drawn out or spindle
(36) Trimming by cutting away the outer edges
(37) Architecture
(38) Testing of silver jewels
(39) Metallurgio-micrology
(40) Knowledge of jewel colouring
(41) Mien knowledge
(42) Botanical use
(43) Ram-cock-quail fighting
(44) Wailing & lamenting of parrot & sārika
(45) Cleaning an person with perfume or scented fluids
(46) Hair cleaning skill
(47) Saying with undestructible fisti-cuffs (closed palms)
(48) Spoken-poetic context barbarously
(49) Knowledge of local or national language
(50) Skill of flower made toy-cart
(51) Astronomical diagram
(52) Applying symbolic diagram of divinity
(53) Expressible-cum-cross debating
(54) Skill of secrecy
(55) Liking treasure-space
(56) Skill of multi action
(57) Fine arts use
(58) Sparing skill of garments

(59) Gambling with dice for prize winning
(60) Attractive sporting skill
(61) Kids sports
(62) Obstacle-removing skill
(63) Skill of wars victory
(64) Skill science of demonic-defeat

Here on account of varied tastes there are many straight or serpentine paths leading to the vast potentialities as the rains through different courses leading to the ocean as seen in the Nature.

The Almighty is like a complete distilled water The Absolute One. If it falls down to the Arabian side of the ocean it becomes Israel's God and is called Heavenly Father. On the other side we call Allah. If it falls in the Himalayas we called Him Shiva. So the supreme one is just like a common term generally approved by all sects: The Hebrew, The Arbic, the English utter in worship – "Omine";. The Greek utter,"Omega" and all are analogous to "Aum". In the entelechy of different cults we find the same source- Cosmic power or Intelligence. While addressing to the parliament of Religion in Chicago in 1893 Swami Vivekanand reiterated few lines- "As the different streams having their sources in different places mingled their water in the sea. So O Lord! The different paths which men take through different tendencies, various thoughts appear, crooked or straight- all lead to thee." Thus human beings of freewill take recourse to poly-path leading to the one goal; so water from all courses of rivers flows to the same ocean through different zig-zag and straight streams.

Now it is relevant to quote in-faith harmony that some of the Muslim scholars who paid respect for Hindu mythology viz-

(a) Md. Shalidullah of Bangladesh
(b) Vedantist Darashikoh translated Atharvveda, the Geeta,Yoga Vasistha, Upnishads and etc.
(c) Shāyistā-Khān (Son-in-law of shāhajahan) was a great skt scholar.
(d) Emperor Akbar- got Valmiki Ramayan translated into parsi by Vaidyuni Nakib Khan.
(e) Faiz Muslim- translated the master piece Bhaskaracharya "Leelavati" into parsi.
(f) Waris Shah- author of epic "Heer – Ranjha". To his views "there is no cleavage between Sufi saint & Hindu Yogi. Because both believe that God is within all human beings and invocation is a step towards salvation".

Such literary efforts are commendable steps towards fraternity and amity. So in a liberal view Secularism is to recognize and promote all religions, cult and discern unity underlying in them. Since all denomination and instincts have the common vedic basis, Shree Adi Shanker underlined the essential unity of all traditions. In common parlance the Dharma of a man is of being true to the dignity and worth of humanity, of offering reverences for life, love, compassion and adequate regards for fellow-feeling.

(g) Muiuddin Chisti- "The highest form of devotion to God is to redress the pains of the aflicted persons and fulfills the requirements of the helpless being". He asked pupils to imbibe the nature of the river, the sun and the earth for their generosity, uniformity and hospitality respectively.

Categorically all religions have only 03 essential truth as their basis-

(i) We are by nature divine image of God.

(ii) To realize and experience that divine nature we must purify our hearts.

(iii) To achieve purity of hearts we must lead a selfless and dedicated life.

However we may conclude eastern dharma & western religion – in practical perspectives.

(1) Eastern Dharma – is cosmic, eternal, transcending, human history in cyclical mode.

(2) Western Religion – is historical, beginning with a prophet or events, human history is linear never to be repeated.

However all religions of the world may preach the philosophy of brotherhood to bring about fuşion with the East and the West through dialogue, group discussion, prayer-meet and spiritual discourses or satsanga.

In order to get rid of chaos, commotions and complications of multi-approaches to religion Lord Buddha did not talk about God, rather he called Him to be Cosmic Consciousness averting such crisis of chopping off one another. So Dharma is a multi-disciplinary approach evolving from all conceptions and formulations of blended attitude to the Almighty. It is the spirit of Universal tolerance and acceptance which enabled Indian culture to survive and prevail in the Vedantin brain with Islamic body of the Secular tradition of India. Lastly all cults preach coalescence in human beings to fuse with the Great Supreme Being.

So in the absence of such legitimate knowledge of the Ultimate Reality (Cosmic Consciousness), We compete for the name of deities. Such types of thoughts are responsible for disturbing world's peace to the extent of riot and bloodshed. Sectists damage emotional integration by playing of rituals words compiled in variorum. Narrow codes, wasteful virtuals make us forget the vital lesson of Universal amity which every religion teaches basically. So one of the biggest tragedies of the world is the dogmatic approach to religion and faith intervening unifying and peaceful force.

Thanks to our Indian tradition which liberates religion from all dogmatic and creedal approach and survives with the spirit of modern Science. Such spiritual approach deepens the scientific humanism of Universality. That is why our Indian Constitution is committed to secular approach to religion and honours all religions of the world in a secular democracy based on composite culture. So the world should adopt Indian views on religion to cultivate cosmopolitan spirit as in the Mahopnishad (Sām Vediya branch)-

अयं निजः परोवेति गणना लघुचेतसाम्
उदारचरितानां तु वसुधैव कुटुम्बकम्–4 / 71

Ayam Nijah paroveti garnā Laghuchetsām.
Udārcharitānām tu Vasudhaiv Kūtūmbakam./4/71

U.K. poet S.T. Coleridge wrote also – "He Prayeth the best who loves best things both great and small".

2(D) Cut Culture & Global Tincture

We should call upon the education to play vital role- the role of balancing technological flights with cultural pulls. It has been essential for us to humanize the science in these days of rapidly growing arsenals and rate-race of nuclear armaments piled by Super powers. History reiterates that countries with political culture have failed; nations with military might have been destroyed; races with absolute power have disappeared. But a country with cultural heritage based on affinity has eternal existence.

Further we cannot survive through vicissitudes of life, the accidents of history and ravages of Time. Whereas the world's hope of survival lies only in sober influence of scholar, philosopher, thinkers and writers. So it has been imperative to hold the sword under the control of cultural spirit. Because culture is the 'pran' of the Nation. On the other hand over-shadowing influence of torn culture and rapidly growing nuclear arms are responsibile for inefficiency to maintain for sufficiency in our cultural heritage.

Further culture is the custom of life which gives a special quality of thoughts, behaviour in social perspectives.

It does not abide by particular faith or religion or tradition. That is why Indian culture is not the heritage of a particular section since Vedic period. It has its ideal harmony in multiplicity or disharmony. It gave wise to all sections with mutual connection or conjunction. It has furnished a lot to the Universe in the fluid of knowledge. Arts, faiths and humanity. Now it has been the trait of glorious tradition in the whole history of human civilization due to its radical anonymity.

In this way culture is the source of Ultimate Values held by particular society which seeks to express in its institution, feeling and artistic creation. It ransoms the man who is born barbarous from the condition of beast by being cultivated. Culture means not only faith, religions or tradition but also "the Arts of living which gives new form of organization, behaviour and thinking way." A German Monk-Theologist and Protestant Reformer Martin Luther pointed out – "the prosperity of a country depends neither on abundance of its revenues nor on the strength of its fortification, but it lies in the number of its cultivated citizens, in its men of education, enlightenment and character."

So culture is, in essence, the development of human power- the upheaval of the body, mind and spirit by training a man with experience. It brings to the awareness of the inflexible value of life bestowed with basic traits of everyone. Such values ensure the stability of each cultured heritage spontaneously for good unexposed to the cyclone of changes.

Thanks to the millennia of our ageless cultural heritage which, even today, provides link between India and her neighbours having allied culture. According to research made by India & foreign historians, The Indo-south East Asian culture included the following lands with their ancient names in the brackets as chips of the old block –

(1) Vietnam (Champa)

(2) Java Island (Javadwipa)

(3) Cambodia (Kumbege)

(4) Borneo Island (Varundwip)

(5) Ceylon (Tamraparni) or Shrilanka

(6) Burma (Indradwip)

(7) Malaya (Malaydwip) (Peninsula)

In a bid to advocate broad vision of India Swami Vivekanand, while addressing the Mammoth meeting in Chicago 1893 said - "I challenged the world to find, through the whole system of Sanskrit Philosophy, any such expression as that the Hindu will be saved and not others. Because there is no discrimination between the East and the West. East and West are two possibilities which every man in every age carries within himself two moments of human spirit.

This is the very reason that despite being severed of trails and tribulations for themselves for thousands of years, India in her sacred land, has given birth to enlightened moral thinkers and at par in other regions of the universe. They all guided human beings with nuclear life-cycle of the universe. Even now Orientology is the repository of culture-history and treasure trover of life values. The prominent among them are being reminded here-

(1) Adi Shankaracharya – World's greatest Hindu Philosopher and Thinker of the 8th century. He was an ardent Vedantist and monist to have identified soul with universal one. He says in Ishāvā syopnishads – (Yajurveda)

यस्तु सर्वाणि भूतान्यात्मन्येवानुपश्यति
सर्वभूतेषु चात्मानं ततो न विजुगुप्सते–40 / 6

Yastu sarvāni bhutānyātmanyevā nu pasyati.
Sarva bhuteshu chātmanam tato na vijugupsate. /40/6

"He, who perceives all creatures in his soul and perceives his soul in all creatures, does not hate anyone due to cosmic vision.

(2) Gautam Buddha – founder of Buddhism and his tenets are –

(a) Human sufferings are caused by endless desires.

(b) Salvation lies in right conduct and non-injury .

(c) Further he laid stress on the 4 Noble-Truth viz –

i. Existence is suffering

ii. Suffering is born of desires and

iii. Desires once fulfilled lead to rebirth of desires.
iv. When rebirth ceases – that is the highest good (Nirvāna)

Further his observation of the 10 commandments –

i. Not to killing
ii. Not to stealing
iii. Not to conceit
iv. Not to adultery
v. Not to tell a lie
vi. Not to speak ill of others
vii. Not to indulge in fault finding or profane language
viii. Not to obtain covetousness or Avarice
ix. Not to hatred
x. Not to enjoy Ignorance

His 8 fold-path of instruction –

i. Right belief
ii. Right thought
iii. Right speech
iv. Right action
v. Right means of livelihood
vi. Right execution
vii. Right remembrance
viii. Right meditation

In this way Buddhism with all efforts of king Ashoka, the Great, ushered a renaissance in religious movement.

(3) Vedavyās – The great religious and moral codifier of the Hindus.

(4) Bhagvan Mahāvir – The last of the 24 or the 24th Tirthankars (spiritual teachers). His concept laid also stress on the unity and universality of life and hailed the aim of life is the development of all good talent in human soul.

(5) Shree Nārāyan Guru – was a social reformer and philosopher of Kerala. He was placed next to Shankar; He worked for meditation of untouchability and installation of social equality on caste; he was the first to propagate the idea – "one caste, one religion and one God".

(6) Gurunānak – Shikha saint, being the philosopher of cult movement of Islamic faith upheld by Hindu Theory. He preached the Muslims

– believe kaba be your conduct, truth be your 'peer' and Mala be your divine desire and Almighty world ensures all existence.

(7) Nadu – founder Bhakti movement in which Ram, Rahim, caste or creed and backward – forward –all constitute to be an integral cult.

(8) Rāmānujāchārya – Vaishnava teacher of Tamil launched Hindu-Muslim ties movements in the south of India.

(9) St. Kabir – A disciple of Rāmānand made an earnest attempt to foster the spirit of harmony between Hindu and Muslim in U.P. He avoided caste discrimination, class-hatred for universal brotherhood.

(10) Ramdeo, Ramdas and Tukaram in Maharastra advocated social harmony.

(11) Chatrapati Shivajee – Indian patron of communal harmony and common culture gave fatherly treatment to handome daughter-in-law of Mulla Ahmad Navāyat, ,The commander of Kalyan fort. When she was brought to the Court of Shivā-jee –

प्रसीद वत्स। पुरतो मयि स्थिते न देहलीशोऽपि तवाप्रिये प्रभुः
पितृगृहं प्राप्य दुहितृवत्सलं कथं विषादैः परितप्यसेऽधुना।

–Chhatrapati Charitam–3/121

Praseed vats! ! purto mayi sthite na dehlisho api tavāpriye prabhuh.
Pitri gr.ham prāpya duhitrivatsalam katham visadaih paritapya sedhuna.

O daughter! Be cheerful, even Delhi Emperor cannot hurt you in my existence. Father's house is the filial lap for a daughter. Why do you disconsolate yourself? Further he ordered instantly his court mate to take her back to her kith & kin with due respect due to cultured personality.

(12) Chaitanya Mahāprabhu - Begal-Vaisnava cult

(13) Aurbindo Ghose – An exponent of Hindu Nationalism, poet & saint. His work – life divine, essay on the Geeta and "Basis of yoga".

(14) Achārya Manu – Ancient law giver to India. His tenets an compiled in "Manusmriti".

(15) Khwāza Moninuddin Chisti – The preceptor of Sufi-cult (Indo-Islamic). In his views there may be differences in language and thought, but both resemble the drop of the same ocean basically, he, further, laid stress on the Code of Conduct and peaceful life. He preached – One may divulge the clue of Allah, attain Allah

or Parmatma by virtue of simple, pure and temperate livelihood. He further advised to believe the monism and serve humanity with liberal sentiment; Because the number of Path to God is as numerous as there are being created" – Quran – XXIV, XXXV.

(16) Kutub Shah – Muslim saint who preached Hindu and Muslim to honour religion with same fidelity.

(17) Muslim st. Amir Khusaro, Hazarat Nizamuddin oliya, Babu Farid, Firdausi, Silsila, Khadari Silsila and the like enriched Indian culture with Arts, music and literature.

(18) Altaf Hussain Hazi, Nair Ahmed, Md. Hussain Azad, Dr. Sir Ikwal and other lit the Candle of secularism and humanism to common benefit to the society in general.

(19) Chandra Bhan Brahman (Gazal Urdu Singer)

(20) Pt. Ratan Nath Sharkar (1845-1902)- writer of Fanāse-A-Azād

(21) Daya Shanker Nasim - Translator of Arabian Nights in Urdu.

(22) Pt. Brija Narayan Chakabasta (1882–1926) – Penned Urdu Ramayan.

(23) Munshi Premchandra (1880–1936) – Wrote 16 novels and stories in Hindi and Urdu and the 1st of which was – "So zāye Vatan" (1910) seized by the British Ruler to Thwart loyalty for the Nation. Surprise to note here that there were many Sanskrit scholars among 9-gem in the Court of Monarch Hitler and Indian Emperor Akbar.

Thus due to Indian cultural heritage Urdu works were developed in the edifice of tolerance, taming trust and true understanding.

Foreign thinker at par – Voltaire, Zoroaster, Confucius and the like preached above the trivial impulse of life for global welfare.

Such is the majesty of Indian culture to recognize the chequered phenomena of world culture. But some spiritual freelancers with devilish brain apply their spirit in churning mundo-milky ocean; and the cream is felt by them while the whey is left for the innocent under misconceptions.

Unlike alien culture, our Indian culture tones up the heart while cultivating the mind. To me if a fissure lies between the mind and the heart, the intellect confined to the ken of reasoning fails to premeate into the highest goal of spirit for inner sensation.

The balanced development of the both (mind and spirit) should be brought about by the cultivation of creative culture. In other words, noble characters nurture our pristine culture whereas well tailored designs display alien culture. Because the gross materialistic view of life tends towards outer space in the vastness of void when our spiritual urges tend towards inner space in the fullness of affluence.

Further, in order to cope with our oriental culture. We, the people, are given octave sacraments as purification for life through action, speech and mind from the birth to death. They are served with spiritual, cultural and physiological purposes to confer privileges of social and religious heritage as follows –

(1) Nāmkaran – Name giving ceremony within 15 days of birth in which father whispers good name in infant's right ear.

(2) Annaprāshan – First feeding of solid foods.

(3) Karnaveda – Piercing ceremony to ears giving to both boys and girls to have health and wealth through this ritual.

(4) Chudākaran – The head is shaved and smeared with sandal wood-paste before the age of 04.

(5) Vidyārambha – Official beginning of primary education.

(6) Upanayam – Ceremonial rites to put on sacred thread to consider as dwija (twice-born).

(7) Vivāh – The marriage ceremony for life time with rotation of 07 times around ritual fire by the couple simultaneously.

Here 07 rounds stand for the complete conjugation of life in the universe full of Nature's phenomena –

1. **07 Ocean** – Pacific Ocean, Atlantic Ocean, Indian Ocean, Arctic Ocean, Mediterranean Ocean, Caribbean Ocean, the Gulf of Mexico or Arctic, South Atlantic, North Atlantic, North Pacific, South Pacific, IndianSouthern Ocean.
2. **07 Mountains** – Mahindra, Malaya, Sahya, Pariyatra, Shaktimān, Rikshavana, Vindhya.
3. **07 Rishis** – Bhāradwaja, Jamdagni, Atri, Vasistha, Viswāmitra, Agastya, Gautam.

   Or

   Mārichi, Vasiṣtha, Angiras, Atri, Pulastya, Pullah and Kratu. But 07 Richis as classical luminaries in different Manvantars are used to be re-enlisted by Acharya Manu as the Head.
4. **07 Gods (Bible)** – His Holiness – Tetragrammaton, EL, Elohim, Eloah, Elohai, EL Shaddai, Tzevaot.
5. **07 Spirit of God (Bible)** – Wisdom, Understanding, Counsel, Fortitude, Knowledge, Piety, Fear (Delight of God).

6. **07th part of the Bible (The book of Revelation)** – deals 07 churches, 07 angels, 07 seals, 07 trumpets, 07 Stars.

   Now 07 Rishis (Hindu) resemble 07 Rishis (Christian)

Hindu	resembles	Christian
Kratu	a Uma	Dubhe Alpha
Pulah	ß Uma	Merak Beta
Pulastya	Y Uma	Phecda
Atri	Delta Uma	Megrez
Angiras	YUma	Alioth Delta star
Vasistha	YUma	Mizar zeta-star
Marichi	YUma	Alkaid of knowledge

7. **07 Island** – Jamboo, Plaksha, Shalmalya, Kush, Krauch, Shaka, Pushakar.
8. **07 Colours** (Rainbow) – Red, Orange, Yellow, Green, Blue, Indigo, Violet.
9. **07 days of creation of world (Bible).**
10. **07 days** – Sunday, Monday, Tuesday, Wednesday, Thursday, Friday, Saturday.
11. **07 forests** – Dāndkaranya, Khandāranya, Champkāranya, Vadāranya, Naimisāranya, Brahmāranya, Dharmaranya.
12. **07 Circles in human body (Yogic conception)**
13. **07 world (Hindu)** – upward (Highter)

    07 world (Hindu) – downward (lower)
14. **07 steps (Buddhism)** – A new born baby rises and takes 07 steps.
15. **07 Men of God (The old Testament)** – David, Elijah, Samuel, Moses, Igdaliah, Shomaiah, Elisha.

Thus the number 07 is positive and auspicious one in world's Mythology Collectively.

07 round (Muslims) – in Mecca walk around 07 times.

8) Antyesthi (cremation) - Funeral rites to release the soul for the next habitat or world.

Lastly the culture encompasses norms, languages, festivals, rituals or ceremonies, pastimes, food, fashion, architecture, craft, trade, economics, lifestyle, belief, traditional skill, Arts, historical games, trending, renaissance Art, historical Art, Social & political organization. Culture reflects the moral and ethical faith to interact with others. It provides means to have a sense of integrity and safety. Culture is an important architect of our personality. It enriches music, art, recreation, costume, folk lore, environment and attitude among people. It develops on the cultivation of cultural, linguistic, archeological and biological Anthropology.

2(E) – Industrial Relation & Oriental Role

Industry is the force to the economy of the country to develop capital goods in large quantity at resonable costs. It promotes the growth of agriculture, transport and communication. It is to produce commodities which can be exchanged for values in which an individual or groups of individual is/are involved.

It is an organization which is understood as an integrated agreement with the idea of "one good family" wherein management and staff-member share a common purpose by expressing mutual venture.

The Industrial policy of the country deals with the ideology of the current political minds. Its strategy is of official endeavour to impress growth and development of all parts of the economy in the manufacturing sectors. A country's infrastructure is a vital booster of wider economy. It aims to promote emerging technologies and builds an innovation-driven economy to encourage high quality industrial infrastructure providing access to affordable capital.

It is a part from macro-economic policies as searching credit and taxing capital gains.

Conventionally Industrial policy referes to subsidize export and import industrialization. Where trade-bars are imposed on some key-sectors temporarily. In keen competitions such bars are lifted to expose the selected industries to the international market.

However industrialization is needed for fast economic growth of the country. It also enhances agriculture, transport, home-trade, foreign-trade, services and social sector of the economy. Further it grows employment opportunities, national income, per capita income and living standard of the people. It helps the country to make it self-sufficient and successful.

Thus it builds up a sound tradition of industrialization prone to the ideology and objectivities of the concerned Govt.

The main objectivities of I.R. –

1. Developing of natural resources - It helps to identify, collect and use of resources purposely to augment national income of the country.
2. Increase in Industry and industrial growth.
3. Modernization – It helps to grow industrial output and productivity.
4. Balanced industrial policy – It eases balanced industrial development of many sectors of economy.
5. Balanced regional development – It makes provision for facilities or discounts for fast development in industrially backward regions of the country. According to Acharya Kautilya in "Artha Shastra" – "A balance is a key of component to enjoy the essence of life. Excess of everything is bad. Extreme and sensitive goodness should be kept away for the needy. So life should have balance between good and bad pursuits, weal and woe, pains and pleasure cries & laughter etc."
6. Coordination between foundation and consumer – It encourages to develop foundation and key industries while paying heed to the development of consumer industries to the extent of providing a platform for economic growth of the country.
7. Coordination between large and small scale industries – These industries can be helpful to one another.
8. Area determination – It determines the area of operation under public and private sectors.
9. Sincere industrial relations – A wide industrial policy is needed to build up harmonious relationship between workers and management for sustainable industrialization.

   Thus it accords relations between works & mgt. with proper utilization of domestic/foreign capital

   The mutual corporation between the Govt. & the Industry lies in the following interweaving –

   (a) Technology transfer and industrial upgrading.
   (b) Coordination of resources across multiple economic system.
   (c) Organisation including clusters, financial services, university research facilities and good-economic planning agencies.

When we talk about industry, we come to know about commercial life based on business perspectives. Because business is viewed as an integral part of the society through manufacturing of domestic goods, distribution, foreign trade, financial investment and other related activities. It entails to work on economic structure based on Sarvalokahitam (for wellbeing of all stakeholders) to boost up the benefit of business. Further it needs to gain all round excellence when maintenance of quality becomes the main object.

Our Vedic philosophy provides a good platform for building business excellence by undertaking relevant clues to control quality of highest order. Upnishadic philosophy may be applied in business industrial training, economic and others fields. A better understanding of managerial issues of life like quality management through our oriental objectives of life should be inculcated as–

(1) Dharma (performance of occupational duty)

(2) Artha (material affluence)

(3) Kām (happiness of good product & relation)

(4) Moksha (feeling of liberation on entrusted manufacturing of goods)

We are confronted with the quality control problems. Because of being aloof from Vedic objectives of life as Achārya Chānakya has illustrated –

(a) Vasudhaiv Kutumbakam (The world is one family)

(b) Samarpana (Dedication)

(c) Loka Samgrah (Welfare of all)

(d) Shubhalābha (Ethical profit)

(e) Niskām Karma (Work without greed)

(f) Ativarjayet (shunning utopian ideas to avoid dystopia.)

These are the key- objectives which the Chief or the CEO should observe among the workers and within himself. He should not overpass righteousness and economy to satisfy his latent intention rather he should enjoy in an equal degree within 03 pursuits of life. Wealth, charity and fair intention.

If anyone excels to enjoy any one of the 03 it would hurt not only the other but also oneself. Undoubtedly wealth is important. But it is as important as charity and fair intention. For this conception we have to apply wealth of knowledge enshrined in our oriental commerce.

2(E) – (a) Industrial Management & Control

So far as I. M. is concerned, it deals the base of knowledge, self-knowledge and leadership. The CEO should draw on all knowledge and observation of humanities on philosophy, economics, history, ethics, physical science and sociology. He should have to focus on such effective knowledge and results to build up a bridge of design, sale and user-friendly software programme.

While Heads of the modern management cling to profit making at first and social welfare secondly, So they would incure corporate scandals, insolvency and the like and still are haunting to increase sustainable business practices. Because we forsake Ethics and fail to make ethical consideration in business transactions. So we should not avert mistakes in management decision driven by avarice and erroneous reporting of the financial scenario of the company; rather we ought to have simultaneous emphasis on profit and welfare. The foundation of business hovers round the customers who create employment. In avoiding such notion, Stake holders suffer a huge loss owing to ethnic failures. Thus we should integrate the modern management with ethical values amplified in the Upnishads, The Geeta, Kautily's Arthshāstra, Patanjali's Yoga Darshan and other oriental scriptures – viz

"The practice of management should start from yourself through moral values and ethical principles."

Only then we are able to manage our intentions and senses being the essence of leadership. It is though such leadership we are apt to connect well with broader society and start sharing a common goal for social advantages. So it is the moral duty and responsibility of an organization to encourage sense of truth through properly managing relationship with the society as a whole and consumers in particular. We, then, move towards addressing the triple bottom lines viz. –

i. People – In the form of suppliers, distributors, bankers, employee's agents and the like to constitute our living stakeholders.
ii. Planet – Constitutes the natural resources and larger environment, the non-living or abiotic ingredients of our stakeholders' estate.
iii. Profit – Proportional to the real cost on manufacturing the commodities.

Here the living and non-living stakeholders are interrelated to one another through our organizational system. Hence we use the term – business eco-system on the web of interrelationship.

We, often, use the term global citizen in the formation of common goal culture of various countries in the context of globalization and international trade. So from the level of self management to the creation of uniform world order is feasible through exchange and transfer of knowledge at various levels. This knowledge is instrumental with the individual to the larger society or universal order with such relations allied to the Vedantic School of thought when the ultimate goal of a man is to connect through "Atman". (Individual self) with the Brahmā (universal self). Such conception of the Self constitutes 06-step successively -

I. Jnāna Srsti (Knowledge-creation)

II. Jnāna Prāpti (Knowledge acquisition)

III. Jnāna Parivaham (Knowledge transfer)

IV. Jnāna Sahabhāgan (Knowledge Sharing)

V. Mukta Navarachanā (Open-innovation)

VI. Adhyatmic Sāmanjasya (Metaphysical balance or Propriety)

According to the RigVeda, such cosmic order governs the entire universe to achieve the goal of excellence through the common vision, Universal brotherhood and equitable property. Such perspective of excellence for society is willing to sacrifice for lower level of needs through higher moral values for all. Such a balanced objective makes us happier and healthier based on self- management and self-discipline to the tune of Vedic concept of growth. Such growth can be obtained through integrating the optimo-global products and their equitable distributions in the society. Thus it entails business leaders to devise and adapt to a common theory based on achieving business excellence constituting policies, techniques, tools and system suitable to the companies.

Excellence is more than competence. It signifies quality of higher order. As per Indian scripture, self-ethics or organization's value systems are synonymous to quality which is the ability of product or service to meet consumers' expectation for implied needs. In Indian Mythology the super excellences have 14 to 16 dimensions. Whereas modern management conceives 08 dimensions of quality –

1. Performance – Main features of the product/service.
2. Aesthetics – Appearance, Smell, Feel and taste etc.
3. Special Feature – Extra traits.
4. Confirmation – Now well the product/Service confirms to customer's expectations.
5. Safety – Risk of injury.
6. Reliability – Consistency of performance.
7. Durability – Indirect evaluation of quality such as reputation, goodwill ...
8. Service after sale – Handling of customer complaints and checking customer's satisfaction.

Now I conclude that isolated techniques will not be enough to change the industrial world. But the integration of Vedic studies with modern Science and technology is essential for industrial chemistry.

The above philosophy of works and integration is condensed in the Geeta –

बुद्धि युक्तो जहातीह उभे सुकृतदुष्कृते
तस्माद्योगाय युज्यस्व योगः कर्मसु कौशलम्–2/50

The stoical stakeholders do not bifurcate between good and bad manufacturing of commodities rather they perform their duties with equal tenacity. So take on integrated work. such integrated approach to work is the co-efficient of pursuits to dispose off their own responsibility.

(b) Industrial Relations

The philosophy of I.R. is to facilitate –

(1) Production and productivity.

(2) Protect rights and interests of labours & management by their cooperation.

(3) Achieve sound, harmonious and mutually beneficial labour management relations.

(4) Avoid any kind of work breakdown.

(5) Establish and maintain individual democracy

(6) Organization & practice of multi-skilled relationship between workers and management.

(7) Union workers & management.

Today the modern Industrial society is marked by rapid change, industrial unrest, conflicting ideology in national and international arena. It is a dynamic concept that depends upon the pattern of the society, economic system, political setup and changes with socio-economic order.

Further it consists of the network of institutions like Trade Unions collective bargaining of employees, laws, States to sustain social well being and industrial growth.

It is not a Science but Arts consists of –

(a) A set of individuals and organizations for interaction to generate industrial relations.

(b) A structure of institutionalised conduct which provides collective procedures, grievances, settlement and etc.

(c) An output that saves to govern future relationship of the parties.

(d) External institutions for Trade Unions and their growth on market forces.

(e) Internal institutions which govern work-rules, wage-structure, joint consultations and grievance resolutions.

To sum up there are 03 factors affecting I.R. –

(1) Socio-Ethical relations – Technological advancement, market conditions, economic conditions and political parties.

(2) Investors' Relations – It referes to the responsibility of managing communication between company's corporate management and its investors. Such relationship provides feedback to normal mgt. and crisis mgt.

(3) Employees' Relations – The focus is on how to manage effectively and strengthen such relationship.

Thus a systematic approach to I. R. fits in with specific needs and objectives of the particular Enterprise.

(c) Labour & Management Relations

Now the term "labour mgt. relation" refers to interaction between employess as represented by labour Unions and their employees. Labour Unions are organization of employees in a particular company, industries or a group of companies or industries that join together for workers' interests. Negotiations between labours and mgt. have been instrumental in determining such issues, wages and salary levels, working hours, working conditions, hiring procedure, training programs and benefits such as health insurance and retirement benefits.

In brief the objectives of labour welfare are –

1. To promote economic development.
2. To provide efficiency
3. To provide proper human conditions for work and living.
4. To minimize hazard.
5. To supplement wage in mandatory terms.
6. To prevent social evils.

Besides there is ILo (International Labour Organization), which has many approaches such as –

1. Psychological approach
2. Sociological approach
3. Human relations approach

4. Marxist approach
5. Gandhian approach

Here Gandhian approach to employers-employees relationship is based on truth, non-violence and non-possession. Such approach to labour problem is completely new and refreshingly human–

(a) He held definite views regarding fixation and regulations of wages.
(b) Organization and function of trade unions.
(c) Necessity of collective bargaining.
(d) Use and abuse of strikes.
(e) Labour discipline.
(f) Workers participation on recognizing mgt &. condition on work.
(g) He emphasized on recognizing each worker as a human being.
(h) He believed in non-violence commission. He realised that relations between labours and Mgt. can either be a powerful booster to economy or social progress.

Accordingly industrial peace is an essential condition not only for the growth and development of industry itself but also in great measure for the improvement in the condition of workers and wages.

He advocated voluntary arbitration and mutual settlement of disputes.

He also pleaded for perfect understanding between capital and labour, mutual respect and recognition of quality.

To him means and ends are equally important.

He supports strikes as a weapon, if there is a valid grievance under non-violence and non-malice against non-strikers.

He assumes employers' as a role of trustees and not owners.

Industrial peace is essential both for growth of industry and improvement of workers' conditions. Thus such approach is suitable to current dynamic Industrial development in India and abroad.

Its roles are –

1. Adoption of instrumental standards.
2. Creation of international standard of labours.
3. Employment promotion
4. Collection and distribution of information & publication.
5. Research & studies.

(d) Corporate Mgt. & Govt.

I deal "Corporate governance" which refers broadly to the rules, process and laws to operate, regulate and control business affairs. This may refer to internal factors defined by the Chiefs, stakeholders and constitution of corporation as well as external forces-consumers' groups, client & Govt.

In oriental perspective," Bṛhdaranyakopnishad" deals about corporate governance" on ethical philosophy in the following dimensions –

1. Self-control
2. Charity
3. Compassion
4. Truth
5. Austerity
6. Sense-control
7. Tranquility of mind
8. Righteousness
9. Mercy
10. Renunciation

In Corporate mgt., the Geeta specifies 15 values which are pertinent to any Manager to have business excellence in companies or industries.

अमानित्वमदम्भित्वमहिंसा क्षान्तिरार्जवम्
आचार्योपासनं शौचं स्थैर्यमात्म विनिग्रहः–13/7

Amānitvamadambhitvam himsām kshāntirājavam.
Achāryopāsanam shauchan sthairyamātma vini-grahaḥ/13/7

Or

इन्द्रियार्थेषु वैराग्यमनहंकार एव च
जन्ममृत्युजराव्यधिदुःखदोषानुदर्शनम्–13/8

Indryārthesu vairāgyamana hankār eva ca
Janmamṛtyujarāvyādhi dukhadōṣanudarśanam–13/8

1. Amānitwam – Modesty
2. Adambhitvam – Non-arrogance
3. Ahimsā – Non-violence
4. Kshānti – Patience
5. Arjavam – sincerity
6. Achārjyopasanam – Seek and service to Boss intent
7. Shaucham – in-out honesty and purity

8. Sthairyam – stability or constancy
9. Ātmavinigrah – Self-curbing or control
10. Idriyarthesu – Sense-gratification or worldy enjoyment
11. Vairagyām – Aversion or absence of mundane passion.
12. Anhankāram – Non-conceit
13. Janma mrtyu jaravyādhi – Life-death, old-age, Physical ailments
14. Dukhadōsa – afflictions and faults
15. Anurdaśanam – Non-infatuation

Gist – (13/7 & 13/8) – A Manager of the company or the industry should have modesty, non-arrogance, non-violence, patience, sincerity, serviceable nature, inner and outer honesty, stability, self-control, non-infatuation to sense-gratification or worldly passions. So that he might not face grave affliction in life, old age and death time.

(e)- Human Resource Mgt.

H.R. mgt. has administrative, operational and strategic roles to processing & record– keeping activities. Its function in manufacturing companies are –

1. Talent acquisition/ Recruitment
2. Compensation Mgt.
3. Benefits of administration
4. Training appraisal
5. Performance appraisal
6. Employees and labour relations
7. Compliance mgt.

(f)- The goals of HR Mgt. –

1. To get people for production
2. To corporate through mutual interests
3. To gain satisfaction with their relationship

Such approaches highlight techniques to improve employees' morale, efficiency and job satisfactions. The management encourages small-work-groups to exercise and control over improvement and thus connive at offensive labour relations with warning.

Lastly the industrial mgt. should organize periodical seminars, webinars or symposium on oriental scriptures regarding valuable suggestions for cohesive team-works, transparency in target, infrastructural growth, business strategy mutual relationship, sincere responsibility, friendship and ultimately aiming to cultivate collective character-confidence in organization.

People in general, are reluctant to spare their costly time to be indulged in old know - how which are deemed to be obsolete for our Computer Age. We are sure to avail own pomp and pleasure in life by dint of modern techniques uncaring for global relief. We must be aware of fact that most of us would have to reap the outcome of amoral and intellectual break-up and repent for decaying days after the fair. That is why financial solidary or personal minting is not enough at the loss of intellectual integrity and safety. Because professional values are captioned under intellectual integrity which is rarer than financial integrity.

History reiterates that comprehensive knowledge of Nature's Laws has led more powerful technology with wider application. During the 19th century the knowledge of mechanical level of Nature's Laws led to industrial renaissance and knowledge of deeper level of electromagnetic has resulted in the electronic and Computer Technology of the 20th century. During the 21st Century the total potential of Cosmic Computer stands committed to human amity and safety and homosapiens are made to enter the Era of Creative Evolution. So the responsibility has been heavy on us to fashion a society geared to justice, freedom and happiness secured through social laws.

Here it should be borne in mind that trial and error method of mercantile enactment on papers only does not solve the baffling problems until renaissance in human thoughts and potentialities be ushered. So what we need, today, anything else is moral leadership based on enterprises, intellectual integrity, discipline and sense of mutual cooperation bristled in Oriental scriptures and axioms.

Chapter - 3

Micro-Metaphysical Feature & She-State

3(A) - Nature & Human Feature

Nature is the original source of serene world in which we survive. The whole atmosphere is ours. Men and women residing in India, Russia, America, Japan, China, England, Germany and the like breathe under the same Either regulated by God. Incense breathing Himalayan breeze and sea-wave are ours. God or the Almighty has endeavoured the living beings with Cosmic machinery to produce a sound within the living organism through inner vibration. The sound produced with this machinery is the Articulate One. Since God has chosen to settle with phonetic machinery in every image is the very height of prefection. Further Respiratory System proves that we breathe O2 (oxygen) and emit CO2 which is further inhaled by plants emitting O2 (oxygen) into the presence of chlorophyll. On the very such give-n-take relationship our great seers have advised to worship the plants to the extent of supposing to be 10 descendants in the "Matsyapurāna" –

दश कूप समा वापी दशवापीसमो ह्रदः
दशह्रद समः पुत्रः दशपुत्रसमो द्रुमः–52/53

Dasha kūpa samā vāpi dasha vāpi samo hardah
dashahrada samaḥ putraḥ dashadutrasamo drumaḥ.

10 wells resemble pond and 10 ponds resemble lake and 10 lakes resemble son and 10 sons resemble plant, plants excel sons. Because sons of the family care for their own and family. But plants care for the being within & outside the family. Further planting own tree in one's family is a wonderful and creative art of love for the mass better than a child of the family. If we cut plants, we do cut our children, as it were. A person is able to maintain homeostasis of the environment. He/she should execute plantation yojana (Yajna) to harbour birds and animals which help us to cleanse the climate as insecticides. That is why Scottish novelist & poet Robert Louis Stevenson advises – "Do not judge each day by the harvest you reap, but by the seeds that you plant".

Again the Rigveda speculates to shower the affluence of sweetness over living and non-living entities by the Nature –

मधुमतीरोषधीर्द्याव आपो मधुमन्नो भवत्वन्तरिक्षम्
क्षेत्रस्य पतिर्मधुमान्नोऽस्त्वरिष्यन्तोऽन्वेनं चरेम–4 / 8 / 97 / 3

Madhumatirosadherdyāvā Āpo Madhumanno bhavatwantariksham.
Kshetrasaya patirmadhumānnośitvarisyanton'venam charema.

The herbage be filled with the pleasing or sweet property, The Earth be filled with cereals. Rivers let flow sweeter fresh water, the Space let nourish Nature's phenomena with rains. The authority of the land be sweet or favourable. Thus we should be favourable and sweet to all, hurt none and favour all.

Such favourable identities with wild life were perceived by great poet Kalidas on the eve of Shakuntala's departure to her husband's abode.

उद्गलित दर्भकवला मृग्यः परित्यक्तनर्तनामयूराः
अपसृत पाण्डु पत्रा मुन्चन्त्यश्रूणीव लताः–4 / 12

Udgalita Darbhakavalā mṛgyah. parityaktanartnāmayurāḥ
Apsr.ta pāndu patrā muncantya śrooṇeeva latāḥ–4/12

Hinds have poured morsels of grass, pea –hen or peacocks have left dancing and creeps are let falling eye drops, as if, dropping off yellowish leaves. Here leaves have been personified as sisters. Further the wild life in general is grieved with pangs of her ceremonial departure to her husband's house. Here priyambadā speaks O dearest! you are not the only one to feel the biting of separation. As the time of separation for husband's house is approaching, the whole arbour seems to have share your anguish as the herd of deer has forgotten to browse, peacocks on the lawn have ceased dancing, the very trees around shed off their pale leaves like tears upon the ground.

We may come across many tales in the Panchatanra by Pt. Vishnu Sharma wherein trees or the like are projected to behave as human beings exposing their feelings and emotions. Because the Botanical kingdom is used to be vibrated with their chloroplast contained in protoplasmic cells (cells).

Again Shree Madbhāgavata purāna asserts to protect wild animals like our own sons-

मृगोष्ट्रखरमर्काखुसरीसृपखगमक्षिकाः
आत्मनः पुत्रवत् पश्येत्तैरेषामन्तरं कियत्–7/14/19

Mṛgos.trakharmarkākhusarisṛpkhagamakṣikaḥ
Ātmanah putravat paśyettaires.āmantaram kiyat–7/14/9

One should treat animals and birds such as deers, camels, asses, monkeys, mouses, snakes, birds and flies exactly like our own sons. the little difference lies among the children and these innocent animals. Here all animals have claim to be of God's property and let enjoy their offsprings and assets freely.

Again Nature's phenomena take care of the creations as token of benevolence and charity with suitable lessons-

पिबन्ति नद्यः स्वयमेव नाम्भः स्वयं न खादन्ति फलानि वृक्षाः
नादन्ति सस्यं खलु वारिवाहाः परोपकाराय सतां विभूतयः।

pibanti nadyaḥ swayameva nāmbhah swayam na khlādanti phallāni vṛkṣāḥ
nādanti sasyam khalu vārivāhaḥ parupkārāya satāmvibhutayaḥ

Rivers don't take water by themselves ,trees donot take their fruits by themselves, clouds donot devour cereals by themselves because the elite are prone to well –wishing temper or charity.

We are indebted to Nature to have accommodated all the creatures in her lap as they are skilled to do well within. They enjoy the beauties and sports of life in greeny and serene atmosphere. All are let engaged in their own likings. So many of our great personalities have emphasized to enjoy the restorative power of regular walk in woods .This life giving discipline never fails to yield a bounty of welcome results.

If you get tedious of trading and trying life, you should take in Nature's surroundings to receive solace and serenity as I feel–

"When I suffer from mental and physical fatigue
I sleep into the woods and pick up a chip of herd's hunt.
Like the little found forming its way through the lichened chinks,
I am also still and turn crystal cleaṛ"

Besides gentle rays of the morning The Sun give us a chance of new life.The young but long trees in woods soothe our physical and mental miseries by kissing the rising Sun.

English poet Thomas Gray has portrayed the springs of life regarding morning breeze. Wherein migrating bird's chirping, chit-chating and cock's high pitch sounding from their shelter are pictured lively-

"the breezy call of incense breathing morn,
the swallow twittering from the straw built shed,
the cock's shrill clarion or the echoing horn
no more shall rose them from their lovely bed.

Further Shakespearean lyrics suggested Duck's prefect delight and happiness which he has experienced in the stillness of the forest –

"Under the green wood tree
Who loves to lie with me
And tune his merry note
Unto the sweet bird's throat"

So Nature teaches us the lesson of benevolence suited to be a global citizen. Because it acts on without moving, it strives for the effortless, it enjoys simplicity in complexity and achieves geatness in little quantity.

Nature's phenomena teach good lessons as are dealt here elaborately-

1. **The Earth-** it does not lose patience and pardons even in excess hurricane.
2. **The Air-** It flows and goes to many places ,but does not imbibe the flaw of the objects .It carries bad smell or odor and still remains pure and healthy.
3. **The Ether-** The sky has one and integral entity in spite of being seen sundry due to checkered/chequered tendencies.

   Further the sky or the Brahma is omnipresent as the Self in all gross-subtle bodies. The Self is unbroken or in entirety as the threading of garland with crystal beads. It remains untouched with scared fire, scared water and scared cereals.
4. **Water-** It is pure, transparent, smooth and sweet. So we should be pure, sweet- tongued, smooth and holy.
5. **Fire-** It is lustrous and starry. It has no pot for accumulation or storage. It is disinfectant and disentangled with demerits despite engulfing all impurities. Here is to say that the person should be Pure, bright, vincible over senses, enjoyer of food stuff and possible affairs.It is seen long, breadth and curved or straight in

burning wood. But it is not in multiforms in reality. Likewise the all pervading Self is related to the vast paraphernalia of the world as sundry. The flames of the fire or the lamp continue to be high and low in moments and not perceived pertinently. likewise the physical entity of the jivas takes birth and decay by the dynamic Time as water waves. But we avoid such experience out of ignorance.

6. **The Sea-**ever open and deeprooted.Its nature, or thought, emotions is immense shoreless & fathomless. It is pacified within tides and waves. It doesnot diminish in winter and increase in summer i.e. it never gets overjoyed in wordly opulence nor gets paled in its negation.
7. **The Sun-** It draws water from the earth and rains on times. So a person should take up mundane affairs in the nick of time and discard or donate when the situation needs. The Self is like the Sun whose reflections are seen to be sundry in several pots of water due to discriminative entities, attributes and peculiarities.
8. **The Moon-**Its waning characters incurs mythical remarks of being indecent entity who was liberated from waning character physically in succesive fortnights (dark & bright). But the prowess and dignity of the moon is sanctified. All increasing and decreasing trends are attached to the body and not the Self.
9. **Deer-** It gets fascinated with songs of flowers and hunters. Sage Rishi Sring, born of the womb of hind turned into a puppet at the hands of the fair sex and mixed with her dancing and singing affairs. So be aware of fascinating agents lest we should ruin ourselves.
10. **Elephant-** It gets fastened in a ditch to copulate with she-elephant made up of wood and black paper putting within the ditch. So a person should not treat with fair sex as an ever organ of enjoyment inflicting termite-like damage to the physical body prematurely. So even gigantic stalwarts get ruined by the other fascinating agents out of greed.
11. **Python-** Ajgar-It is satisfied and not grieved with dried-rough-sweet-tasty-sour stuffs in a litle or a large quality for life's sustenance.
12. **Serpent-** The hermit should wander alone not in the company. He/She should depend on none and be laconic in speech. A serpent does not build houses for itself. The construction of high Tech Towers under amoral avarice is the morass of extravagance for decaying body.

13. **Pigeon (Columbidae)-**It does not dive deep into house holderness. It is honoured by many religions-Hindu, Islam, Christian and Sikhs .It has the ability to return to its home after flying to long distance. So we should maintain balance in our peaceful life and not fly as vulture.
14. **Fish-**It loses its life for the greed of pieces of flesh bored to fish –hook. Likewise the silly get overtaken or caught for self appeasement of fleshly appetite affecting life to premature death. So in order to be subduer of senses we have to subdue carnal flavour.
15. **The Bee-**Suck the essence of big and small flowers. So the intelligentsia should extract essence of all the discipiles,scriptures or works or treatises. The pious should not beg till the night and store for the next day.

    They might fall in trouble to collect cereals of the same householder till night as the bee happen to be decayed in distress to enjoy honey within the striking or closing tubular pollen of flowers at night. Secondly bees teach us the way of transformation and fertilization in bare need. They hover between the pollen and sweetest honey. They taste the nectar to feed on. They are optimistic to divine order of life in a peopled kingdom. They cooperate with their workers and male drones to defend homeland-a great lesson to mankind today. Their deep-black beauty imbued with intelligenc longs for the best endeavour in life.
16. **The prostitute or the whore** – They live on the thread of hope for the lewd to be entangled. Sometimes they get disappointed or sometimes they may enjoy appointment. Here acute expectations might have acute agony and self dependence does have encouraging and cheerful experience as the Shreesmadbhagāvada purana says–

    Expectation is extreme woe and frustration or nonexpectation is final felicity.

    आशा हि परमं दुःखं नैराश्यं परमं सुखम्–11/9/44

Āshā hi paramam duhkham nairashyam paramam sukham–11/9/44

17. **Moths or fireflies-**Moths or fireflies get attracted to light with their positive phototaxis and are burnt to death by kissing the glow of fire. A person defeated with sense organs get overwhelmed with glow of the fair sex causing decay as fireflies suffer deadly.

Now I have focused on valuable lessons by Nature's phenomena of which we are not keen to adopt them in our day to day life. We must be aware of the fact that we do learn more and more lessons suitable to human facility and fun of life from innumerable Nature's phenomena. As human beings are social animals first, they should mend social life before venture to earn livelihood in peace and prospect. It is easier to ponder over the characters of Nature's phenomena without any investment or coach. The above narration shows the affinity between the Nature and the Creature. So we should enjoy our global phenomena with friendliness and good hearts. So while breathing the air of the world we should assume that whole knowledge, principles, power, thruth, happiness, sorrows, doctrines, Krishna, Mohammad, Ram, Christ and Buddha and Sikh belong to ourselves. Because they are just like drops and waves of the ocean bearing the same potentiality wherein the same of the drops bear the potential ocean and the base of the waves be the infinite ocean. In this way we should take lesson from Nature's phenomena as teachers to improve human feature in friendship.

3(B) - Metaphysics and Monism

The Hindu mythology is cofronted with multi-theory of the Atma or the Self as called-

1. Ontology
2. Cosmology
3. Dipthology

As Physics, Chemistry, Biology and the like have no Hindu & Muslim editions, So the Metaphysical Science has no Muslim & Hindu notions. We have to revive global amity to avert human holocaust. The Hindus, the Muslims, the Christians, the Jews, the Buddhas, the Sikhs and the parsis – all class of cults of human folk of the universe have the same spiritual phenomenon within to let lead a peaceful and prosperous life under fostering care based on the Theory of Cosmology.

As the ideal mindset of our oriental precepts is based on Metaphysics, it's a device in which there is constant awareness of unity with the world covering all aspects of bio-life. Every relationship is guided by the recognition of oneness between the Self and the Universe.

Inner and outer chambers of life are united and as such anti human drives which people impose on one another cease to reoccur. These tenets are non- negotiable. They are both ethical and biological .They are ethical because experiences have shown that harmony leads to improve human to the state of fulfilment where the Self-call of the heart sends powerful vibration to the Cosmos and create a magnetic field to sustain cosmic harmony. Our oriental tenets are biological because experiences have shown that disharmony tends to stressing, straining, suffering and delay at all levels of human beings. Our ceaseless disharmony on the increase would surely lead to the vicissitude of mankind and perhaps of the planet. So, at present, internal Self- realization is the surest safeguard against the collapse of the living creature. Whereas the goal of life according to Lord Krishna – "the integration of the embodied consciousness of the individual with non- dualo-cosmic consciousness of the PARMĀTMĀ (The embodiment of the existence + wisdom + bliss = Sacchidanand). Here Sacchidanand's composition is being tried categorically as-

(a) Sat(existence) derived from the root "अस् भुवि" stands for the past, the present and the future continuation.

(b) Chit(Wisdom) derived from the root "चिति संज्ञाने" stands for universal consciousness & sub consciousness in all species.

(c) Anand(bliss) derives from the root "टुनादिसंमृद्धौ" stands for the glad giver for the pious. Thus I mean that ADHYĀTMAVĀDA helps to poise the two different aspects of life and the living. To its view, life is different from the living. Here life is like a flow of water incessantly moving towards its ultimate goal. Whereas living is the daily mundane section of one's life. Life does not depend merely on 'MATTER' and does not cling to the obscure presentation of mental "ACROBATICS". It has to cling thoroughly on CHETANĀ–SPIRIT. Without such Energy source life has to cease itself. Therefore life and spirit (The Self) are the most inseparable identities.

MATTER though belongs to material, cannot exist without SPIRIT. All the 5 senses, i.e. visuals, audible, olfactory, lingual and cutaneous cannot work at all without their Spark called SPIRIT. Hence the MATTER mismanaged by human being is an insult to the SPIRIT.

Therefore, spiritualism (ADHĀTMAVĀDA) strongly adheres to the balance of the MATTER, Intellect, Sense and SPIRIT. Any imbalance in them causes spiritual disturbance. For example, suppose I am having a lot of money and so I am having quite material amenities and comforts. But I often fail to take care of my precious ornaments, TV, cars, video and other sophisticated appliances. In due course they get disordered out of unmindfulness - here I am insulting the DIVINE SPARK that was instrumental in the invention of these sophisticated materials Without that DIVINE CHETNA(SPIRIT) into the minds of inventors, nothing so high and exalted materials could have been invented. Thus spiritual practices consist in the proper care and preservation of the material pieces. In addition to one's own body and senses the Self synthesizes external memory-experience and preservation of human body with inner personality, So Metaphysics plays vital- inevitable role in the richness of human being. Talking to inner strength of Indian mass, Economist John KEN GALBRAITH (CANADIAN-AMERICAN) observe "there is richness in the poverty, despite distress our inner strength which enables them to dignity and hold their heads - is the outcome of age-old tradition of spiritual excellences" With this very notion William Shakespeare opined- "sweet are the uses of adversity". To be more explicit ,human personality remains always in a state of flux. Nobody knows whether a man is strong or weak until and unless an occasion comes to test his/her strength of character. Virtues deserve to be called virtue only when they can resist and overcome temptations. Indeed, adversity alias adjustment with one's own circumstances is the best discovery of the virtues and charms in human beings. For example a man passes gold metal to the sufferings of fire to regain purity and charm in it. Likewise the bright and brilliant character of human beings focuses through the feel of adversity which corrects and checks them. Whereas self-centered prosperity discovers vices of avarice leading to mental agony and uneasiness. Thus we cannot ignore the fact that spiritual progress is bound up with material well being. That is "SWARNA PRABHA SUTRA" (Golden Light Sutra) a colonial work on Buddhism edited by Japanese prof. HOCKEY IZUMI advocates also – "spiritual life is rather the richness of abundance". The whole world is illumined with the only Self as "Bṛhdāranykopnishad" commands–

आत्मानैवायं ज्योतिषाऽऽस्ते

Ātmānaivāyam jyotis.āste

Again the Kathopnishad defines–

अंगुष्टमात्रः पुरुषो ज्योतिरिवाऽधूमकः
ईशानो भूतभव्यस्य स एवाऽद्य स उ श्वः एतद्वैतत्–2/1/13

Angus.thāmatrah purus.o jyotirivādhumakah.
Ishāno bhubhavyasya sa evādya s au shwah. etatdwetat–2/1/13

The Self or the Supreme Being (Puruṣa) seated in the heart lotus within thumb size (equal to 8 barley corn) is like the light being smokeless and darkless; and the inner controller of the past, present and the future under definite unvariation and constancy is called Brahma.

But I am not agreed to the conception of Kathopmishad regarding mass – magnitude (thumb size due to Its Light property).

The Brahma has varied synonyms due to its eternal flow such as- Our great philosophers and thinkers conform synonymous axioms in the following propositions-

1. The Rigveda (True vision of The Supreme Being)–Prajnānam Brahma (Super Wisdom) that super wisdom presents in the living and non-living body, the mind and the Self. Here प्रज्ञानम्" means–

   सुषुप्तावस्थायां आनन्दं उपभुज्य मानं चैतन्यम् प्रज्ञानम्

   Suṣuptāvasthāyāṃ ānandaṃ upbhujyamānaṃ caitanyaṃ–prajnānaṃ.

   Super wisdom tends to whole consciousness perceptible to the Super natural or divine object within living and non-living entitles. The Super wisdom is knowledgeable and beyond attainable by the understanding. It is crystal pure, intelligent emancipated from the bonds of the worldly existence and undecaying. We can attain salvation with meditation of its great lustrous feature. It is whole and all prevailing within which the creatures see, hear, smell, speak and have the experience of the taste-distaste.

   The Super Wisdom and the Brahma are synomonus to each other and Omni-present or all pervading in the Cosmos or the universe or the Space.

2. Such is the perception of the Hindu mythology also as depicted by Shree Madbhāgvatapuraṇa-

   ज्ञानं अनन्तं ब्रह्म (Jnānam Anantam Brahma)

   the Brahma or the Super Self is the Infinite Wisdom. Its axiom may be classified as the intrinsic properties of the Brahma ItSelf.

   1. The ocean of wisdom
   2. The ocean of bliss
   3. The ocean of love
   4. The ocean of peace

   Thus these 04 attributes fall under the substratum-The Wisdom or Consciousness

(a) In words of Udayanacharya in "Nyāyakasumānjal" there are 07 organic features in the Super Being such as –

Omniscience

Satiety

Eternal intelligence

Freedom of will

Independence

Power of manifestation

Infinite power

(b) In Yoga Philosophy it is defined as–

क्लेशकर्मविपाकाशैरपरामृष्ट पुरुष विशेषः

Kleśakarmvipākāśairaparā mṛṣta Puruṣa viśeṣaḥ

Detached with

(a) Nescience

(b) egoism

(c) passion

(d) grudge

(e) attachment

3. Yajurveda (vision of ceremonial rites)– अहं ब्रह्मास्मि "Aham brahmāsmi"

I am the Brahma-vision of the ceremonial rites-Bṛhdaranyakopniṣad–1/4/10

Here 'I' stands for Ātma (the Self) that pervades around the "Consciousness" in all beings and oversees the multi-verse as witness. Specially 'I' or 'the Self' within me is the eternal witness attributed to the Brahma who is anxious to get back his friends by virtue of KARMA account or KARMA DATA_BASE- .Such Sanskrit aphorism is the central essence of the Advait Philosophy which explains the unity of macrocosm & microcosm as the core of the whole Vedas for KAIVALYA_MOKSHA.

4. Sāmaveda – (vision of religious meditation) तत्त्वमसि "Tattwamasi" That thou art "here 03 words may be explained–

(a) तत् (Tat)– That Super Self

(b) त्वम् (Twam)– The Self within

(c) असि (Asi)– Art

Here identical equation between The Super Self and the Self within has been expressed.

Tenor–that'you' and 'I' become 'we-ness' averting polytheism & dipthesism to ascertain monistic view of the Self and Super Self being the same. This "Tattwamasi" Chhadogyopnisada" has classified in श्यामात् शबलं प्रपद्ये शबलात् श्यामं प्रपद्ये "Shymāta śabalam prapadye or śablāt śyman prapadye "the inner Self and the outer world are interdependent or integral.

5. Atharvaveda (proficiency in the worldly science)– अयमात्मा ब्रह्म Ayamātmā Brahma

   That the Self is the Brahma. Here O3 words may be explained.

   A. अयम् (Ayam) the person that you feel yourself

   B. आत्मा (Atma) the person whom the other person feel

   C. ब्रह्म (Brahma) the person that feels you really

Tenor- the Self works as the witness of the both the body and the mind-consciousness where our body works and the mind muses over under the witness of the Self.

Now **Upnishadic propositions-**

1. The Self prevading or conquering the universe. Chāndogyopniśad–

   सर्वं खल्विदम् ब्रह्मं–आत्मैवेदं सर्वम्–3 / 14 / 1

   sarvam+ khalvidaṃ brahmaṇ–ātmaivedaṃ sarvaṃ

2. The whole universe or the space is nothing but The Absolute-Mundopniṣad–

   ब्रह्मैवेदं सर्वम्

   bṛahmaivedaṃ sarvaṃ

3. The Self being the Brahma-Bṛhdaran-yakopnisada–

   आत्मैव ब्रह्म

   ātmaiva brahma–***

   Here the Brahma does not admit the existence other than the Atmā. The above theories proclaim that the human body is not the components of physique, sense-organs and the mind but the Body (Being) above birth and death geared to weal and woe cycle. So the human beings are seers and scenes of the universe mentally or spiritually.

4. The Bhagavadgeeta- with 700 verses within 18-chapter may be divided into O3 set of each 06 chapters explaining Vedic aphorism as-

   1. Ist set of 06 chapter explain– त्वम् (Thou the Self within)

2. 2nd set of 06 chapter explain– तत् (that the Supreme lord)
3. The 3rd set of 06 chapter explain– असि (art)

   The Soul + The Supreme soul = unified Soul of ecstasy through meditative measures under the course of cognition (Jnānamārga)

5. Brahmapurān(235/40/42) आनन्दं ब्रह्म (Ānandan Brahma)–

   The Brahma is Divine or Spiritual or Delight or Bliss ItSelf and not Delight in Brahma as needless to quote water (property) in the ocean.

6. The great sage Yāgyavalkya (precursor of Advait Philosophy) termed शिवोऽहम् (Shivo'ham) "I am the blessed Self". All have the true Self within identified with Super Self pervading the Cosmos.

   Now The Kathopanishada (1:2:8) & Mundkopnishad (2:4:14) under micro-macrocosmic study of the Self reveals that it is just like the Atom being the prima potency & cosmic consciousness which is the ultimate indivisible particle of the world or the ultimate state of the manifest universe akin to modern Science of Atomism. Here the Atomic feature of the Self and the Brahma has cognate character as fire with flame or heat with temperature.

Now the subtler study of the Atma or the Brahma

The Brahma sutra –starts with query अथातो ब्रह्म जिज्ञासां (athāto Brahma Jijnāsā)–1/1/1

Here "Athato" Opines the extinction of physical, mental and prudential errors or mistakes before quest for the Brahma. On subduing the flaw of reflections one may visualize Atma by virtue of sravana (hearing) Manana (meditation) Nidhidhyāsana (practice of incessant meditation with mind or Purification in all aspects is essential to realize the Self).King Bhartrihari in Vākyapadiya proclaims-

कायवाग्बुद्धि विषया ये मलाः समवस्थिति.........

Kayabāgbuddhivis.ayā ye malāh. samvasthiti........

Human beings suffer with physical, languaging, mental flaws or pollutions which can be kept off through O3 devices-

1. Physical impurities –with stars gems and pharmacology
2. Decisive impurities–due to passion and emotion with Metaphysical Science
3. Flaws of language –Communication of words or sentences with grammatology

In guiltless gaiety I should step forward to inquire about the Ultimate Truth i.e. the Brahma alias Atma the root base of all the disciplines and knowledge.

Such inquiry causes upheaval in physical and metaphysical field. there are tri-system or prasthān to realize the Brahma

(a) Nyayaprasthān (hearing) that which represents philosophical or vedantic thoughts through hearing

(b) Srutiprasthān (Meditation) through being heard

(c) Smr.tiprasthān (incessant meditation with condensed mind-practice through being remembered

These tri systems are illustrated by the Vedanta, the Sruti and the Smriti by Adishankarāchārya Rāmānujāchārya Nimbārkāchārya and Ballabhāchārya. Now let me dive deep into the perception of The Self or the Brahma as in The Brahmasutra-

(a) Gross perception–Cerealness which is produced to bring up the body and lastly transformed or terminnated into one of these –05 Matter or Substance.

(b) Subtle perception- Life Energiness–one living being gives birth to another living being. All senses work due to life-energy and at last the life-air flies away into the Space .

(c) Subtler perception–Mindness being the control of senses. A living entity through biological drops gets impregnated in mother's womb with one's mental momentum.

Because the mind inspires our senses with eyes, nose, skin, tongue and impregnation.

(d) Subtlest perception–Spiritual Consciousness as the Enlightened Self. A body cannot survive without the Self i.e. blissful in the innermost vesture of the body.

Great scholar Pt. Vachaspati Mishra of "Mithla" paraphraser of hexa-philosophy wrote "Bhāmati" sub-commentary on "Brahmasutra–Shankar-Bhāsya." Wherein he also affirms the philosophy of the Self, being the Brahma based on fire and flames or part-share by share-relationship as heat and temperature. The perception or wisdom or cognition or the enlightened Self controls–

A. Krodha(Anger)-through the mind

B. Spr.hā (Lust)-through desires

C. Manvachan (Mind + Speech) through conduct to protect sublimity

D. Bhaya (Fear) through constant vigilance to shed off

E. Abhimān (Vanity) through wise service to control over

In this way the perception of the Self paves bypass way to fly over the ocean of worldly existence or life before total ruin or decay as affirmed in Kathopnishad.

इह चेदशकद् बोद्धुं प्राक् शरीरस्य विस्रसः
ततः सर्गेषु लोकेषु शरीरत्वाय कल्पते–2/3/4

Ih cedaśakar boddhum prak śarirasya visrasaḥ
tataḥ sargeṣu loke ṣu śariratwāya kalpate–2/3/4

Again the "Barhmasutra" also affirms the only upward motion of the Self or Life Energy with mega potentiality–2/3/4

Whereas the 05 primary or Great Elements have downward as well as upward motion.

Here the living Force or the Self is eternal as air within and outside or without the body. When the external covering (material body) is decayed the living spark like the Air within the body continues to adjust by the direction of Lord and the living entity is at once granted the spiritual body with Lord in the manner of

(a) Equal bodily features (sārupya)

(b) Equal facility to live on the same planet (Sālokya)

(c) Equal possession of opulence (Sṛiṣti)

(d) Equal affinity with the Lord (Sāmarthya)

It should be borne in mind that the living entity is not the body but separate as driver (Atma) who knows the assembling process of the parts of the body (the senses, the mind and qualities of material modes). Further Atma is spiritual ignition or sparking as part and parcel of the Super Self. We are unknown or careless under the spell of illusionary Energy in the morass of the mortal planet. The light or the Atma does not off only the material body turns into complete ruin. More clearly I mean the Atma or the Self as chip and the Super Self or Consciousness as CCTV to witness and supervise the Karmdātā of the living beings.

(A) The nature of the Self

It is non-chemical and immaterial having O3 immaterial components (the mind, the wisdom and the impression) opposed to the heart, being organ of the body. Wherein the mind commits among tri-mental hedges (good, bad & worse). The wisdom contemplates in tri-dimensions and the impressions ever-change with material and immaterial tracks or trainings. The Self riding and driving the body – chariot is the receiver of impressions or operations. Its habitat centre is the Great Matter within which internal Light sparkles through consecrated meditation.

(B) The state of the Self

Māṇdukyopanishad states–

(a) The Self or the Brahma-being universal consciousness is related to gross body at awakening state.

(b) The Self or the Brahma-being consciousness is related to subtle body at dreaming state.

(c) The Self or the Brahma being super consciousness is related to causal body at deep dream state.

(d) The Self or the Brahma being supreme consciousness is related to immaterial or transcendental spirit at ethereal or radioactive state.

Such abiotic amplification to salvation is possible by human being having 5 cocoons

(a) Cerealness

(b) Energiness

(c) Mindness

(d) Wisdomness

(e) Blissfulness

Concerned with

(a) Udbhija (cerealness)

(b) Swedaja (cerealness + life energiness)

(c) Andaja (cerealness + life energiness + mindness)

(d) Jarāyuj (cerealness + lifeness + mindness + wisdomness)

(e) Blissfulness (abstract experience possible to all Jivas)

(c) The property of the Self

According to Kathopnishad

अशब्दमस्पर्शमरूपमव्ययं तथाऽरसं नित्यमगन्धवच्च यत्
अनाद्यनन्तं महतः परं ध्रुवं निचाय्य तंमृत्युमुखात्प्रमुच्यते–01 / 3 / 15

Ashabdamasparśampupamavyyaṃ tathārasaṃ nityamagandhavacca yat
Anāndyanantam nahataḥ param dhruvam nicāyya tanmṛtyumukhātpramu cyate–1/3/15

1. The Self is Ashabda (not audible with ear organs or indescribable)
2. The Self is Asparsa (not known with skin touch or untouchable)
3. The Self is Arupam (cannot be seen with outer eyes or incorporeal)
4. The Self is Avyayama (unwasted, imperishable, and eternal)
5. The Self Arasam (insensible to taste)

6. The Self-Nitayan (constant or everlasting or not perishable at the death of the living being
7. The Self-Agandhavah (unsmellt with nose organs)
8. The Self-Anādya (eternal)
9. The Self-Mahatahparana (the Supreme Self or The utmost Holy)
10. The Self-is dhruvarn (unchangeable or uniformable or constant)

And takes off from death–mouth invariably. In this way the Self is the Absolute Brahma as liberal beyond mundane weals and woes.

Here according to Neo-logician (Udayanācārya of Mithila) –there are 09 abstract features applicable to the Supreme Being as depicted in "Nyāyakusumangali"–

1. Omni-associate
2. Omnipresent
3. Omniscient
4. Saturated state
5. Eternal Intelligence
6. Independency
7. Undecaying power or ever performing
8. Infinite potency
9. Omnicontroller of ever action in nuclear motion

Again "Āpastambadharmasutra"

सर्वभूतेषु यो नित्यो विपश्चिदमृतो ध्रुवः
अनंगोऽशब्दोऽशरीरोऽस्पर्शश्च महाच्छुचिः
स सर्व परमाकाष्ठा स वैषुवतं स वै भाजनं पुरम्–1/8/22/7

Sarvabhuteṣu yonity o vipaścidmṛto dhruvah.
anango'śabdo'sariro'sparśa sca mahacchucih.
sa sarvam parmakastha sa vais.uvatam sa vaibhajanam puram–1/8/22/7

Here Eleven properties of the Self have been deciphered-

1. Constant – not perishable in all states
2. Endowed with wise consciousness
3. Nectar of immortality (un-decaying character)
4. Uniformable
5. Non-organic
6. Indescribale
7. Untouchable

8. Incorporeal
9. The utmost Holy
10. The highest extremity
11. The Supreme Spirit as Vaisuvat in samvatsar (year).

Here the super-excellent properties of the Self have been exposed .

(b) The vision of the Self

Now the "Kathopanishad alludes-

एष सर्वेषु भूतेषु गुढोऽऽत्मा न प्रकाशते
दृश्यते त्वग्रय्या (त्वग्रमिवाग्रया) बुद्धया सूक्ष्मया सूक्ष्मदर्शिभिः–1/3/12

Eṣa sarves.u bhuteṣu gudhoaatma na prakaśate
drśyate twagrayyā (twagrmivāgrayā) buddhyā sukṣmaya suks. madarśibhiḥ–1/3/12

The secret Self or the Super Self is not visualized by all beings, it may be visualized by sharp or micro-sighted being with mental acumen.

Besides, Yāgyavalkya explains in Bṛahadaryakopnishad–

आत्मा वा अरे द्रष्टव्यः श्रोतव्यो मन्तव्यो निदिध्यासितव्यः–4/5/6/15

Atmāvā are drstavyaḥ srothyo mantrvyo nididyāsitavyaḥ.

The purport is to be visualized or experienced directly through the process of audio–debate charged with inner reflection and constant meditation. This is verily the achievement of immortality or cease-pain. This pristine proclamation of Yāgyavalkya is the fons et origo of all schools of Indian Philosophy. It is the ultimate base upon which the edifice of philosophical intelligence of India has been built. It is worthy of note that his spouse "Maitrey" chose the life of reclusion on such typical message of Yāgyavalkya to obtain Bliss. The immedediate realization of the fair and flawless Self culminates into the final cessation of pains of human life- is the ipse dixit of Yāgyavalkya.

(c) The conservation of the Self

The Geeta says–

देही नित्यमवध्योऽयं देहे सर्वस्य भारत
तस्मात्सर्वाणि भूतानि न त्वं शोचितुमर्हसि–2/30

Dehi nityamavaddhyo yamdehe sarvasya bhārat
Tasmātsarvāni bhutāni na tvam sochitumarhasi. 2/30

The Self remains inviolable. So any lamentation and infatuation are not needed for the whole beings.

Again the Geeta says-

नैनं छिन्दन्ति शस्त्राणि नैनं दहति पावकः
द चैनं क्लेदयन्त्यापो न शोषयति मारूतः–2/23/

Nainam chhidanti śastrāni nainam dahati pāwakaḥ
Na cainam kledayantyāpo na śoṣyati mārutaḥ–2/23

Weapons cannot cut it, fire cannot burn it, water cannot swallow it and air cannot dry it away.

Because the Geeta says again-

अच्छेद्योऽयमदाह्योऽयमक्लेद्योऽशोष्य एव च
नित्यः सर्वगतः स्थाणुरचलोऽयं सनातनः–2/24

Achhedyo'yamadāhyo' yamkledyo'so s.ya eva ca
nityaḥ sarvagataḥ sthān.uracaloyam sanātanaḥ

Since the Self is un-performable, un-burnable, un-swallow-able and un-dryable. The Self is constant, omnipresent, static and eternal

Again the Geeta says-

न जायते म्रियते वा कदाचिन्नायं भूत्वा भविता वा न भूयः
अजो नित्यः शाश्वतोऽयं पुराणो न हन्यते हन्यमाने शरीरे–2/20

Na jāyate mriyate vā kadācinnāyam bhutvā bhavitā vā na bhuyah.
Ajonityaḥ śāśvato'yam puran.o na hanyte hanymāne śarire–2/20

The Self never borns, dies and is not emerge-able nor being nascent.

Since, it is unborn, constant, eternal and primeval. It does not die on the death or demise of the body. Only the body is ruined and not the Soul.

The same conception of the Geeta has been supported in Kathopnishad (Krishna Yagurveda)

न जायते म्रियते वा विपश्चिन्नायं कुतश्चिन्नायं बभूव कश्चित्
अजो नित्यः शाश्वतोऽयं पुराणो न हन्यते हन्यमाने शरीरे–0/2/18

Na jāyate mriyate vā vipaśinnāyam kutaścinnāyam babhuva kaścit
Ajo nityaḥ śāśwatoyam purāṇo na hanyte hanyāmane sarire–0/2/18

The enlightened Self does not born nor dies. It does not emerge out and not cause to bring forth. This Self is unborn, constant and void of wane –gain.

Thus the Upnishadic discourse on the revelation of the Self, as an abode of bliss, is neither born nor does it die.

It is primal Puruṣa, un-decaying, ever-young, un-dying or immortal, nectar of immortality and fearlessness.

Like The Atomic Theory of conservation. The Atma has been deciphered in The Geeta- Cream of Upanishads.

Also British theologian and preacher of Biblical message –Peter Lewis has affirmed the soveriegnty of the Almighty to treat the world of God around the law of Conservation of the Self.

(d) The sanctity of the Self

Now it poses another question as to how does the eternal, pure and universal Self abiding in impure and finite creature enshrines its sanctity and perfection. To me the only sun is the cause of the vision of everybody's eyes and the focus of the sunlight does not imbibe the flaws of the eyes. Further everybody looks yellow to jaundiced eyes. Here the yellowish vision of the individual falls flat on the purity and sanctity of the sunlight. So the immaculate Self abiding in creature does not imbibe the flaws of the flesh as the "Brahma sutra" advocates-

प्रकाशादिवन्नैवं परः–2/3/43

Prakāśādivannaivam paraḥ–2/3/43

As the sunlight and the like, so the Supreme Being or the Brahma is uncontaminated with flaws of the flesh of the jivas.

According to the Bible-God is the Supreme light as lit-up candle in the church. Out of 15-point of Ethics of the Chinese preacher Confucius-in the 09th century- reads as- "human soul is just like a mirror, because the mirror does not imbibe or retain any impression of the different objects focused on it. Further it maintains its stainlessness as it is."

Besides, the Self does not imbibe the flaws of the universe. So it is out of worldly flaws while living in the world. Just as water drops do not suffer sticky flaws of leaves of lotus rather roll on them. Its scientific reason is the natural anointing of wax like chemical which prevents drop breaks as physical cause of their hinder or back tension.

(e) The exclusive excellence of the Self

After interpreting the sanctity, infinity and integrity of the Self now the Supremacy of the Self having exclusive excellence is quoted in The Geeta–

इन्द्रियाणि पराण्याहुरिन्द्रियेभ्यः परं मनः
मनसस्तु परा बुद्धिर्योबुद्धेः परतस्तु सः–3/42

Indriyāni parānyāhurindriyebhyaḥ param manaḥ
Nasastu parā buddhiryo bhddheḥ partastu saḥ–3/42

The 05 senses are superior or subtler to corporeal body, the mind is superior to those senses, the intellect is superior to the mind and this Self is superior to the Intellect. Further it never gets contaminated as The Sun, being the universal eye-sight, is unstained with outward ophthalmic flaws.

Kathopnishad adds the same view on the supremacy of the Self-

इन्द्रियेभ्यः पराह्यर्था अर्थेभ्यश्च परं मनः
मनसश्च परा बुद्धिर्बुद्धेरात्मा महान् परः–1/3/10

Indryebhyaḥ parāhyapthu athebhyaśca param manaḥ
Mansasca parā buddhirbuddherātmā mahān paraḥ–1/3/10

Monism

Oriental Great poet and Vedantist Shreeharṣa in his book "Khadanakhanda khādaya (खण्डनखण्डखाद्य)" on Advait Philosophy has asserted the axiom of non-dualism disapproving the Nyāya school of the notion of Causality. He was influenced with doctrine of Nihilism or non-existence of Nāgārjuna(Buddhist). According to Philosopher S. Radhakrishnan on Indian philosophy Vol-1 – "The Brahma and the Atma, the cosmic and the psychic principles are looked upon as identical i.e. the Brahma is the Atman.

Western Philosopher like Pluto and G.W.F. Hegel have not differentiated between the subjective and objective thoughts.

The Sufi cult (Persian) also conforms the Vedantic Philosophy of the Absolute Monotheism. Like Indian Bhakti culture Sufis adopted their own track of philosophical speculation between Him and His creation.

An American philosopher, Ralph Waldo Emerson who led the transcendental movements in the mid 19th century was impressed with the speculation of the Advait Philosophy, the Geeta and the Kathopnishad and composed the poem "Brahma" with Metaphysical approach to the Ultimate Reality in the cosmic principle-Monism. Such approach is the single binding unity against adversity. The Brahma is identical to the Self which is divine spark, eternal, everlasting, never ending (Atma) omnipresent, omniscient and omnipotent. The Self or The Brahma is qualified as satchitāanand (truth-consciousness –bliss). The Brahma is both far and near, remembered and forgotten, shadow and sunlight, vanished and appeared, shame and fame.

In the realm of pure Consciousness there is no state of duality. At the deepest or the ultimate level one transcends duality of thoughts waving in ones mind. Inside each living being there is the existence of mutual connation in spiritual oneness as the 2nd stanza of the poem "Brahma" speaks-

Far and forgot to me is near.
Shadow and sunlight are the same.
The vanished Gods to me appear.
And one to me are shame and fame.

Here the Advait Vedanta advocates the validity of all the disciplines of human expression on the pleas of-

(a) Workmanship (Karmayoga)

(b) Devotional path (Bhakti mārg)

(c) Wisdom channel (Jnāna mārg)

Which ultimately lead towards the realization of the non-dual Brahma. Therefore the Vedant intends oneness with each and every entity in the spiritual context. It fosters the ultimate ideal of democracy i.e. unity in adversity.

But the philosophy of (Achintyābhedābheda)-inconceivable differences, non-differences (oneness) proposition of Caitanya Mahāprabhu proposes – a logical inconsistency between the seer and the seen, the complete whole and its part to thwart the monistic view of the Self and the Super Self (The Brahma). But the underlying enlightenment ratifies the oneness of the quintessence simultaneously and not two entities as the ShankarVedānta asserts-

नित्य शुद्धाविमुक्तैकऽखण्डानन्दमद्वयम्
सत्यं ज्ञानमनन्तं यत्परं ब्रह्माहमेव तत्–36

Nityam Suddhāvimuktaik Khandānandmadwayaṃ
satyam jnānamantaṃ yatparaṃ Brahmāhamevatat

- The Supreme Brahma is eternal, pure, fully liberated, oneness, unbroken bliss, non-dual and the truth-wisdom-infinite.

Thus a close investigation reveals that both Upnisadic Brahmvāda and Buddhistic Vijnānvāda are interconnected system of thoughts.

We are non-dual in sentiment also. If we play on the Piano near any quasi –instrument. We find the untouched quasi-instrument is let waved by the musical vibration caused with the piano played on.

In drama the spectator imbibe the same tragic or comic sentiments displayed by the dramatis personae. Thus we are all united psychologically and spiritually by virtue of Telergy. These illustrations advocate that all the creatures (jivas) are one in the Eternal One and whoever kills the creature hurts the eternal heart. It is owing to the fact that the essential requirements of mortal existence are not dissimilar even if we move around the world. Among such optimist Pt. Nehru (Ex P.M. of India) while referring to the wide ranging talk on universal approach to "one world" said-"such concept must bear fruits or else this would go the pieces."

This concept of oneness in the world was also propagated by American preacher Wendell Wilkins, while convening theme on" Religious Liberty

in the workplace "in 2018 asserted- a world Govt. must and will come because there is no another remedy for global ailments, after all there is basic unity that runs through all human societies."

So at the sea base-observation of all the modes of expressions we find the same innate, property to be called a global identity citizen. Wherein we are of the universe and the universe is ours.

Moods or thoughts or reflections or discernments or decisions or determinations or circumspections void of space and motion evolve immaterial intent in Nature and not chemical object. Further it is distinct from time, place, space, gravitational and photo-natural energy which are material objects. Such reflection of the mind is adjusted or harmonized with cerebral hemisphere to express global feelings in consciousness being incorporeal in nature. Such incorporeal consciousness dwells in all living entities of the world irrespective of caste, creed, sex and nativity. We on the globe are fraternal with one another. Physically we are the hetro-offsprings of our parents. But spiritually we all are the offsprings of the same Supreme Being. Such cosmopolitan spirit causes simplicity, satisfaction, soundness, softness, sympathy, submission and sentiment to lead a life of peace and prosperity. In this way we should behave with fraternity and kick off colour contest, lingual contest, land contest, sovereign-contest and the like. So lastly shed hatred and not blood for global bloom – "Vasudhaiva Katumbakam". On the other hand the skimmed intellectuals mistake metaphysics for inability to solve mundane problems of bio – beings. But they should be aware of the fact that metaphysical devices play vital role to suppress fissiparous drives imposing grave threat to mankind. History reiterates that whenever the curse of problems on national or international. level occurred, Material science could not furnish a readymade solution in the short span of its operation. Since no chemical or physical contrivances can indicate as to how much, O2, CO2, H2, atom, electron and blood cells are needed to enlighten our inner human (personality) which is just a lighting force for the universe. It is the spiritual integration or emotional urges which could be helpful to solve those problems with the passage of time. That is why spiritual leaders of the world paraded the domain with flying colours and preached the policy of cosmopolitics by virtue of their illuminative knowledge on philosophical polemics. Now it has been quite evident that Metaphysics is a dynamic force expressing ItSelf as a ceaseless efforts towards the acme of integration of the embodied soul with mono-cosmic-Consciousness. Bliss lies in the spirit or soul and not in the material indulgence. In common partance it transforms our life and civilization on the earth into high pedestal of felicity, congruity, development and tranquility. Further its illustrations are based on human doctrine – that the happiness is the only good, justice is the only worship, humanity is the only religion and love is the only priest.

Metaphysics is the best key to achieve eternal bliss free from weal and woes of life. Further human beings are the only source to avail such felicity of life. So do not miss for the privilege of the salvation within human life full of weal and woes.

We are the masterpiece of Nature's creation. That is why Indian new logicianGadādhar Bhattacharya has initiated with "अखंडानन्द बोधाय" in his Didhiti treatise with spiritual intelligence because–

"ऋते ज्ञानान्न मोक्षः"

Ṛte jnānānna mokṣaḥ.

Here it is the fitness of thing to clarify that woes or sufferings in our human life consist of O3 types which engulf our righteousness and corrupt our nature utterly such as-

1. Inevitable or accidental reaction of the Nature i.e. cold, hot, rains, earthquake etc.
2. Material or physical inquiries or harms due to men, animals, birds, lions, mosquitos and other beasts or jivas.
3. Self impurities due to negative nature (anger, lust, disease and pains of sense organs.

Further "Yogadarsan" of Patanjali states of O3 types of suffering also–

1. Consequential (Parinām) any effortful activity to feel joy insantly. the result is nothing but damage to the doer in terms of loss of the stamina and memory in cohabitation.
2. Tormental (Tap)-insatiable enjoyment and envied inflammation comparatively.
3. Conceptual (Sanskār) The enjoyment reposed in the hearts gets deserted but remains of memory are left only in terms of wife, son, assets or apartments etc.

Thus we may conclude that we do feel anxiety while enjoying due to simultaneity of the tri-components of the Nature (Sat, Raj & Tam)

While listening to the discourses on Sattva property we get disturbed with worldy or weary load. In order to erase such woes "Yogadarshan" of sage Patanjali formulates–

हेयं दुःखमनागतम्

Heyaṃ Duhkhamanagataṃ–2/6

That is to say that woes and pains in the past life have gone away and those of the present life are going away. But the sufferings in future are to be liberated by untying the knot between the embodied Self and the Supreme Self in the next perspective. Because the Absolute being, being abstained from woes, is the realm of salvation or bliss or contentment as is dealt successively-

(a) Nāyāyasutra of sage Gautam

तदत्यन्तविमाक्षोऽपवर्गतः–1/1/22

Tadatyantavinokṣopavargah.

The absolute abstinence from grieves is called salvation.

(b) "Yogavāsistha" of Maharshi Vālmiki (Mumuksha Vyavahārchapter)

संतोषः परमोलाभः सत्सङ्गः परमागतिः
विचारः परमं ज्ञानं शमो हि परमं सुखम्–16/19

Santosah parmolābhaḥ, satsangaḥ paramāgatiḥ
vichāraḥ paramam jnānam śamo hi paramam Sukhaṃ?

Contentment is the highest benefit, good accompaniment is the highest resort or shelter, Self thought (circumspection) is the highest wisdom and satiety is the highest bliss

3(C) - Phonetics & Aum photon

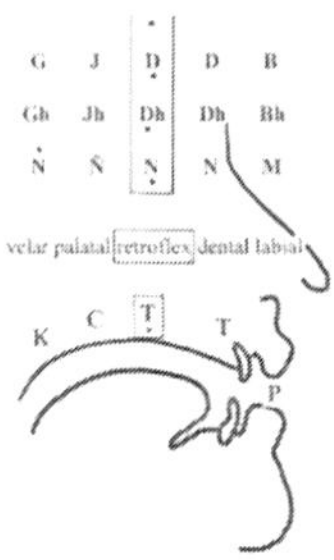

Phonetics is the scientific study of sounds of the human speech. The study of the sounds (Shabda) begins with properties of sound waves in O2 types

1. transverse

2. longitudal

Normally longitudal waves frequently ranges 20 HZ to 20000 HZ of human beings. This is differentiated by the way in which waves are propagated. Further it is the branch of linguistics that examines the languages silent or have multiple pronunciations.

The 1st phonetic examination occurred in 500 BC in ancient India. It is a vocal sound from phonates or phonautagraph of verbal adjective of phoneme (set of smallest unit of speech that distinguishes one syllabic sound from the other) or abstract cognitive unit. This voice gram or phoneme is the least part to differentiate speech sound as

क (Ka)

म (Ma)

च (Ca)

प (Pa) and etc.

This is the psychogramic process in which each sound falls under each phoneme due to vowels and side sounds. This phoneme tends to differ in between the similarity of the place and manners such as

प (Pa)- not vibrated

'व' (Va)- slightly vibrated

फ (Pha)-frictional bottom lip into contact or near contact with upper teeth.

Segmental phonemes of the skt. Vowels are

	Forepart	**Middle**	**Back**
High	इ (i)	ऋ (ṛ)	उ (u)
Middle	ए (e)	-	अ (A) ओ (O)
Low	ऐ (ai)	-	औ (ou)

Pure vowels according to Pānini octavo-chapter-(A, I, u)–अ, इ, उ

Phonetics has O3 branches–

1. Articulatory phonetics–to study the production of speech sound.
2. Acoustic transmission–to study the transmission of sounds between speaker and listener.
3. Auditive perception of sounds- to examine as to how sounds are perceived by the listener

Now the sounds of human speech are very complex. All small and big organs of our vocal cavity are mechanized to utter phonemes that distinguish one syllable from the other with the loco biological organs seated in Maheshwar Sutram of Pānini Vyākarana.

These phonemes or abstract cognitive units, observe or record the simplest phenomena of language and receive knowledge from verbal testimony. Our vocal cavity works as a piston which moves back and forth under compression and rarefaction due to high and low density of the region. This disturbance from the different seats of alphabet (Skt. Grammar) travels within vocal cavity to produce longitudal sound-wave; and ears detect wave- vibrations of such a small amplitude(vocal cavity)

When one utters a mixture of sound wave length (syllable) it exerts positive interference through potential vibration to the listener.

Firstly the divine feature of sounds was generated by Lord Shiva who echoed 14 times with a double drum to redeem the will of ascetical society and adjuged aphoristic collection of each individual sound of human speech at the end of dancing-

नृत्यावसाने नटराजराजो ननाद ढक्कां नवपञ्चवारम्
उद्धर्तुकामः सनकादिसिद्धानेतद्विमर्शो शिवसूत्रजालम्

Nṛtyāvasane Natarājārajo Nanād Dhakkām Navapanchavāram
Uddhartukāmaḥ Sankādisiddhānetadvimarśo Shivasutrajālaṃ

The 14 times stand for 14 planets in the vast universe echoed with–

अइउण्, ऋलृक्, एओङ, ऐऔच्, हयवरट्, लण्
ञमङणनम्, झभञ् घढधष्, जबगडदश्
खफछठथचटतव्, कपय्, शषसर्, हल्–14

Here I want to point out that these imperishable syllables are not merely monosyllabic symbols of sound but signify poly connotations with multi effects as in "Ekākshari Kosa" of Purushottamdeo-

अकारो वासुदेवः स्यादाकारस्तु पितामहः
पूजायां चापि माङ्गल्ये आकारः परिकीर्तितः–01
इकार उच्चते कामो लक्ष्मीरीकार उच्चते
उकार शंकरः प्रोक्तः ऊकारश्चापि लक्षणम्–02

Akāro vāsudeoh syādākārastu pitāmaḥ
Pujāyām cāpi māngalyo ākārah parikirtitaḥ–01
Ikār ucyate kāmo Laxmireekār ucyate
Ukāra sankaraḥ proktaḥ ookārascāpi Laxanaṃ-02

or

कश्चात्मनि मयूरे च कः प्रकाशः उदाहृतः
कं शिरो जलमाख्यातं कं सुखं च प्रकीर्तितम्–07
पृथिव्यां कुः समाख्यातः कुः पापोऽपि प्रकीर्तितः
खमिन्द्रिये खमाकाशे खः स्वर्गेऽपि प्रकीर्तितः–08

Kascātmani Mayureca Kah prakashaḥ Udāhrtaḥ
Kam Shiro Jalmakhyātaṃ Kaṃ Sukham ca prakirtitam-7

Prthivyām Kuḥ Samākhyātaḥ Kuḥ pāpo 'pi' prakirtitḥ
Khamindriy Khamākāsh Khaḥ swarge 'p' prakirititaḥ-8

Now in Shree Madabhāgvatapurāna-

रपर्शरतस्याभवज्जीव स्वरो देह उदाहृतः
उष्माणमिन्द्रियाण्याहुरन्तःस्था बलमात्मनः–3/12/46
स्वारा सप्त विहारेण भवन्तिस्म प्रजापतेः–3/12/47
Sparśastsyābhavajjivaḥ swarodeh udāhṛtaḥ
uśmāṇamindriyānyāhurantaḥsthā balmātmanaḥ–3/12/46
Swarāsapt vihāreṇa bhavantisma prajāpate–3/12/47

Further Lord Brahma's own Embodiment was expressed or manifested as-

tangible consonans of 05 class alphabet-	25
His Body manifested as vowels----	13
His senses are sibilant alphabets----	04
His energy as intermediate alphabets---	04
Total-----	46

In other words His pursuits of pleasure in garden of music as classified

Vowels----	13	13	
Tangible consants –	25	25	33 Consonants
Intermediate----	4	04	
Sibilant-----	4	4	
Nasal sound marked by dot (.)		01	not included but treated as alphabets.
A mark by 02 perpendicular dots (:)		01	
Representing hard aspiration-------		48 total	
Whereas traditional lessons----		46	
Comprehensive lessons---		48	
Pānini Shiksha (Euphonic) lesson –		60	

So the syllabic diversity is illustrated here.

Now let me narrate the vast feature of verbal sound reposed in the Ether out of 05 primordial masses in Charaka Samhita-

महाभूतानि खं वायुरग्निरापः क्षितिस्तथा
शब्द स्पर्शश्च रूपं च रस गन्धाश्च तद्गुणाः–1/26
Mahābhutāni kham vāyuragnirāpaḥ ksitistathā
Sabda sparśsca rupam ca rasa gandhāśca tadguṇāḥ–1/26

In "Tarkasangraha" of Annam Bhatta (pratyaksakhanda)

शब्द गुणकमाकाशं–शब्दगुणकमिति / गुणपदमा–
काशे शब्द एव विशेषण इति द्योतनाय न तु अतिव्याप्ति वारणाय।
śabda guṇakamākāśam–Sabdaguṇakā miti/gunapadamā–
kaśe śabda eva viśe ṣaṇa iti dyotanāya na tu ativyapti vārṇāya

Thus the sound is the property of the Ether and the sky is the subtratrum of the property "sound" and is produced with other elements & instruments. Where the 1st H(ह) and the 2nd H(ह) is hard and soft sound of the cloud (Ether) respectively in Maheśhwar Sutra of Achārya Pāṇini. So when we utter syllabic sounds consecutively, the prior gets adjoined or settled in the Ether. But their essential nature of vibrating sounds settled in the Ether generate impression to let connect with the last syllable of word or sentence through the Theory of Sphotvāda(Sproutism or articulatism) propagated by Skt. Grammarians on the foot of "SABDA BRAHMA".

Further the word "sphot" means that which sprouts up senses or meaning.

Here it is pertinent to note the Sphot formula of Archarya Mammat of Kashmir (India) in "Kāvyaprakash"-

बुधैव्याकाणैः प्रधानभूतस्फोटरूप व्यंग्यव्यञ्जकस्य
शब्दस्य ध्वनिरिति व्यवहारकृतः
Budhaivyākarnai pradhānbhutas photrupa vyangyo
vyanjakasya śabdasya dhwanirity vyavāharkṛtaḥ

"The learned grammarians used the sound of word by suggesting of suggested sense in the form of 'sphot' mainly. Acharya Anāndvardhan 's Theory of "Resonance" or "sound" (Dhwani siddhānt) in "Dhwanyāloka" called it sound or wavelength (process of suggestion).

In brief the' sphot' is the inseparable cause or existence with the last word mechanized through prior to prior words due to impressive arrangement systematically for verbo-collective cognition of suggestion-

पूर्व–पूर्व वर्णानुभव जनित संस्कार सहितान्तिम
वर्णानुभवेन स्फोटो व्यज्यते
Purva purva varṇānubhava janita sansakār sahitāntim
varṇānubuavena sphoto vyajyate

According to Bhartṛhari in "Vākyapadiya"- The "sphọt" is a spontaneous process in which a latent idea or thought arising out of consciousness or the mind of the speaker is manifested by sounds(dhvani) of the spoken words employed in the sentence. And it is directly grapsed through intuition by the listener.

Now life air issuing from the heart and colliding with seats of sound – instruments in vocal cavity creates multi sounds. And the life air's touching points are seats of utterance of particular groups of syllables.

Seat organs of utterance	Skt. Alphabets
(a) Throatal a guttural (kanthya)	A, AA (अ, आ), K-class (क–वर्ग) Visarga (a mark of 02 perpendicular dots (%))
(b) Palatal-(Tālavya)	I, EE (इ, इग), C-class (च–वर्ग), Shi (य, श)
(c) Cerebral (above tounge)	R, R (ऋ, ॠ), T-class (ट–वर्ग), R, Sh (र, ष)
(d) Dental (dantya)	LR+, LR+ (ऌ, ॡ), T-class (त–वर्ग), La, Sa (ल, स)
(e) Labial (Osthya) or Labial	U, OO (उ, ऊ), P-class (प–वर्ग), aspirate visarga.
(f) Nasal (Anunāsika)	ञ, म, ङ, ण, न, (marked by dot) Where the air is totally diverting from throat and is directly through the nose to produce 'N' sound wherein the tongue, lips and teeth are positioned differently.

Throat palatal- (e, ai) ए, ऐ

Throat Labial (o, ou) ओ, औ

Dento –Labial (va) व

Sibilant (sh, ṣ, s- warmth) श, ष, स

Tongue –common helping organ for uttering.

Here we see that all Skt. Alphabets are uttered with the help of different seats-organs of human vocal cavity. Therefore multi reflection, accent and impression of syllabic sounds are meant for physical or biological cure of lisping and the like ailments at the early age. It is a proven fact that the amplification or the proven range of resonance in Skt. Syllables has bio-scientific structure to have unified effect on the body and the mind through vibrating nasal sound en route to nucleo-semicircle (.). Such sounding in the form of mechanical energy is produced through vibrating particles of the medium (not vacuum) in our body.

Again such speech- sound is arranged at O3 levels -

(a) Phonetic feature- an attribute of sound such as voicing, place of articulation and tongue height with philological features.

(b) Frictional(+)

(c) Consonantal(-)

There are 10 places of articulation having O2 categories-

1. Active Articulator

   (a) Bilabial–p, b, m, w

(b) labio-dental
(c) Dental
(d) Alveolar
(e) Post-Alveolar

2. Passive articulator-
   (a) Retroflex
   (b) Palate(root of the mouth)
   (c) Velar
   (d) Uvular – fleshy soft plate over the roof of the tongue
   (e) Pharyngeal – (guttural consonant -throaty)

Besides-

1. Pulmonic consonants are produced by air pressure from the lungs as opposed to impulsive like clicked consonants.
2. Utterance- is a stretch of sound between 02 adjacent pauses with no pause in the middle.
3. Setting- is a stretch of sounds with a tendency towards some particular state as jaw position.

It can be as long as utterence and as short as segment. Now the life wind or vital air of different kinds is seated and issued from the following regions of the body-

Region of the body	**Types of life wind**
(a) Heart	Breathing for life(prāna)
(b) Anus	Breathing downwards (apān)
(c) Navel	Breathing to digest friendly (samān)
(d) Gullet	Breathing upward(udān)
(e) Physical body	diffusion through veins / arteries (Vyān)
Emetical	Life wind expelled by eruption(Nāga)
Blowing region	Farting(tortoise)
Sneezing	Changing(chameleon)
Yawing	X-wind

Further we are prone to automation of our mouth, tongue, teeth and throat to various seats of utterance or place to induce some types of resistance in the air flow. The various obstructions help produce various sounds.

There are O5 internal and pre- sounding mechanized with seats of utterance classified as–

(a) Touching effect from- क (KA) to म (MA)
(b) Slight touching effect-य (Ya), र (Ra), ल (La), व (Va)
(c) Bare open effort- all vowels
(d) Slight open efforts श (Sha), ष (Ṣa), स (Sa), ह (Ha)
(e) Hidden effort –Short akār

Besides these are 08 external and ending sound mechanized with utterance classified as-

1. Open throat breathing 2. Sole air breathing 3. Soft air breathing	The 1st & the 2nd syllable of class consonants + श (Sha), ष (ṣa), स (sa)
4. Obscure articulation 5. Contraction of throat 6. Hard sounding	The rest of consonants + all vowels
7. A low air breathing – consonant without ह (ha) sound	
8. A high air breathing – consonant with ह (ha) sound as Kh, gh, dh, etc.	

So the more we recite conjoined sound avoiding catachresis, the more life winds get stirred to excrete impurities through ears, eyes, nose, tongue, teeth, navel, nails, anus, reproductive organ, head and pores of the body resulting healthy life.

These conjoined sounds are seed mantras (productive organs) of the body-universe which has unique sound with nasal character marked by lunar point on the head line-

(a) one unit of a foot of the nasal modification of vowel gets uttered in the heart
(b) Half of the unit gets uttered in the forehead
(c) Half of the unit gets uttered in the nose

Whereas the mind affects the digestive fire of the abdomen and that digestive fire activates the life breathing or the breathing of life.

That life breathing generates deep and gradual sound or voice via transmission through the heart –region-.

(a) Because heart is the repose of the grave vowel accent.
(b) The forehead or cerebral is the repose of high vowel accent
(c) The ear root is the repose of the mid accent vowel
(d) The whole mouth (nasal effect) is the repose of the increased grave accent vowel.

Such techniques of the utterance are felt or heard in the following creatures-

Indigo sparrows--- single footed sound

Crow-------double footed sound

Peacock-----tri-footed sound

Mongoose----half- footed sound

Further When we fall in woes the lunar symbol on the head of the alphabet lessens our weal and woes in utterance or recitation.

As we have come to know that God has endowed the living beings with internal mechanism which is capable of producing sound by means of inner vibrations produced by the element of air in the region of the ethereal cerebral. The sound produced through each mechanism is Articulate one. The air- reach plays a vital role to collide with at least O2 sound-components (intermittent pause) from aerial resistance which exerts audio- expressions as the Articulate sound. Such conjunction occurs between tongue + palate, tongue + teeth, lower and upper lip and etc. According to phoneme scientist, the tongue being the common helping organ of utterance, plays a vital role to differentiate speech-sound due to its o5 vowel parts phonemically-

(a) Apex tongue

(b) Fore tongue

(c) Sub-fore tongue

(d) Middle tongue

(e) Back-root tongue

It has O2 status also –

(a) Horizontal called fore, middle and back parts

  (i) इ, ई,, (I, ee, e)–fore parts

  (ii) अ (A) -----middle part

  (iii) उ, ऊ, ओ, औ, आ (u, oo, o, ou, Ā) back part–

(b) Vertical ---lower, middle, higher or manifest, half manifest, concealed & high concealed

  (i) (EE, I, OO, U)----high ई, इ, ऊ, उ

  (ii) (E, O, A)----Middle ए, ओ, अ

  (iii) (Ā, Ai, ou)----Lower आ, ऐ, औ

Besides tongue and lips play a vital role in vowel utterance on the basis of each other global diffusion, non-global diffusion and indifference or passive. Meaning thereby while uttering vowel phonemes, our tongue generates varied foot measures towards back portal of soft palate or fore portion of hard palate resulting (OO, O, Ou)- circular (ऊ, ओ, औ)

A (अ)-Passive.

Some of the conjoined syllables are being illustrated for biological tone-up as-

बं (Baṃ) to cure acidity, gas trouble, rheumatic pain and lisping

खं (Khaṃ) to cure B.P. (high-low), heart attack and hepatic disorders.

सः (Saḥ) breathing in for healthy hygiene

हं (Haṃ) breathing out for healthy hygiene

एं (EṂ) toning of throat, palate, nose, sense of appetite

ह्रीं (Hriṃ) toning of throat, palate, nose, cerebral

श्रीं (Shreeṃ) toning of palate, cerebral, nose

क्रीं (Kreeṃ) toning of teeth, nose, palate

स्वाहा (Swāhā) cure of illness and complications

So the conjoined syllables generate potential energy which has dynamic effect on the mind to heal up. Further the mystical seats of articulate sounds may be channelized to vitalize our body as dealt in PARAMLAGHUMANJUṢA of M.M. Nagesh Bhatta who gave philosophical thought on Skt. Grammar to identify the eternal sound-world with the Brahma (pratyagātma)–

परां वाङ्मूलचक्रस्था पश्यन्ती नाभिसंस्थिता
ह्रदिस्था मध्यमा ज्ञेया वैखरी कण्ठदेशगा
वैखर्या हि कृतो नादः परश्रवण गोचरः
मध्यमया कृतो नादः स्फोटव्यन्जक उच्यते–P-27

Parām vānmulchakrasthā paśhyanti nābhisamsthitā,
Hṛidisthā madhyamā gyeya vaikhari kanthadeśhagā.
Vaikharyā hi krito nadaḥ paraśhravan gocharaḥ,
Madhyamayā kṛito nādaḥ sfotvyanjaka uchyate. -P-27

The inner vibration to induce Articulate sound gets mechanized through faculty-organs in terms of परा-parā (below navel region), पश्यन्ति-pashaynti (navel-region) मध्यमा-madhyamā (intermediate-heart rgion) and वैखरी-vaikhari (throatal region) for vigour and vitality of body. In its sequence, the Vedic chanting of the Mantras (verbal formulas) with phonetic feature like pitch, accent, conformity and congruity plays a vital role in our physical, psychological and spiritual aspects of life and Cosmos. Such inner vibrations due to tonal accents are channeled through 04-steps of Yogic mechanics as -

(a) Parā (b) Pasyanti

(c) Madhyamā (d) Vaikhari

articulation of which vaikhari is expressive. Although they all are too intricate to express through speech, music, literature and spirituality as follows -

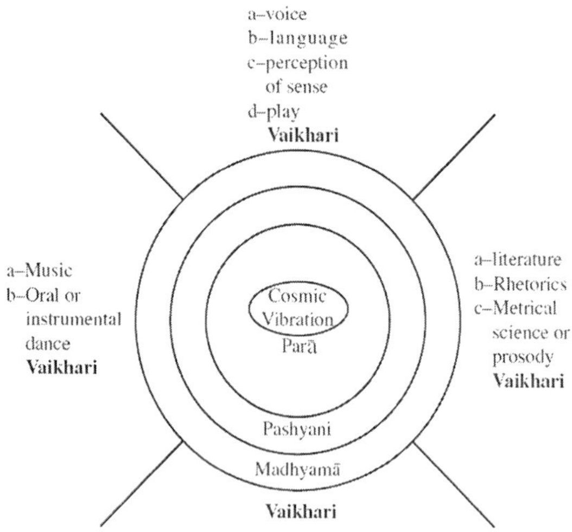

05-Gross Elements (space, air, fire, water, earth) responsible for cosmic genesis have subtle 05 elements on spatial attributions related to the sense of acoustic treatment as -

Space – Sound

Air – Tangible + Sound

Fire – Shape + Tangible + Sound

Water – Taste + Shape + Tangible + Sound

Earth – Smell + Taste + Shape + Tangible + Sound

Space – Space-chamber plays a vital role to commune between deities & human beings. The common chanting invocation is performed in house-chambers, temples, churches, Gurudwaras, Mosques and etc. These shrines are made up of stones and bricks which are highly onomatopoeic or echoing or vibrant to enhance spiritual aspect of the devotees. Such shrines have womb-chambers connected to semi-chamber to resound sacred sound of AUM in uniformity.

Besides chanting of Mantras, the playing sound of Conch-shell (Turbinella pyrum), ringing sound of bells and chiming gong match AUM resonance.

Now step on the Indian gamut having 07 Notes - सा, रे, ग, म, प, ध, नि - hinted with lord Brahma as identified earlier.

This hepta note or reverberating sound determines the fullness of perceived tones in acoustic excellence. It fills up with the sense of optimism and renewed energy. Further this hepta-group of sound starts from the imageful or shapeful identity of lord Brahma and ends with imageless or shapeless identity of God Brahma. So the eternity of words like the Brahma is asserted here.

According to Nārdiya Shikshā- of sage Nārad, each syllabic note stands for a particular character of sound as –

सा (Sā) for षड्ज (Khadaja) – derived from 06 organs (nose, throat, chest, palate, tongue & teeth) + Articulate sound between high & low – Swarita.

रे (Re) for ऋषभ (Rs.abha) – as bull or cow – grave accent – accentless – Anudatta.

ग (Ga) for गंधार (Gandhar) – acutely accented sound – Udātta.

म (Ma) for मध्यमा (Mashyam) – Intermediate or moderate sound or articulate between high + low – Swarita

प (Pa) for पंचम (Pancham) – Derived from 05-faculty organs of the body (air, navel, chest, throat, cerebral)

ध (Dha) for धैवत (Dhaivate) – Grave accent or accent less – Anudātta

न (Na) for निषाद (Niṣadā) – Acutely accented sound – Udātta

So out of 07 notes we have – 02 – Udātta
02 – Anudātta
03 – Swarita

Total = 07

Such sound notes of the Indian gamut are claimed to have diffused among those of sea-tides, air, leaves (autumn), fountains, dew-drops, birds, clouds, cows, rivers, glaciers and etc. So such sound is the semi-circle notes of the Selfculminating into the Super Self.

There is a deep relation between classical music and brain. While listening to classical music, neurons of the brain get activated with electro-magnetic wave through vacuum. Such listening works on EEG (Electro-encephalo-Gram) mechanism to avert tensions and tears of life in musical concerts. While listening to Indian music, a beam of buoyancy is reflected on our mind and heart. It is to bring beauty of harmony and expression of emotions. Music can lift up our mood and put smile on our face with soothing effect of Ragas at prescribed times between day and night. Its charming notes buzzing in the Nature's hive sweeten the Self and cure the body. Further such music expresses that which cannot be said and while it is impossible to be silent. It is the spontaneous over flow of powerful feelings and hummed in tranquility.

Again musical therapy helps ease the anxiety and stress of pregnant women with MAPS device (Music Sound-Assisted Pre-natal Sonography). This device is applied to detect foetal anomalies in the womb. Further we are provided to listen to musical notes in the Nature. Wherein we feel pleasure, peace, patience and silence among -

(a) Humorous sound of wind

(b) Feathering sound of leaves

(c) Streaming sound of mountains

(d) Rolling sound of dew-drops

(e) Buoyant sound of sea-tides

(f) Hovering sound of clouds

(g) Cuckooing or chirping sound of birds

(h) Deep sound of glacier

(i) Bubbling sound of rivers

Our classical music is based on melody which trills the heart from within. But western music is based on harmony which trills the heart from outside.

Let us observe the average frequency (Hz) of Vedic instruments -

<table>
<tr><td colspan="2">Instruments</td><td>Frequency (Hz)</td></tr>
<tr><td colspan="2">Chanting of Vedic Mantras (alone)</td><td>147.5, 302. 440</td></tr>
<tr><td colspan="2">Conch shell sounding (alone)</td><td>327.5 – 2292.5</td></tr>
<tr><td colspan="2">Bell sounding</td><td rowspan="4">1265.5-2877.5</td></tr>
<tr><td>Its basic</td><td>1292</td></tr>
<tr><td>Its hand belling</td><td>200 (maximum)</td></tr>
<tr><td>Hanging bell</td><td>3200 (maximum)</td></tr>
<tr><td colspan="2">But simultaneous sounding of Vedic chants, conch. shell. bell and chiming gong</td><td>327.5 – 3002</td></tr>
</table>

But such frequencies may vary with hearing range also.

Now I turn to treat 07-lotus circle with Skt. Alphabets which are annexed to vitalize or awaken our body and soul for spiritual enlightenment through seed Mantras (cosmic connectivity). These Mantras as inner controllers are specified to each petal of lotus emerges from morass and blooms out of glooms, as if, to flower into the Cosmos –

1. मूलाधार (Mulādhār) – The mystical circle below navel between anus & generative organs. This is earth-element, being the foundation

of our bodies located at the base of the spinal cord for self-preservation as physical entity. It motivates dynamic existence, good health and elevation with charging of Skt. Syllable –

i. व (Va)	
ii. श (Sha)	04 Mantra - लं (seat-organ=teeth)
iii. ष (Ṣa)	
iv. स (Sa)	

2. स्वाधिष्ठान (Swādhisthān) – 3"or 8.62cm above the panis-root near abdomen – it is water element oriented to Self satisfaction or saturation as an emotional identity. It connects others through feelings and sensational movements. It motivates liquidity and sensual fulfilments with the charging of –

i. ब (Ba)	
ii. भ (Bha)	
iii. म (Ma)	06 Mantra - वं (lips + teeth)
iv. य (Ya)	
v. र (Ra)	
vi. ल (La)	

3. मणिपुर (Manipur) – Navel-root. It is a fire element and ego-oriented to self-definition. It motivates metabolism and will-power spontaneously with charging of –

i. ड (Da)	
ii. ढ (Dha)	
iii. ण (Na)	
iv. त (Ta)	
v. थ (Tha)	10 Mantra – रँ (Cerebral)
vi. द (Tha)	
vii. ध (Dha)	
viii. न (Na)	
ix. प (Pa)	
x. फ (Pha)	

4. अनाहत (Anāhat) – Unbeaten heart-region. It is an air element having social identity oriented to self-acceptance. It adjoins opposites in the psyche, the mind and the body, person and shadow, male and female, ego and harmony. It motivates deep love, mercy and peace with charging of –

i. क (Ka)
ii. ख (Kha)
iii. ग (Ga)
iv. घ (Gha)
v. ङ (Yan)
vi. च (Cha)
vii. छ (Chha)
viii. ज (Ja)
ix. झ (Jha)
x. ञ (Yan)
xi. ट (Ta)
xii. ठ (T_h)

12 Mantra - यँ (palatal)

5. विशुद्ध (Vishuddha) – Throatal region. It is a sound element having creative and communicative identity oriented to self-expression. It motivates vibration of sound through speech or voice to treat worldly life with charging of –

i. अ (A)
ii. आ (Ā)(AA)
iii. इ (I)
iv. ई (Ee)
v. उ (U)
vi. ऊ (Oo)
vii. ऋ (R.i)
viii. ॠ (R.ee)
ix. लृ (Lr.)
x. लॄ (Lr)
xi. ए (E)
xii. ऐ (Ai)
xiii. ओ (O)
xiv. औ (Ou)
xv. अं (Am)
xvi. अः (Ah)

16 Mantra - हँ (Breathing out)
Total - 48

6. आज्ञा चक्र (Āgyā Chakra) - Between eyebrows or forehead. It is light element or quintessential element oriented to Self-reflection.

It motivates psychic chambers to attic wisdom with charging of -

i. हं (Ham) | 02
ii. सः (Sah) |

7. सहस्रार चक्र (Sahasrāra Chakra) – Thousand petalled at the crown of the head. It is cognitive having global identity oriented to Self-realization or recognition or consciousness. It motivates our wisdom, cognition and spirit to connect with the Super world for the bonanza of Bliss with charging of –

i. उँ (Um) | 02
ii. ॐ (Aum) |

GRAND TOTAL = 52 (48+2+2)

Here it is worthy of note that these lolus-circles have vital electric energy and boi-flesh to rejuvenate the entirety of the body by reciting particular groups of alphabets.

Someone has classified alphabates in different groups –

(a) Vowels A, AA, I, EE, OO, R., E, AI, O, OU
(अ, आ, इ, ई, उ, ऊ, ऋ, ए, ऐ, ओ, औ) = 11
(b) Consonants K-Kh to, Śa, Ṣa, Sa, Ha
(क.ख to श, ष, स, ह) = 33
(c) Combined consonants Ks., Tra, Gya, Ś (क्ष, त्र, ज्ञ, श्र) = 4
(d) Semi-circle (चन्द्र बिन्दु– ँ) = 01
(e) Aphas (विसर्ग–:) = 01
(f) Binary Consonants D, dh (ड़, ढ़) = 02
Total = 52

AUM Photon

Now the Acoustic Science deals the mechanism of the Mantras (divine formulas) and their dynamics are being displayed globally.

I want to focus on the eternal property of Akshar (indestructible syllable) under oriental perspective. Bṛhdaranykopnishad says –

अक्षरमन्बरान्तधृते–3 / 8 / 11
Aksharamabarāntdhrte–3/8/11

Here the Akshar (imperishable) is Brahma. Because it supports everything up to Akāsa (The Ether)

Etymologically it means syllable and therefore it represents the syllable 'AUM' which is also an act of meditation to have neurobiological changes without physical stimulations. This Sutra says –

The Akshar stands for the Brahma viz the Ether woven like warp and woof. Akshar is neither gross nor minute, neither short nor long – all relative properties are absent in it. Therefore Akshar is Brahma.

We have vision of the word "AUM" in Brahman portion of the Vedas as Shruti-smriti states rules, codes of employment or explanation or illustrations to perform ritual sacrifices.

In the Geeta lord Krishna says –

अक्षरं ब्रह्म परमं स्वभावोऽध्यात्ममुच्यते
भूतभावोद्भवकरो विसर्गः कर्मसञ्ज्ञितः–8/3
Aksharam brahma paramam swabhāvoahyātmamuchyate,
Bhutbhavodbhavakaro visargaḥ karmsangyitaḥ./8/3

The Monistic approach (not to be broken or divided) to Akshar has enlivening identity of Supreme Being or Consciousness in Metaphysics.

On the other hand, the Mantras (being the essence of the verbal Brahma) are the unique sound of the Brahma. The word 'AUM' has a nasal character marked by lunar point on the head of the line. So when we fall in woes this lunar symbol lessens our weal and woes in utterance. So one should utter a nasal sound in the way of neither inarticulate nor hard (broken). Because the proper technique of utterance gets consecrated to the world of The Brahma as in Rikṣprātisākya Samhita of Shounkāchārya –

The Mantras (transcendental sound) have dual aspects –

सर्ववर्णाः प्रयोक्तव्या नाव्यक्ताः न च पीडिताः
सम्यग्वर्ण प्रयोगेन ब्रह्मलोकं महीयते
Sarvavarṇā hpraytoktavya nāvyktyāh na ca peeditāh
Samyagvarṇa prayogen brahmalokam mahiyate

(1) Verbal

(2) Acoustic

So our navel to throatal sounding should harmonize with ours & Nature or the universe. As we observe to have harmony between the recital and playing on the harmonium.

Here we should know that the verbal Brahma is the spiral Energy of the embodied Soul. The whole world is the epithet of this Energy in the form of sound, light, water and etc. under verbal force. Because the soul or the Self and the verbal force is the Eternal or the Ethereal Brahma being the substratum of sound. Jagdish Tarkālankār in "SHABDASHAKTI PRAKĀSHIKĀ" has elucidated the verbal testimony to be the force of divine light characteristic of capacity, significance and verbal excellence individually or collectively as–

योग्यतार्थगताकांक्षा शब्दनिष्ठानुभाविका
प्रत्येकं वा मिलित्वा वा नैते लिंगमसिद्धितः–4
Yogyatārthagatānakānkshā shabdanisthānubhavikā,
Pratyekam vā militvā vā naite lingamasiddhitaḥ. – 04

Further 'AUM' is abridged with coalition of tri-syllable culminating into monosyllable. Such condensed pervasion is observed in "Taittiriy Brāhman"-

वाचं देवा उपजीवन्ति विश्वे वाचं गंधर्वाः पशवो मनुष्याः
वागक्षरं प्रथमजा ऋतस्य वेदानां माताऽमृतस्य नाभिः–2/8/8/45
Vācham Devā Upjeevanti vishve vācham gandharvāḥ pashvo manushyāḥ,
Vāgaksaram prathamajā ṛitasya vedānām mātāmṛtasyanābhiḥ /2/8/8/4 or 5

"all living beings, the Brahma, animals, Gadharvas, Rudras, 8-vasu, Adityas (Sun) and the like reside and recognize their existent identity in the sacred syllabic hymn of the cosmic/universal elegance (AUM). And 1sly the syllabic Goddess of universal connectivity or voice or speech came into existence to be the syllabic Mother of the Vedas and syllabic nucleus of the Immortal nectar.

It is resound-able or vibratile in all planets. So it is for the learned to dive deep into the Divine sound – AUM and realize Its Space-wide excellence. Modern scientists have proved global connectivity to be air-wave and what we see is the light-wave radically. These both waves vibrating in the same motion admit that the root cause of Cosmic Creation is the vibration due to motion in billowing nature under unequipoise among Sat, Raj & Tam as depicted in "Mantra yoga samhitā" on Vedico mystical Science.

कार्य यत्र विभाव्यते किमपि तत्स्पन्देन सव्यापकम्
स्पन्दश्चापि तथा जगत्सु विदितः शब्दान्वयी सर्वदा
सृष्टिश्चापि तथादिमाकृतिविशेषत्वादभूत्स्पन्दिनी।
शब्दश्चोद्भवत्तदा प्रणव इत्योंकाररूपः शिवः।
Kārya Yatra Vibhāvyate kimapi tataspanden savyāpakam,
Spandshchāpi tathā jagtsu viditah shabdānvayi sarvadā,
Sristiśchāpi tathādimākṛti vishesatvādbhutspandini.
savdaścodvaavattadā pranav ityonkāraroopaḥ shivaḥ–1

When there is work, there is a vibration and where there is vibration or thrilling there is verbal connectivity. Because vibration is based on global connectivity (shabda). Cosmic Creation is a type of work. Such conception as echoed - एकोऽहं बहुश्यामः (Ekoham Bahusyamah) refers to pro-motion propulsion.

The Mimansā school of Indian philosophy deems syllable to be verbal Brahma or God.

Further All Mantras take birth in the womb of this Supremo – sacred formula (AUM)-mantras being the epithet of the Supreme Being in "Vogasutra" of Maharshi Patanjali -

तस्य वाचकः प्रणवः–1/27

Tasya vācakaḥ pranavarḥ– /1/27

'AUM' signifies resonance to enliven spirit through mild breathing process.

According to "GopathaBrāhman" (Atharvaveda) the word 'AUM' has tri-prosodial metre or foot as –

I. Brahmā

II. Vishnu

III. Mahesha

The word "AUM" contains 02 vowels and 01 consonant classified as –

1. (a) अ (A) – the accent of the 1st metre or foot (Brahma) of vowel vibration phonetically through Vaiswānar (fire God) to sparkle in waking state.

   (b) उ (U) – the accent of the 2nd metre or foot (Vishnu) of the 5th vowel vibration through Tejas (fire energy of the Supreme Being) to flame in dreaming state.

   (c) म् (M) – the accent of the 3rd metre or foot of the 25th consonant through pragyā (wife of the Sun) in deep repose.

   The root or the origin of nasal point is dispeller of distress and deems to be the base surface of the creation of the Cosmos. Later on a triangular shaped organ was sprouted or sprung out of the origino –nasal point (M) for linear diffusion of the Universe.

   To be more clear, this tri-syllabic mono-syllable indicates

(2) 03 connotations as –

   i. अ (A) - for the creator – Brahma

   ii. उ (U) - for the sustained soul – Vishnu

   iii. म् (M) - for the dissolution of our woes and the world – Mahesh

(3) 03 properties of all created objects –

   i. अ (A) - Sat (Cognitive power)

   ii. उ (U) - (raj) – executive or operative power

   iii. म् (M) - (Tam) - objective power

(4) 03 Vedas –

   i. अ (A) - Rig Veda

ii. उ (U) - Yajur Veda

iii. म् (M) - Sām Veda

(5) 03 World (Loka) -

i. अ (A) - Heaven (paradise – स्वः)

ii. उ (U) - The Space (Bhuvarloka)

iii. म् (M) - Terrestrial world – the earth (Bhur loka)

(6) 03 Stages of life -

i. अ (A) - The womb (40 weeks)

ii. उ (U) - The earthly (80 years)

iii. म् (M) - The Spirit world – eternity or ultimate destination

Thus this mono syllabio- verbal connectivity from A to M is merged with egg- shaped universe to perceive infinite worlds. In this way such divine hypothesis helps to charge our whole bodily – universe with monosyllabic circuit.

Elaborately Lord Shiva (Maheswar) descended 52-54 deities upon The Earth representing 52-54 skt. Alphabets as verbal Spirit ItSelf by playing the small drum (Damru). We find in the event of Satyayuga that 52-54 seats of the Female Force or Creative Potency were consecrated to install with the cut-fall of Body parts and jewels of the corpse of goddess Sati accompanying Kalbhairava as Her consort being the manifestation of lord Shiva – pervading India, Pakistan, Bangladesh, Sri Lanka, Tibet, China and Nepal etc. I mean the allusion of 52-54 cut falls signifies 52-54 skt. Syllables as well as 52 astrophysical exoplanets or squares in exosolar system. Further Her celestial or divine or universal Body in brazing lustre might have tallied with 52 celestial or galactic bodies which are billions of times brighter than the Sun. There are 10s of billions of solar system in the Milky-way Galaxies which radiate mass energy every second.

In other words, number 52-54 may be seen as its significance digitally –

52 = 5 & 2 where 05 = gross elements for creation And 02 digits stand for-

(a) Religions & spiritual or

(b) Purusa & prakriti or

(c) Assimilation & dissimilation of the universe or

(d) Faith & courage in romantic love, harmony & union or separation

or 54 = 5 & 4 where 05 = gross elements

(a) 04 = Vedas

(b) Four faced Lord Brahma

(c) Four headed Lord Vishnu

(d) Four sides of directions (N+E+W+S) and

(e) Resonating vibration of energy of practicability or biblical significance of the 4th day of the Creation of the material world in weekend Creation.

We have varied accounts of seats of creative potency mentioned in global myths as in–

(a) Tantra Cudāmani – 52 seats

(b) Devi Purāṇa – 51 seats

(c) Devi Bhāgvata – 108 seats

(d) Devi Geeta – 72 seats

Out of which 04 – Adi Shaktipeeth

18 – Mahā Shaktipeetha

To avoid such complexity of numerical conceptions I want to portray 52 skt- syllabic manifestations of The Supreme She-Force to proclaim the perception of Shabda Brahma (Verbal Brahma) on the basic ayllables of skt. Alphabets –

Shaktipeethas

1. अ - cut fall spot of vulva of SATI – Kāmrupa (Assām)
2. आ - cut fall spot of left breast – Jalāndhar (Punjāb)
3. इ - cut fall spot of Anus – Pashupati (Nepāl)
4. ई - cut fall spot of left eye – Kolhāpur (Mahārastra)
5. उ - cut fall spot of left ear – Parvat (Laddakha or Kashmir)
6. ऊ - cut fall spot of right ear – Vishālāxi (Vāranasi U.P.)
7. ऋ - cut fall spot of Nose – Sugandha peetha (Bangladesh)
8. ऋ$_{\varepsilon}$ - cut fall spot of left cheek – Arbudānchal
9. लृ - cut fall spot of right cheek – Gandki peetha (Nepāl) or Godawari kabitar (A.P.)
10. ल$_{\varepsilon}$ - cut fall spot of nails – Ekamvapeethe
11. ए - cut fall spot of tri line above naval – Trisrot peeth
12. ऐ - cut fall spot of naval – Kāmākshi Amma Temple (T.N.) or Uttakal (Odisha Yagpur)
13. ओ - cut fall spot of fingers – Kailash peetha (Himalaya) or Prayag peeth (U.P.)

14. औ - cut fall spot of teeth – Jagdambā devi (Telangana) or Panch sagar peetha
15. अं - cut fall spot of right breast –Ramgiri parvat Maihar (U.P.)
16. अः - cut fall spot of neck – Mallikārjuna or shree shailan (A.P.)
17. क - cut fall spot of head skull – Hinglaj (Baluchistan – Pakistan)
18. ख - cut fall spot of upper skin – Jyotishmatha
19. ग - cut fall spot of bosom (heart) – Baidyanath dhām (Jharkhand) or koneshwar temple (Sri Lanka)
20. घ - cut fall spot of left shoulder – Mālvā peetha
21. ङ - cut fall spot of right armpit – Pushkar (Rajasthan)
22. च - cut fall spot of left armpit – Ketugram Bahulashakti (W.B.)
23. छ - cut fall spot of womb region – Gokarna peetha
24. ज - cut fall spot of 1st skin fold on upper part of the belly – Matureshwar peetha
25. झ - cut fall spot of 2nd skin fold on the upper part of belly – Attahas peetha
26. ञ - cut fall spot of 3rd skin fold of the upper belly – Ambujā Junagadh (Gujrat)
27. ट - cut fall spot of pelvis – Rājgrih peetha (Bihar)
28. ठ - cut fall spot of buttock – Amarkantaka (M.P.)
29. ड - cut fall spot of left thigh – Jayanti (Meghalaya)
30. ढ - cut fall spot of right thigh – Patneshwari (Patna, Bihar)
31. ण - cut fall spot of left upper thigh – Kaulgiri Peetha
32. त - cut fall spot of right knee – Jayanta peetha
33. थ - cut fall spot of left knee – Ujjaini peetha (Avanti M.P.)
34. द - cut fall spot of left lower thigh – Raksha peetha Samisti peetha or Saharsa (Bihar)
35. ध - cut fall spot of right lower thigh – Ratnāvali (T.N.)
36. न - cut fall spot of right ankle – Tripursunsdri (Tripurā) or Ujjain (M.P.)
37. प - cut fall spot of left ankle - Tristeta (Jalpaiguri-W.B.) or Ekveerika Temple Mahur (M.S.)
38. फ - cut fall spot of body fluid – Prayāg peeta (U.P.)
39. ब - cut fall spot of right heel – Kasheergram (W.B.) Daipayan Sarovar (Haryana)

40. भ - cut fall spot of left heel – Māyāpura Peetha
41. म - cut fall spot of blood – Malayapeetha (Island)
42. य - cut fall spot of spleen – Vaishnava or Shreeshail peetha
43. र - cut fall spot of marrow – Merupeetha (Himalaya)
44. ल - cut fall spot of langue – Jwālāmukhi (Kangra H.P.)
45. व - cut fall spot of tissue – Mahendra peetha
46. श - cut fall spot of right thumb – Vāman Peetha
47. ष - cut fall spot of left thumb – Hiranyapur Peetha
48. स - cut fall spot of glazing luster – Mahālaxmi Peetha (Mumbai)
49. ह - cut fall spot of artery – Nalhatti (Bolepur W.B)
50. क्ष - cut fall spot of hair lock – Chamundeshwari Temple (Karnataka) or Kali Temple (Kali ghat W.B.)
51. त्र - cut fall spot of right foot – Vimalā Temple inside Jagannathpuri (Odisa)
52. ज्ञ - cut fall spot of left foot – Kukkuteshwar Swami Temple (A.P.)

Now the Beej Mantra (Seed Mantra) generates divine force in human life. As a seed grows into a strong tree, blossoms and produces a mass of fruits. It has immense power of nourishment to enrich by itself. Likewise The Mantras have spiritual vibration to enliven static consciousness. The practice of Mantras sanctifies consciousness (the mind) and cleanse our negativity as regular foot-steps on weeds. The Mantras are the causal power to create spiritual vibration within us to connect with Cosmic vibration for proper evolution. Even Botanical researches have concluded that certain syllabic vibration of sound, audible or inaudible, enriches the growth of plants also. Further vibrational energy influences the subtle elements to the extent of spiritual enlightenment.

There is no syllable without mystic – sacred formula and there is no herb without medicinal property. Hence is essential to experience its significance and experiment on medicinal secrecy. All Zoological and Botanical phenomena are the product of seed Mantras. So the essence of the Vedic Mantras is supposed to have sacred syllabic base to meditate for power & potency; and the Mantras themselves help to generate the higher power to push up souls above material murk in order to connect them with the SuperSelf. Further they also still our body and instil a novel faith. In this way there are the proven healing devices for better clarity and calmness by defeating negative energy around us. Thus we receive permanent peace and pleasure with chanting, meditating or memorizing the Mantras. Such is the mystery of the syllabic Science. Further the biological effect of the Seed Mantras (Algebraico- mystical Syllable) combined with vowel and consonants vibrate en route to cerebral nerves. And the generated wave-velocity catalyses inner secreting glands like pituitary, thyroid and para-thyroid ones. In this way such process enhances resistant power to cure diseases of the body. Further –

- अ - to initiate mouth for connection
- उ - to channelize elementary canal
- म् - to close our mouth

So the utterance or accenting or sounding of 'AUM' can cure throaty dysphonia along with stenosis in lungs, heart and neurotic disorders.

So utterance causes to emit CO_2 & inhales much O_2 to activate blood circulation for vitality. So much so it heals up skeletal system, nervous system, digestive system, urinary system, respiratory system, reproductive system, ophthalmic system, psychiatry and nightmare. The Mantras are more useful to activate systolo- diastolic air pumping and exhausting device for glowing health.

Again Gayatri Mantra & Mahamṛtyunjay Mantra cure lisping problem and the uttering sound reflects much on tongue.

Now the sacred- Supreme syllable 'AUM' is modified in the following seeds –

1. Yogabeej (योगबीज) – Pericarp (Seed vessel of lotus)
2. Tejabeej (तेजबीज) – Kindling or energetic seed)
3. Shantibeej (शान्तिबीज) – Tranquil seed

Which are known as -

ऐं, ह्रीं, क्लीं, क्रीं, हूं, हं, गं, क्ष्रों, ह्रों, दूं, श्रीं, स्त्रीं
AIN, HṚEEN, KLEEN, KREEN, HOON, HAN,
GAN, KSHROUN, HROUN, DOON, SHREEN, STREEN, etc.

Now the mystical significance and healing effects on living beings are being dealt as follows –

i. ऐ (Speech Seed) -ऐ - Goddess Saraswati
   Nasal Sound – Universal mother
   Nasal Point – Distress Destroyer
ii. ह्रीं (Prakriti Sound) - ह् - Goddess Bhuvneshwari
   ह्–Prakriti fire world (Material energy of Supreme Lord)
   र्–Universal Mother

ई–Semicircle point (ँ) – dispeller of griefs

Meaning – Bhuvneshwari (Prima potency) dispels my sorrow.

iii. क्लीं (Krishna Seed) - क - Yogi Shree Krishna

ल्–Divine luster

ई–Yogeshwar

Above dot- Semi-circle-power-destroyer of distress

iv. क्रीं (Kali Seed) - क - Kāli Goddess

र–Prakriti – fire Brahma

ई–Mahāmāyā – material energy of the Supreme Lord

Nasal-above dot- Nasal Sound – Universal Mother

Semi-circle point – Dispeller of darkness

v. हूं (head lock) - ह् - Shiva Lord

ऊ–Bhairava

-Nasal Sound – The Supreme Mother

-Semi-Circle Point – Dispeller of distress

vi. हं (Hanuman Seed) - ह् - Lord Hanuman

अ–freedom from danger

-Semi-circle Point – Dispeller of distress

vii. गं (Ganpatibeej) ग् - Lord Ganesh

अ–avoiding obstacle

Above-nasal dot Point – dispeller of distress

-He grants fearlessness, riches & knowledge.

viii. क्ष्रौं - (Nrsinghbeej) क्ष - Nrsingh lord

र्–Brahma

औ–divine lustre

Above-nasal dot-Point – distress destroyer

- He grants foe futility, all protection, bravery and Self- confidence.

ix. ह्रौं (Shivabeej) -ी - Shiva

र्–Brahma

औ–Sadāshiva (ever lasting happiness)

Nasal Sound – Universal Mother

Point – dispeller of distress

x. श्रीं (Laxmi Seed) - श् - MahāLaxmi Lordess

र्–riches

ई–Great Prakrti

-Nasal Sound – Universal Mother

-Point – Dispeller of darkness

xi. स्त्री (Mahāmāyā) - स् - Liberation of distress

त्–Saviour

र्–Salvation

ई–Super energy of the Supreme lord

-Nasal Sound – Universal Mother

-dot Point – Dispeller of distress

The operational devices of the Mantras are –

1. Through Writing – Likhit
2. Through Vocal – Vaikhari
3. Through Whispering – Upānsu
4. Through Inner recitation – Unceasingly Ajapā
5. Through Meditation – Mānas

Lastly if one does not discern the true state in eternal or divine syllable "AUM" containing all sacred formulas and all gods; what does to speak of not receiving the desired result as in the Rigveda –

ऋचो अक्षरे परमे व्योमन् यस्मिन् देवा अधि विश्वे निषेदुः
Ṛco akṣare parme vyoman yasmin devā adhi vishve niseduḥ

यस्तन्न वेद किमृचा करिष्यतिय इत्तद्विदुस्त इमे समासते–1 / 164 / 39
Yastanna veda kimṛcā kariṣyati ya ittadvidusta ime samāsate–1/164/39

3(D) Zero Zenith & Zen Optimum

In Indian philosophy Zero (Zenith- expansion-radiation-orbit) is the state of total absence or neutrality where nothing is everything with full spiritual havings. It relates to the Buddha philosophy of Nihilism (Shunyavāda) in which a person does pacify in the state of highest felicity or absolute extinction of worldly existence void of 12-anguish (agitation, agony, awe, anger, annoyance, anxiety, apathy, arousal, adversity, acrimory, afflication and apprehension) on cranial nerves of the human world having dual or cranky nature in materialism. The zero (0) or nonentity has no predecessor but successor of one (1) and ends at infinity. It does not have plus (+) or minus (-) value being the feature of the Brahma which in return, is symbolized as 'AUM'- the latent Energy of the Creation. This Energy comes from nothingness to evolve into its next state.

This zero (0) is symbolized as womb, egg or seed from which all life comes out of evolution and completion in circular pattern. Thus zero state is the zenith of life, fall of Self- conceit and seat of salvation.

The Indian philosophy proclaims that all human beings are born to attain the highest felicity or bliss within the span of life-circle instead of crazing for perks and packages usually. They craze for mortal feud than immortality which is like an inside bolt in a room of life to unbolt by themselves. Whereas mortality resembles jail fitted with outside bolt under subjection or custody.

Such infinite state of spiritual repose and nihilism for property of perfection or eternal bliss or neutrality is hymned to the Supreme Being as Its intrinsic nature in Shuklayajurveda–

पूर्णमदः पूर्णमिदं पूर्णात्पूर्णमुदच्यते
पूर्णस्य पूर्णमादाय पूर्णमेवावशिष्यते–3/49
Purnamadam purnmidam purnātpurnamudacyate,
purnasya purnmādāya purnamevāvaśiṣyate–3/49

That (the Absolute or the Prime Spirit) is perfect integer in excellence This (the Potency or the universe) is perfect integer in excellence, the Absolute (the Ravaged or Devouring time) undergoes addition, subtraction (multiplication & division as well) of the perfect potential; and lastly The Absolute (Perfect endowment) remains Perfect or Constant i.e. void of modification or alteration. I, too, abridge such aphorism as अहं ब्रहमास्मि (Aham Brahmāsmi). The circle (0) imbues the image of totality, wholeness, infinity, eternity, perfection, cyclic movement and timelessness. Further the Supreme Being is characterized as circle (0 or dot - .) whose center is everywhere but circumference is nowhere. So if one's centered soul-frequency remains – negative point of Average Dominant Focus (IDF) fails to create conflictions and chaos of life. As a result of which all vexes or peeves disappear within Zero (0) frequency. Such frequency hatches positive gyration into brain to evolve global vision.

Besides the primal-cum-successive twin digit denoting Mono-Philosophy 01 – one (the Supreme Self with cosmic property in perfection being the ocean of multiplicative identity with non-modification) as denominator to nominator zero (0 – state of neutrality or tranquility without mudane property) is equal to zero (0) in fraction-

$$\text{Calculated as } = \frac{0}{1} = 0$$

$$\text{To solve} = \frac{0}{1} \text{ or } \frac{1-1}{1} \text{ or } \frac{0}{1} = 0$$

$$\text{Or } \frac{1}{1} - \frac{1}{1} = 1 - 1 = 0$$

Vice versa - $\frac{1}{0}$ = undefined or infinity being the character of the Brahma.

Here the denominator (0) is devoid of times being non-multiplicative to independent & paradoxical character, beggars definition to the extent of infinity wherein infinite possible values of character are endowed-

Arithmetically - $\frac{1}{0} = \infty$ (Micro-macro character of the Brahma)

Thus divine identity of zero (0) is constant in addition, subtraction, multiplication & division and causes Cosmic Creation, protection and dissolution of The Cosmos.

But of the 04 basic operations in Arithmetic, the no. '01' has multiplicative identity i.e. if you multiply any no. with 01, there is no change in its value. So it refers to homogeneity or passing through own square and square root, own cube, cube root and so on. Further it tends to soar upward in vertical nature (01) which signifies pristine property. Here it is worthy of note that all ascending numbers are incomplete without adding '01' integrated to the material world. That is why Greek philosopher & mathematician Pythagoras (570 BC – 495 BC) espoused the Theory of Metempsychosis (post-mortem transmigration of the soul after death in boitics, human and animal) and held that genuine numbers were the most vital thing to create the world. Besides, Neopythogorean logician Moderatus of Gades was instrumental in developing Pythagorean – numerical philosophy categorizing the spirit as a sort of numerical consistence."

Further zero (0) is the cyclic nature of the world-

- Dissolution (nihilism or nothingness) + assimilation and vice-versa
- Dissolution regulated by the Brahma

In its sequence, the mystic mechanism of the universe enshrined in the sublime solicitation may tally with the life web of the miniature like the spider. It creates orb-shaped or global web (world) with silky thread processed from its spinneret glands located in its abdominal cavity (abyss). The protein fluid (milky oceanic) through series of ducts (instruments) sodifies into a gel (churning) which, later on, hardens into a solid silky fiber. It has the skill to stroll in pleasure within its web (sportive world) and devours its global web by itself in nothingness (dissolution). likewise the Supreme Being weaves the Universe as Transient – web by Itself and absorbes such Universe-web by Itself with the ravage of the Time in cipher or dot form (– nothingness or Absolute Negation). Although zero zenith has been dealt in chapter 2(a)also. Wherein I have tried to clarify its clue on the metaphysical theory of salvation stilled with infinite potency.

However, according to "Brahma-sutra Shānkarbhāśya" of Bādarāyan, the Universe is charged with the grandeur of the Supreme Being who created 05 Gross Elements by the Penta valency of 05 suble elements in prescribed ratio and the resultant of such equation /fraction is – zero (0).

Here, out of 05 subtle elements the element which is to be converted into the Gross one is $= +\frac{1}{2}$ and the rest – 04 subtle ones are $= +\frac{1}{8}$ and each equation resulting to = 0 (zero) – state of Metaphysical within physical flux-

$$\text{Gross Earth} = \frac{1}{2}\text{earth} + \frac{1}{8}\text{fire} + \frac{1}{8}\text{sky} + \frac{1}{8}\text{water} + \frac{1}{8}\text{air} = 0$$

$$\text{Gross Water} = \frac{1}{2}\text{water} + \frac{1}{8}\text{fire} + \frac{1}{8}\text{sky} + \frac{1}{8}\text{air} + \frac{1}{8}\text{earth} = 0$$

$$\text{Gross Fire} = \frac{1}{2}\text{fire} + \frac{1}{8}\text{sky} + \frac{1}{8}\text{water} + \frac{1}{8}\text{air} + \frac{1}{8}\text{earth} = 0$$

$$\text{Gross Ether} = \frac{1}{2}\text{sky} + \frac{1}{8}\text{air} + \frac{1}{8}\text{fire} + \frac{1}{8}\text{water} + \frac{1}{8}\text{earth} = 0$$

$$\text{Gross Air} = \frac{1}{2}\text{air} + \frac{1}{8}\text{fire} + \frac{1}{8}\text{sky} + \frac{1}{8}\text{earth} + \frac{1}{8}\text{water} = 0$$

(Here digit = 08 is the aggregate of 05 elements – earth, water, fire, sky, & air) + The Sun + The Moon + Sacrificing chief = 8

"Kathopnishad" (Katha Branch of Krishna Yajurveda) states –

यदापञ्चावतिष्ठन्ते–ज्ञानानि मनसा सह
बुद्धिश्च न विचेष्टति तामाहुः परमां गतिम्–2/3/10

Yadāpanchāvatiṣthante gyānani mansā sah,
Buddhishcha na vicheṣtati tāmāhuh parmāṃ gatiṃ./2/3/10

Such 05 sense organs resting with the mind and perception, wisdom & consciousness which get stilled is called-final Beautitude.

Such Eternal bliss or Negation of desires warrant the specific state of perfection or salvation as called zero (0) – tension free Infinite potency.

Thus we have seen that zero zenith is the feature of the Absolute Bliss being the highest divine goal of human beings.

3(E) - She – Shock & Global Glamour

Firstly I narrate the chronological status of the fair sex in different Eras –

(a) Vedic period – About 5000 years ago there was The Golden Age wherein women were important organs of the society. They were given education, righteous avenues, and equal rights in patrimony, politics and ritual practices. They were allowed to inherit the virtues of sacrificial rites done by men. Widow – marriage was sanctioned in the society. They were liberal to select their consorts. So their condition was comfortable. Whereas women of the western countries were slave to their consorts as goods for marketing.

(b) Post – Vedic period – Till the fore part of the 3rd century there had been an assault on the freedom of women due to malign composition of texts on religion resulting dependency in their marriage, reduction in female education and prohibition from Vedic recitation. They used to be married at an early age accountable for being unaware of fundamental culture. As a result of which they used to pocket insult and suffer inability to rear up their children properly. Marriage custom in some high breed family used to be customized tediously for dowry system resulting prostitution and Deodasi cult of life. Girls were treated as lifeless substance to consume the robust passion of male figures. Their life was entangled in the clutches of rituals barriers.

(c) Dharmashastra Period – Till the latter part of the 3rd Century, civil and religious codes of law books were composed to correlate the status of women such as guarded by parents in childhood, by husband in puberty and by sons in old age. Their husbands were treated as their lords of life.

(d) Mediaeval Period – Since the 11th till the 18th century curtain-Customs, banned education, widow life, physical offence as penalty for minor mistakes, debarred from patrimony were in practice. Some of their pitiable plights were hearsaid accountable for Greek or Mohammadan Rules.

(e) After Independence – There has been the renaissance in social, economical and political rights to the extent of co-education, co-rituals, co-ordinance, and co-competitions.

Thus in the Rigveda period, daughters were given free to choose their counterparts. The system of widow-marriage was prevalent. There was no example of early or child marriage. Marriageable age in the Rigveda period was prescribed between 16 to 17 years of age. But in post Vedic period, the status of women and their sharing in sacrificial rites began to be questioned by the then society. Although many suitable measures were practised to curb atrocities in conjugal life based on marriage.

That is why in ancient times, the fair sex were annexed with prima potency, intuitive knowledge, Self-sufficiency, affectionate reward, reputation and prestige namely –

1. Ramesha, Urvashi, Nibwari, Lopāmudra, Vishwatarā, Apala having knowledge of Vedic hymms and Economics.
2. In Mahabharat Era – Great lady Kunti, mother of Pandavas, was well versed in Atharva Veda.
3. St. Kushadhwaj's daughter (Vedomati) was Brahma expounder.
4. MAitreyi, pious wife of Yāgyavalkya was philosopher.
5. Kaushalya & Tara were the court member in the regime of king Janaka.
6. Buddha Period – Samedhā & Anupamā were learned monks.

Under the circumstances there may not be husband's anarchy over his wife. She may not be treated as chattel or subordinate falling prey to pros and cons consent of her husband. There may not be patriarchal anarchy over daughter and husband's anarchy over wife. Social exposition of masculine dominance should be averted. She may not be seen as passive body with no will of her own to the extent of legally unfit. Every citizen is the sovereign of his /her own Self. No woman seeks material husband for her protection. Because husband or wife is dependent on his/her Karma Account. The plight of the both is determined by his/her past pursuits.

But alas to mention here that we are confronted with gender violence within global village. Any act of gender-based violence causing physical, emotional and psychological harms is responsible for her deprivation of liberty in private or public life. Violence against women within their houses is a brutal fact in the concerned fields –

(a) Gender based violence against women, refugees and asylum seekers.

(b) Violence in working place including teasing and harassment.

(c) Domestic violence, murder and divorce, rape, battering by husbands and allied male members.

(d) Gender based violence by the police and security forces including torture of female detainees.

(e) Violence connected with trafficking and prostitution.

(f) Genital circumcision.

(g) Foeticides or infanticides.

(h) Traditional practices in male dominated society to violate her rights.

(i) Dowry related violence and early marriage to the extent of burning and tortures which ill-treat her health to higher Maternal Mortality Rate (MMR).

(j) Marital rape and incest etc.

To some extent such plight of the fair sex is accountable for backwardness in education-system from primary to higher level.

Even their influx into schools or colleges act as a prelude to get married rather than risk to higher level in productive dignity of the Nation. In addition to that the traditional system of masculine dominance deep rooted into the mind of the vast community or unequal malpractices are eating into the vitals of our social life. Gandhian dreams of equality and social justice are supressed under cry in wilderness.

English Novelist Thomas Hardy in his novel "Jude The Obscure" says in its preface -marriage should be dissolvable as soon as it becomes a cruelty to either of the parties being then essentially or morally no marriage". He advocates a more rational or saner view of marriage wedlock as Browning

& Dickens. He deals with the question of chastity and monogamy. He believes that a girl who has been raped is thereby rendered unfit for marriage with other man.

As a traditional stream we blame the masculine to have imposed violence on feminine ones. But we should not ignore women of being indulged or interested in adultery in the following ways –

(a) 1st – One who enjoys both her husband and a lover - being faithful to neither and is condemned by the society.

(b) 2nd – Rejects her husband to enjoy with her lover only – also censured by the society.

(c) 3rd – One rejects her husband and enjoys her love with the Supreme Being alone – where bodily perception of life recedes.

(d) Some husband & wives commit suicide due to annoyance of their mischiefs.

(e) Some wives run away with precious assets for lovers.

(f) Old age homes are working for old age couple to have a sigh of relief from Step-daughters or relatives in-law generally

(g) In olden times we came cross the exploitation of male figure by female one as Urvashi Curshed Arjuna (Mahabharat) to be impotent for his denial against her love chain.

Besides the least clad-cum-lewd women of some Hi-Fi society undertake sexual autonomy even after marriage for fair means or foul. No body has rights to override her free will for illicit connection. The youth girl prefer their engagements or jobs as item girls, dream girls, call girls and etc. In support of such sexual autonomy, most countries of the world define "prostitution" a female phenomenon. Most women of the world deny to control over own fertility unwilling to their husbands.

Sometimes we, happen to hear the decrees of the Hon'ble courts to have nullified offence of female harassment or adultery done with dual consent. But it would add a fuel to animal or brutual anarchy in the society. That is why

1. "MANUSMRITI" provided punishment to the extent of banishment for addiction to cross with others' husbands or wives.
2. Apasttamdharma Sutra – Adultery or stuprum is punishable as a crime.
3. Goutamdharmashāstra – If a person commits adultery, he should sustain a life of chastity for 02 years or further on the gravity of crimes.

4. Quran – In An-nur (Name) chapter 24th of the Quran- verse-02 reads – the adulteress or Adulterer must flog each other with 100 stripes without any pity in the presence of believers in Allah as chastisement.
5. Even old civilization 'Sin of Adultery" and Haim Arabia's (Middle East) code of 1754 Be prescribed death by drowning as a punishment for offence by wife or husband.
6. Judian (an ancient religion) i.e. the 10th commandment derived by lord Moses on Mount Sinai (Egypt) includes the 7th commandment thou shalt not commit Adultery set out in the Holy Book of Exodus (departure of the Israelites from Egypt under Moses – 2nd book of the Bible) – The old Testament. Apparently the wage of such sin is – death.
7. The Book – Leviticus in The Old Testament prescribed death penalty for the Adulterer or the adulteress.
8. In Christianity – We find adultery being condemned as amoral sin for both men & women by st. Paul's letter to the Corinthians (Central part of Greece)
9. Jesus, HimSelf, stated that – "a man incurs sin at the moment he looks women with hurtful intent. On the other hand, when the event happened to punish a women for adultering by stoning to death corresponding to Ancient Jewish Law, lord Jesus uttered the famous word – "Let him who has not sinned cast off the 1st stone" to the lewd.
10. In England – In the 17th Century adultery was only a ground of divorce. But it became a Capital offence in Cromwell's Puritanical England in 1670 and later on such offence was nullified as soon as king Charless II. Came back to Monarach. Lord Macaulay also refused to load penalty against adultery.
11. When the penal codes were enacted in yester years 1860 The majority of the Hindu population in India had no official law of divorce as marriage was considered to be religions sacrament & communion and social freedom of polygamy till 1950. Post 1950 the enacted Hindu code does not allow to marry many wives.

    Here it has been the fitness of thing to deal the holy notion of marriage sacrament.

    We come across commotions in conjugal life based on marriage under alien effect. Whereas the holy purpose of marriage is the mutual support with material and spiritual sentiments to the extent of progeny.

Further the term "marriage" connotes the following characters oriently–

(a) As sacrament spiritual union in which men & women utter certain vows reciprocal to bind the both for life and mutual spirit.

(b) As a contract – mutual agreement to live together as husband & wife. He should provide shelter, protection and sustenance and she should care for in-house activities and nurture the progeny.

(c) As an institution – It is a lawful custom in the society to bring stability to the family & social orders.

(d) It is a sacrifice for each Self to the greater good of the family & the society.

(e) The husband must be carrying, understanding, masculine, loving, affectionate and as unselfish provider to the best of his ability through honest means, and the wife is to perpetuate faith and create for fine citizens. She should be more intuitive, emotional, gentle, modest, kind and compassionate for proper care and metamorphosis.

Thus both are equal helpmates in weal and woe despite biological difference between the two. In the Mahabharat (Shanti parva) Bhisma says –

नास्ति भार्या समो बन्धुर्नास्ति भार्या समा गतिः
नास्ति भार्या समो लोके सहायो धर्मसंग्रहे–12/144/16
Nāsti Bhāryā samo bandhurnāsti bhāryā samā gatih,
Nāsti bhāryā samo loke sahāyo dharmasangrahe./12/144/16

12. In 1983 U/S 498A (Amended) of the IPC advocates – cruelty by husband or relatives of a husband is a non-bailable offence. The Dowry prohibition Act 1961 under which give and taking dowry is an offence. whereas U/S 498 IPC – to protect women against cruelty had been notorious as a revenge tool.

13. In 1987-88 – Rajasthan High court passed the state Act which became the Indian Commission on sati (prevention) Act making, committing, altering and glorifying "Satisystem as a crime".

14. In 1997 – The Bombay High court's judgement states – a Christian women can seek divorce on the ground of "physical or mental cruelty" Earlier U/S 10 of the Indian divorce Act, she had to prove that her husband had commited adultery in addition to other charges. But here is a matter of great concern to note that most of women are misusing such codes for skewing their own goals. It

may be enslaving activities on let men pocket insult and blunders causing or revolting furious battles.

But our Constitution protects the natural rights of sexual privacy.

Now I turn to Shakspearean view – "O frailty, thy women" destined to tears and tortures. In India the supersesson of amoral trafficking in girls and women's Act 1956 and anti-dowry Act 1961 fell flat. So it has been the desideratum of the day to cure fair sex of their tortures in social pathology. Here unless and until we follow the foot prints of our oriental seers, we are unable to get them rid of their tortures by mere enactment.

Because law is neither an end in itself nor does it provide end. It is to serve the realization of men's ends ultimate and mediate; it is pre-eminently a means to serve what we think is right. So we should come to human legislation of law and not brooding over omnipotence. It is a systematic approach to human goal of orderliness which is not the helpless silence but the genuine justice of the last and the least, the lowliest and the lost.

Now let me turn to sociological survey of the land Culture-after Independence in India, civil rights, land reforms, common-health, business contract, Bondage labour, anti-dowry Act and other – social laws are lagging behind. The weaker section of the society are almost sailing in the same boat. It is a matter of great sorrow & surprise to note that heinous crimes, suicides and other beastly treatment keep on increasing in India which is acclaimed to be the pioneer of non-violence, rich in human ideal and the preacher of ideoligy to the world. There are many reasons for their failures –

So long as Jurisprudence denies the divinity in human beings and holds the superstitions that human beings are born bad and can be frightened into goodness; as long as the police and prison pose that evil must be met by evil – such inhuman systems making the remedy of the laws aggravate the society.

Here to make the laws effective we have to uproot the evil nature eating into the vitals of our body as a whole and cultivate that divine fervour which st. Sufi receives in this human body as "the golden cage of the birth of spirit". According to st. Luke (Christian) – "Realizing the kingdom of God within him".

Mahatma Gandhi said – "there is court of Ethics than the High court, and that is the Court of Conscience; it supersedes all other courts".

I, also, mean that the mission of laws is to wipe every tear from every eye to remove inhibition in certain practices among people and promote pursuits of perfection by each and every fellow without enquiry to others.

St. Rumi says in the Quran also –

फ आति जल्कुर्बा हक्कहू बल्मिस्की–न–नस्सबीलि–121/30/38
Pha āti jalkurbā hakkahū valmiski na nassabili.121/30/38

"Confer legal rights to the neighbours, the needy and the passers-by without discrimination".

So in order to solve the above problems in the society, we should follow the command of the Vedas – the most fundamental language of the Nature. The Vedas are the kingdom of potential wisdom endowed with the instincts of Nature's law to vouchsafe Creative Consciousness. Because the impulses of the Nature's laws constitute the dynamic principles to control the universe. It is an avowed fact that the National laws allied with Nature's Laws strengthen the Govt. and regulate the destiny of the Nation in ideal and balanced modes.

It recoils that in spite of curbing steps against gender riot, the society may be responsible to let lead a quarter-clad life being the symbol of ultra- modernity and smart living. Here the niche arises that human beings are destined to differ from animal living in free-wheeled style where no complaints are lodged against teasing and molestation. Thus the trends to exhibit maximum body organs through transparency do cause itching incidents subject to automation on the scientific Rule of Polarity in remote sensing devices. But alas to mention here that when question of avoiding such ultra looks arises the fair sex cry to have been encroached of their own freedom in lifestyle. Such social problems get excused on honest love affairs which entail discussions.

It is an axiom that the world is the manifestation of love which attracts molecules, atoms, stars, sex and individual towards gravitational point to sustain natural phenomena. As mother sacrifices true love for her children so we should sacrifice royal love for the land to restore solace to the mankind.

Such principle inspired Jesus Christ (Christian) Confucius (Chinese), Zoroaster (Persian) and Buddha (Buddhist) to sacrifice for human welfare.

At last love has the spiritual consciousness as Bṛhadārankopnishad (Kanva branch of Shukla Yajurveda) states in Rishi Yagyavalkya words to his consort Maitreyi –

न वा अरे पत्युः कामाय पतिः प्रियो भवत्यात्मनस्तु कामाय पतिः प्रियो भवति।
न वा अरे जायायै कामाय जाया प्रिया भवत्यात्मनस्तु कामाय जाया प्रिया भवति।
न वा अरे सर्वस्य कामाय सर्वं प्रियं भवति आत्मनस्तु कामाय सर्वं प्रियं भवति–4/5/6

Na Vā are patyuḥ kāmāya patiḥ priyo bhavatyātmanastu kāmāya patiḥ driyo bhavati
Na vā are jāyāyai kāmāya jāyā priyā bhavatyātmanastu kāmāya jāyā priyā bhavati
Na vā are sarvasya kāmāya sarvam priyam bhavati
Ātmanastu kāmāya sarvam priyam bhavati–4/5/6

O darling! no consort loves her husband for husband's sake rather she loves him for the Self within her husband who is loved.

O darling! no consort loves his wife for wife's sake rather he loves for the Self within his wife who is loved.

O darling! All do not love for all sake but all love for the Self within all.

So love for the Self and not for trade view point. Because I have dealt the Atomic Theory of the Self which is the minutest or subtlemost or the Supreme and The Eternal being the root cause of all.

To be more clear it is not due to love for husband that a husband becomes dear, but due to the love for the Almighty (the Supreme Self) that a husband becomes dear.

Again, it is not due to love for wife that a wife becomes dear; but due to love for God that a wife becomes dear.

Therefore do hear about the Self within the both to think as well as fix your mind on true love. When you understand the clue fully, all this would be understood.

It is not out of need for the husband that a husband is dear; but out of need for the Self that is dear. So we can love others truly when we recognize the Divine Truth in them.

Further nobody loves something for its own sake. All love emerges out of the love in the spiritual Self. This is not the point under the topic. It is the very Universal Supreme Self that is really moving you on of which you are ignoring. If the Self or the life energy goes off you would be non-entity to be repulsive. When the consciousness goes off his/her individuality gets vanished to one of the 05 elements. Further one does not love for salty or sweet beauty nor does one love the mind rather one loves for the Self Light in oneself and this very effort to realize the Self or The Brahma culminates into one's Immortality or Infinite bliss. Such infinite bliss cannot be availed through riches or wealth. So, what's the use of wealth when it is unable to confer perennial bliss in eternal existence. Here Maitreya intended to get the mystery of life devulged with the wise preaching of Rishi Yāgyavalkya.

Nāgārajuna, pioneer of the Mahāyāna school of Buddhism, along with his followers adheres to the principle of God of love and inculcates the need for dedication.

American politician Dean Alford also writes – "God is love" – the New Testament. (2/4/8)

Even M.K. Gandhi advocates the law of love which is based on the Law of truth, without truth there can be no love. Love transcends all animality. Latin dictum –

- Amor vincit omnia–Love wins all. (by English poet Chaucer's "Canterbury Tales" Sanskrit dictum–

  सत्यं शिवं सुन्दरम्

  Satyaṃ Shivaṃ Sundaraṃ.

- Truth is beneficial and good.

Mind that own mother being the living image of maternal or filial affection, transcends all laws i e out-laws (single word-mother-is used) while the next mother is arranged with Latter affection i.e. mother-in-law is used.

So Truth and love are two wheels to run a chariot of life in amity. Further he believes in the sovereign Rule of love which makes no difference. As all have spiritual ties binding all of us in unison. So M.K. Gandhi believed in the inherent goodness of human nature and living faith in God – that was his final device in his struggle to sustain peace-loving-society in the world. Such belief is based on the Truth being the gravitational principle of the universe by which it is supported and in which it inheres. So better to build the ship of Truth in which our soul may sail. To him non-violence is a goodwill towards all.

On the other hand Ethics advocates also – love one another. But it does not clarify as to why we should love one another? I mean since you, he & I are one. Thus oneness and harmonious blend of sentiment tested to infinite felicity makes a person achieve the highest peak. Whereas the transient pleasure begets reaction and the result of which is of competitive nature.

We feel that we are all aloof from the world; but as soon as we come to know that "I am blissful; I be the same", I be the soul of the universe, I be the eternal free – The eternal love springs up. Such love transcends reword, punishment, fear, suspicion and other principles. So it is that 'I' which pleads for thorough examination by Jurisprudes of Jurisprudence and lawyers of the legal system, sociologist and scientist of the human order itself. So love is all evident and pervading.

Further love is a miraculous force to attract each other defying social barriers or parental denial, and arrogance get surpassed on the law of Polarity. Flower does not dream of the bee. It blossoms and a bee comes. So at least a little drop of gentle fluid be poured into love-base account. Such culminated gain of romance is more hearty than cash in one's bank account. Where Mathematics does not teach how to add love or deduct hatred out of one's personality for a balance in life rather it solves arithmetic in life. That is why American Poet Ralf Waldo Emerson said – "Without the rich heart, wealth is an ugly beggar".

Now Russian writer Leo Tolstoy says – "The means to gain happiness is to throw out oneself like a spider to knit adhesive web of love and to catch in all that come". But one has to cross through vicissitudes of life to gain the spring of love – love is a challenge to accept, a candle to light it and a gift to take it. It connects the divine inside with the divine outside. The yearning for union that flows will validate all of existence.

The dignity of love may be depicted in rhythmic mode –

Love is God's will
All are beyond mill
Love is divine all forbade this life
Love is divinity it has its dignity
Love is Almighty it chooses its ability
Love is such God's creation which demands devotion

The equable equation of love may be illustrated as –

Love, the fun of the days
And dense dark of night
Be calm with the wrath of the Sun
Track your trust up in run
When sadness soaks your face
Surmount it with more pace
Let us caress the calm of night
And divulge the mind with inner light.

Such sweet fragrance of divine love may be felt in a better half who longs for her husband's pleasure and vice-versa at the two-in-one state of the spirits in which the wishes of the both are let fused with each other. But we have been indifferent to such pristine conception and as a result of which we have been fallen prey to family repulsion instead of attraction.

But mind that love may be fraud if it is used badly and be boon if it is used nicely. Love should be dignified and generous. It turns into fancy or freak to the plight of subjugation leading to animal heat for molestation. Such freakiness gives birth to brutal behavior and ruin. It works on both the eye-viewer and the blind as well. So a lover or beloved should be firm in judgement or free from hallucination. He/she should withdraw the heat of mind as a tortoise withdraws its playful expansion of the body at risk.

There may be tragedy in love affairs under blind forces. According to Shakespearean tragedy "Othello's love has blind forces to treat the tides and cliffs of the brain, and pleasure & revenge for the effect of the will for the next decision. 'Orthello' as the hero of the tragedy has some inherent fatal flaws in his characer to suffer for credulity and jealousy in his love life.

When beloved Desdemona was strangled to death in sincere & pure love, Othello laments and damns himself to have murdered innocent Desdemona who was quite loyal to him at heart. The whole scene occurred due to malign planning of envious Iago –

"Excellent wretch! Perdition catches my soul.
But I do love thee! And when I love thee
Not, chaos is come again." – 3/3/5

Again English novelist Thomas Hardy in "Tess of D´urbervilles" says that prostitution of the body is not so much amoral as the prostitution of mind and soul. Tess was not at all victim of an inflexible moral law and an inexorable social guilty for the latter crime. She was the purest specimen of womanhood in feeling and purity of her character. But it was all by accident whatever her sins, they are not sins of intention but of laxity and why should she have been punished persistently? Thus Tess remains a glorious example of that love which is the ultimate aim of human life.

Unlike the present plight but on chic and classy track of the fair sex, let me deal our oriental reverence to dilute with the above problem as a step towards global glamour.

1. In course of narrating the glory of women – SARVOTTASA TANTRA says –

स्त्रियो देवाः स्त्रियः प्राणाः स्त्रियश्चैव विभूषणाः
स्त्रिसंगिना सदा भाव्यामभावे
स्वस्त्रियामपि–52/2

Striyo devāh striyah prānāh Striyashcaiva vibhus+anāh
Strisanginā sadā bhāvyāmbhāve
Svastriyāmapi. – 52/12

Women the Almighty, Women the life energy;

and Women the ornament.

We should think of such philosophy of universal gendership also we should coopt own living she-potency of the family in exclusive situation.

2. In Advaitabhāvanopanishad –

अहं स्त्री

Ahaṃ Stri

- "The cosmos is female".

It is the minor Shākta Upnishada that delineated the Tantric outlook and attempted to reconcile with the Vedic approach. It is affiliated to Attharveda. It is related to Tantra-Raj-Tantra of Shree Vidya & Parā Vidyā (transcendental knowledge). Wherein the worship is performed in the Space of one's heart (hṛdayākāsha). Its purpose is to establish relationship between structure of the body and shree chakra (circle of the globe) as the essential character of the universe. Thus it is the process to harmonize the micro and the macro with Shree Chakra being the medium imbibing by Itself each as the characteristic of the Both.

3. In Markandey purana (Devi Mahatmya) –

विद्या समस्तास्तव देवि भेदाः
स्त्रियः समस्ताः सकला जगत्सु–11/5

Vidyā samastāstava devi bhedāḥ,
Striyaḥ samastāḥ saklā jagatsu. /11/5

All learnings and women of the universe are said to be the counterparts of Goddess Durga.

In KOULIKĀRCHANDEEPIKA – While deciphering-

4. The primal Mass –
   (a) विजया (Vijayā) – victorious female said to be Ādya Madya (आद्य मद्य) – primā – spirit or liquor
   (b) अदरख (Adrakha) – (Ginger) – said to be Adya Mansa (prima-flesh)
   (c) जम्बीर फल (Jambir phal) – Lemon fruit - said to be Ādyamin (prima fish)
   (d) खाद्यान्न (Khahdyanna) – Cereal – said to be Ādya Mudra (prima poses or image)
   (e) धर्मपत्नी (Dharma patni) – pious wife – said to be Ādyā Shakti (prima potency)

   Such prima potency charged in creature has been exposed in different ways.

5. Vaisheṣikas (Vaishesic Sutra being one of the earliest texts on Physics) –termed it

- परमाणु (Atom) as-

- शक्तिर्द्रव्यादिस्वरुपमेव (परमाणु)

Shaktirdravyādisvarupmeva (parmānu)

- or The similar dynamo-character of the matter and the Mass.

6. The Buddhists termed it –
   - पूर्णाविद्या (Purnāvidyā)
   - Perfect learning as paragyāparmitā
   - प्रज्ञापारमिता (Transcendental intelligence)
7. Yogi (harmonized soul) – termed it –
   . आध्यात्मिकशक्ति (Ādhyātmashakti)
   - Spiritual power to join embodied soul with the Supreme One.
8. The chemist termed it – "dynamic molecule"
9. The materialist termed it – Energy or dynamic electro-particle fused with proton (+) in equal capacity as essential in the structure of elements.
10. Phychologist – Termed it – "Excitement" applicable to "Mind".
11. Ideologist – termed it – "Consciousness"
12. The Aesthetes termed it – "कवित्वबीजरूपसंस्कार विशेष" Kavitvabijrupsanskār vishes. - Poetic spontaneity.
13. The Charvaka Materialist termed it –

    स्वभावपदार्थानां प्रतिनियतशक्तिः

    Swabhāvpadārthānām pratiniyatshaktiḥ

    Eternal power geared to the nature of the Matter.
14. The westernist termed it – "Idea or Supreme God" So in view of such vast potentialities in marvelous creation of the fair sex, we ought to pay them due respect & honour.
15. Shree Mad Bhagvata purana-deals the majesty of the fair sex -

    सर्वाश्रमानुपादाय स्वाश्रमेण कलत्रवान्

    व्यसनार्णवमत्येति जलयानैर्यथार्णवम्–3 / 14 / 17

    Sarvāshramānupādāya swāshrmen kalatrvān,

    Vyasnārnavamtyeva jalyānairyathārnavam.

    "As one can cross through the ocean with sea-vessels, so one can cross through tragic tides of the life-ocean living with a wife in social system".

    In Hindu mythology (also others) God remains always glorified with His consort. Because without the prime potency (feminine deity), the static force (purusa-male) is inactive.

Further lord Shiva (one of the sacred Hindu trinity) is a corpse without Shakti (dynamic energy). So a powerless God is not God at all. At the same time, both are not detached personalities rather counterparts of the Cosmic Being. The composite nature is Hermaphrodite. Further without the glittering surface (lighting power) a diamond is Just a stone, and without the stone there is no brilliant light liable to be declared as precious gem. So the both are inseparable having equal grandeur. It is something like a dynamo- unmoving it is useless and harmless because it is producing no current; but the moment it starts moving, we immediately put a fence around it "dangers 4000 volts". So god is motionless dynamo and we need the current (power-shakti) to set into motion. So half the talent and half the energy in domestic life cannot be ignored. Both are identical as the Moon and its lustre.

Such cognate conception is coined in KulārnavaTantra–being the foremost Tantra of Kaul school. This Kaul system is the equipollence of Shiva (static) & Shakti (dynamic). This composite image is just like incoming and outgoing respiration (e, ie, Ha, Sa). Such union or wedlock of delight rests between ascending power and the presiding Lord.

The Tantra draws upon Ethics, religion and philosophy to elevate human life marching towards the level of godly one for conjugal commitment. So this pristine knowledge inspires us to maintain harmony in our conjugal life of which the immoderate society is bereft.

16. The Rigveda says that each female carries within herself the male pranic energy and each male carries wither himself the female pranic energy. So the both (wise male & learned female) should bring up his/her issues scholarly and experience the property, performance and the purport of the substances from the land to the lord. The both should have the character of flower and bees.

स्त्रियः सतीः तां ॐमे पुंसः आहुः–1/164/16
Striyaḥ sateeḥ tām aumme punsaḥ aahuḥ–1/164/16

Mutual efforts be undertaken for upbringing of children scholarly. Reciprocal relationship in conjugal life has been avowed in the Shree-Mad Bhāgvat Purāna –

कृतमेकतरेणापि दम्पत्योरूभयोरपि
पत्न्यां कुर्यादनर्हायां पतिरेतत् समाहितः–6/19/18
Kṛtmekatarenāpi dampatyoruvayorapi,
Patnyām kuryādanrhāyām patiretat samāhitah–6/19/18

A person is enough to perform devotion or spiritual service between wife and husband. They both enjoy reciprocal relationship for good. So if a wife is unable to perform such activities, her husband should do so carefully and vice-versa. This way the faithful wife would share the fruits of action. I may annex mutual fedelity with techno-Wi-Fi Alliance to run bicyclic Ethernet of wordly life on Telergy (wireless system of psychic force). Although there is much ado about his/her fidelity and infidelity. But true emotional ties can go beyond such issues. At the same time, our civilization is advancing towards Self-standing mode to receive more means for life-run.

In Indian perspectives 04 kinds of sacrificial rites are executed from birth to death for virtuous version in human life such as –

i. Rishi-sacrifice
ii. Ancestors' obsequial sacrifice
iii. Guest hospitality
iv. Scarifice for living beings

These sacrifices cannot be performed without wife's sharing. These sacrifices have the sublime goal in 04 dimensions –

i. Birth of child
ii. Rapture with certain constraints in chastity
iii. Collective or organized life
iv. Moral binding

In Sarbollāsa Tantra by sarvānand Nath –

स्त्री मात्रे हरपत्नी स्यात् पुमान् मात्रे च शंकरः
विवाहं बन्धनं ज्ञेयं वर्तिस्थो वह्निवत् प्रिये–34/14
Stri mātre harpatni syāt pumān mātre cha shankaraḥ,
Vivāham bandhanam gyeyam vartistho vahnivat priye–34/14

"All ladies are lord Visnu's consorts and all gents are Lord Shankar. Holy wedlock in marriage deems to be flame (fire) in a wick". Here non-difference at base between Lord Har & Shankar is hinted at also.

Akin to this Cosmic theory it is puerile to underestimate the fair sex in comparison with the sterner one.

Further women are viewed with debility, frailty and war-shirker. But we cannot ignore the fact that women are as zealous as men. Both apply their intrinsic qualities in their own ways. Men seldom foster their children with proper tenacity and filial affection as women do. Further if men have enhanced their efficiency women do enhance their tolerancy. Men lack in painstaking whereas women lack in onerous pursuits. However women have risen to the higher level of sacrifice for heroism at national borders. Their contribution to nationality throughout the history is not lesser than that of men. In modern days women play marvelous role in administration, architecture, medical Science, Space-research, National Security, Music, Theatre, Politics, Mass-communication, I.T., social reforms, cosmetology, Meso-therapy, legal practices, Journalism, divine preaching and the like.

But alas to mention here that the rude and metallic society relishes women as cesspits to dive deep into sports of love. Further the indiscreet people use them as sweet media to propagate generation only. Such beastly behaviours with the fair sex entail fighting against their back and call service together with cultural backwardness thrust upon them.

Now I give a clarion call to pay honours for wives as co-heirs for the grace of life. We ought to erase hurts in congugal hearts. They should be freed from selfish regards and carnal pretences. They must be allowed full freedom for their proper development. To make such practices effective more than God's grace, the mood of the society needs to be changed with Acharya Manu's remarks of right respect –

यत्र नार्यस्तु पूज्यन्ते रमन्ते तत्र देवताः
यत्रैतास्तु न पूज्यन्ते सर्वास्तत्राफलाः क्रियाः–3 / 56
Yatra nāryastu poojyante ramnte tatra devtāḥ,
Yatraitāstu na poojyante sarvāstatrāfalāḥ kriyāḥ. 3/56

Gods dwell where women are honoured, all efforts end in a fiasco where women are dishonoured (Krishnayajurveda).

Our Taittriya Brāhman (KrishnaYajurveda) conveys also –

अयज्ञियो एष वा योऽपत्नीकः–9 / 4 / 66
Ayagyiyo eṣa vā yo!ptnikaḥ–9/4/66

"Husband minus wife and the like is unfit for sacrificial rites".

Apastambadharmsutra conveys one to help women in deserted solitude i.e. woods –

अरण्ये च स्त्रियं नासंभाष्य व्यतिब्रजेत्–1 / 4 / 14 / 29
Aranye cha striyam nāsambhāsya vyatibrajet./1/4/14/29

"Do not go away without inquiring about women in the forest i.e. frightened spot. The purpose is to support them and not to get the better of their helplessness to the extent of mass rape or stuprum or disgrace as heard frequently today.

Further in The Geeta Lord Krishna, being colossal character, feminized Himself to be Kirti, Shree, Vāk, Smriti, Medha, Dhṛti and Kshamā for

7 divine wives with their verbal or literal senses –

1. Glory
2. Prosperity
3. Speech Goddess
4. Divine or deistic memory
5. Divine intelligence
6. Self content
7. Patience or forgiveness-

कीर्तिः श्रीर्वाक्य नारीणां स्मृतिर्मेधा धृतिःक्षमा–10/34
Kirtih shreervākya narinām smṛtirmedhā dhṛtiḥ kṣamā–10/34

Lastly in order to avoid atrocities committed with women, we should follow the footprints of our oriental sacred canons or conceptions with fidelity. Wherein one behaves with anyone as one would behave with oneself. Hitherto I have dealt sad plights and their remedy for feminine upheaval. But it is frequently seen that the ultra-fashionable lady despises her husband if he fails to follow her whimsical commands. She wants to see him as a puppet in her hands to meet her own ends. But she should be aware of the fact that –

नारीणां भूषणं पतिः
Nāreenāṃ bhuṣanaṃ patiḥ

The husband is the real ornament of her celebrated life. Only then a sweet relation may prevail between the two hemispheres.

The report in the Science research Journal published by the University of Groningen, Netherlands, in 2004, reveals the inherent merit of feminine figures. When they are in tensions they secrete "Oxytocin hormones which lessen the effect of Cortisol hormones" to transmit positive mood & emotions. As a result of which they are not liable to be severed of affinity with their family. Whereas the masculine figures transmit negative results –

Further the magnanimity of the mother (female) is being focused here-

नास्ति मातृ समा छाया नास्ति मातृ समा गतिः।
नास्ति मातृ समं त्राणं नास्ति मातृ समा प्रिया।।
Nāsti māṭṛ samā Chāyā, nāsti māṭṛ samā gatih;
Nāsti māṭṛ samam trāṇm, nāsti māṭṛ samā priyā.

No patron (shadow) like mother, no haven like mother, no lifeline like mother and no nice (heavenly) like mother.

Chapter - 4

Holistic Care & Lord Testament

4(A) – Yogic Science & Holistic Therapy

Domestic approach to Yoga teems with superstitions. Yoga resembles recluses who renounce life and living in caves of the Himalayas. But we should know above superstitions that Yoga is life-abundance and not life negation.

Lord Krishna says in The Geeta –

तपस्विभ्योऽधिको योगी ज्ञानिभ्योऽपि मतोऽधिकः
कर्मिभ्यश्चाधिको योगी तस्माद्योगी भवार्जुनः–6 / 46
Tapaswibhyoadhiko yogi gyānibhyoapi matoadhikaḥ,
Karmibhyashchādhiko yogi tasmādyogi bhavārjunaḥ./6/46

"Yogi is superior to ascetics; he is deemed to be superior to those who are versed in sacred discipline; the yogi is superior to those who perform rituals & duties with some motives. Therefore Arjuna, you do become a yogi. Here the very term "Yogi" we should mean Karmayogi (doer of the worldly pursuits and rites).

The Yogic Science was greatly misunderstood as religion for many whereas the Science of Yoga covers a great range of human problems. It solves not only the problems of the spiritual life but also helps to ease the problems of our day to day ailments.

Since the whole body is a composition of prāna and the mind. The pranas are responsible for action or performance and motion in life; the mind is responsible for thinking and feeling; the mind and prana are the great forces in our physical system, if the both lose their balance, corresponding imbalance is created in our mental and physical behavior. This imbalance in individual life hinders to harmonize Creative thinkingwith fertile activities for the good of all.

That is why the Geeta says –

योगस्थः कुरु कर्माणि संगं त्यक्त्वा धनंजय
सिद्धयसिद्धयोः समो भूत्वा समत्वं योग उच्यते–2/48

Yogasthaḥ kuru karmāni sangam tyaktvā dhanajaya,
Siddhyasiddhyoḥ samo bhutvā samatvam yog-uchyate./2/48

"Here the uniformal balance should be maintained through the state in Yoga whether the actions are fulfilled or unfulfilled. The purpose is to perform one's duty or rites ignoring one's thirst of infatuation for consequences. Because the instant attainment of will forbids one's bliss. Such balance of the prāna is to be practised with Asanas (postures) and Prānāyam (breath control). Whereas mental forces are to be balanced by the practice of dhārana (Concentration). & Dhyāna (Meditation). Yoga practices insert more pressure on mind being the resolutionary power of the Self. We can sanctify our Self with the mind, cognition, concentration or sanctification. Here I want to clearify that the heart is the body oragan but the mind is soul-organ. But both organs are interdependent on the outcome of positive and negative ideas. If our Wisdom is impure or indulged in lust, anger, longings, selfishness, haughtiness, we prefer negative or heinous activities. So only the metaphysical yoga devices would bring better impression to avert physical mental and adverse itching. Such Yogic Science would help us to treat ARTHA as pure knowledge of Self, the Brahma, God, salvation instead of ample riches to invite lust, anger or self-love.

To me until our body consciousness under Nescience and Delusion (Māyā) is substituted by our existence in self-faith or self-consciousness, all barriers around the mind would not be averted for unified bliss. Such substitution would relish super sentiment or flavour or elegance, super fragrance or super sensation or feeling and global connectivity. Because body consciousness or heat or thermal energy is the repercussion of negative thoughts which may be absorbed with yogic system at thermal equilibrium by Telekinesis (generating immense energy of the mental arena with strong power of concentration to propel an object without touching as Trātaka practice); where heat is absorbed (+) from its environment and released (-) to its environment. Further we know that our body being the most computer of the planet is the constituent of 5-Matter in which –

- 72% is water (H2O thermal energy in solid, liquid or gaseous state)
- 12% earth
- 6% air
- 4% fire
- 6% space or sky

Here the huge percentage of water, being magical liquid as memory or intelligence forms a tide-wave in objects by vibration due to gravitational force among celestial bodies like- The Sun, The Moon and etc. So it is through yogic meditation in psychic system, we should avail virtues of peace in life. Except the space or sky, the remaining 04 elements need purification to boost up health, longevity and immaterial access. Further the body consciousness is mortal or temporal just like a fruit sprout develops, ripens and rots. But the soul seed within becomes stronger and solid. So immense power of the soul-seed should not be applied to macro-cosmic affairs which recede our highest goal of life – eternal bliss.

Whereas Material Science develops mental complexity, mental imbalance, behavioural defects to the extent of psycho-analysis or psychiatry. Now psychoanalyses or agonies in modern life are being explained at one place to assess their gigantic gamut and avoid them as fallacius oddness or fearfulness in –

(a) Racial relation
(b) Family relation
(c) Neighbour relation
(d) Cultural relation
(e) Religious relation
(f) Professional relation
(g) Linguistic relation
(h) Political relation
(i) Partnership relation
(j) Industrial relation

(k) Consumer-producer relation

(l) Economic relation

(m) Foreign relation

Here only the yogic techniques or practices would suffice to surmount odd-relationship and save even from temper.

Initially let me explain the term yoga as-

युज्यते एतद् इतियोगः
युज्यते अनेन इतियोगः
युज्यते तस्मिन् इतियोगः

Yujyate etad itiyogaḥ
Yujyate anen itiyogaḥ
Yujyate tasmin itiyogaḥ

That is to connect and balance oneself to the Almighty i.e. The Self + Super Self.

हिरण्यगर्भ (Hiranyagarbha) – The Brahma (primeval womb – the Supreme Cosmic Creator) was the foremost oriental proclaimer of the Yoga Discipline which came down chronologically to sage Patanjali who defined yoga as-

चित्तवृत्ति निरोधः Chittavrttinirodhah – categorially –

1. Chitta – is the mind or the instrument that stands between the mind and the cosmos. As a gardener applies tilling instrument to nourish the garden, so a man applies the mind to deal with the world. Acted upon the things of the external world through the senses, the mind prevents a man from the panorama of those things as on the spectrum of the life action. The mind transmits through power into action within the body. Thus the Chitta has 02 functions –

   (a) Receptive or Negative

   (b) Active or positive

   In a vivid sense it transmits from the world to a man within and also from the man within the external world.

2. VRITTI – Signifies eddy or mundane circuit.

3. Nirodha – Signifies restraint or control.

In this way Yoga practice is the control of whirlpool, change of mind or voluntary direction of what is commonly called "Thought".

Further concentrate one's mind into super mind with wisdom, cognition, confidence, consciousness and recognition as between father & son under filial affection. That is to favour the mind, direction and action for super connection. This technical process bridles the fickle flow of the mind to engage the Self with the Super Self.

Now the "Chittavrtti" (the mind and the mudane circuit) are of 05 types –

(1) Pramāna (Testimony of knowledge) which consists of 03 types –

(a) Pratyaksha (Perceptional or ocular evidence) – Intelligence through wisdom, mind and sense organs void of confusion and suspicion.

(b) Anumān (Inference) – Knowledge of the vision indirectly through perceptional device.

(c) Āgam (Sacred doctrine or scripture) – Knowledge through the Vedas, traditional texts and statements of the authority or trustworthy personalities.

2) विपर्यय (Viparyay) – Mịscomprehension as acknowledgement of the pearl in the conch boat. Some scholar treat misconception and Nescience to be the same wrongly. Because misconception happens occasionally. Whereas Nescience retains until final beatitude or identification with the Supreme spirit as योगा दर्शन (Yoga darshan) of sage Patanjali says –

तदभावात्संयोगाभावोहानं तदृशेः कैवल्यम्

Tadbhāvātsamyogābhāvohānaṃ tadrisheh kaivalyaṃ.

- "There has been the negation of union between the Puruṣa and Prakriti by the Nescienc; and the absolute negation of the past and future sufferings through consciousness is the emancipation of the Self in order to connect with the Brahma.

More or less the Brihadaranyakopnishad also gives quasi conception –

यदा सर्वे प्रमुच्यन्ते कामाः येऽस्य हृदिश्रिताः
अथ मर्त्योऽमृतो भवत्यत्र ब्रह्म समश्नुते–4/4/7

Yadā sarve pramuchyante kāmāḥ yeasya hṛdishritāh,
Atha mṛttyomrito bhavatyatra Brahma samashnute. /4/4/7

"When all wishes of the heart get disappeared, the jiva becomes immortal and communes with the Brahma".

(3) विकल्प (Vikalpa) – Contrivance – It is not actual and has verbal-based knowledge or verbal speculation.

(4) निद्रा (Nidrā) – Sleepiness – It acts as a circumference against the negation of the knowledge which gets recollected on awakening.

On awakening a man forsakes laziness and connects himself with sense-organs in active mode.

(5) स्मृति (Smṛti) – Recollection or Reflection – The act of manifesting the experienced factors. Such reflection resides in the heart region as –

हृदये चित्तसंवित् = योगदर्शन (yogadarshan)

Hṛdaye chittasamvit = yogdarshan -3/34

- "Further there is a lotus like holy-cum-ethereal space in the heart region accountable for spiritual knowledge."

Further the Yoga is not a religion but a scientific system which develops brain and brawn harmoniously. It has its own conception on ailments. To its views ailments manifest in the body but do not originate in the body; ailments cause with the state of imbalance between nervous system and hormonal secretion. So Yoga defines ailments in subtle manners and we should treat them accordingly.

There are 08 manners to right or healthy living as –

1. Yama (यम) – Self controlling and observance teaches social ethics which is made up of 05 commandments –
   (a) Non-violence or harmlessness
   (b) True to all beings
   (c) Abstinence from theft
   (d) Non-discontentment
   (e) Non-avarice
2. Niyam (नियम) – (Self-regulatory rules) – is personal ethics consisting of 05

   Rules as –
   (a) Inner – outer purity
   (b) Satiety
   (c) Penance (practice of tolerance or religions austerities)
   (d) Self-perseverance or spiritual reading
   (e) Devotion to God

   These 02 universal principles are worthy of limitation by one and all – whether one is rich, poor, Brahmin, SC/ST, Hindu, Muslim, men, women, old & young- irrespective of time, place or circumstances.
3. आसन (Aasan) – A particular posture or poise of exercise in STHIRASUKHAMAASANAM– स्थिरसुखमासनम् - pleasing posture of the body. It is very tersely put by sage patanjali as –

(a) Right poise

(b) Right attitude

(c) Right position

Therefore Asanas are meant to develop the physical & physiological stability, good health, lightness and agility of the body-mind. Through such techniques a perfect citizen is a fit instrument to the Almighty to dwell within.

4. Prānāyām (प्राणायाम) – Restraining or suspending breath during mental recitation of the attributes of the deity. It has 03 processes –

   (a) पूरक (Purak) – Filling up breath from outside.

   (b) कुम्भक (Kumbhak) – Stopping or sustaining breath by closing the mouth and nostrils with the fingers of the right hand.

   (c) रेचक (Rechak) – Emission of breath. Further it is the right control of life force which mainly consists of suppression of breath, regulation of breath and control of breath.

   Here it is worthy of note that regular Asanas and Pranayam are essential to maintain osteo-system, muscular system, repository system, reproductive system and glandular system for healthy state.

5. Pratyāhār (प्रत्याहार) – Abstraction or right retreat or marching back – It is concerned with restraint of senses. It gives mental stability essential for intellectual clarity, alertness and agility. It, further, eliminates tension. Such alert and agile mind can dispose off day's burden easily.

6. Dhārnā (धारना) – Steady abstraction on concentration at one place or faculty of retaining in the mind.

   Yogadarshan of sage Patanjali says –देशबन्धश्चित्तस्य धारणा–3/1– Deshabandhacittasy dhārnā

7. Dhyān (ध्यान) – Meditation or mental representation of the personal attitude of deity – योगदर्शन (Yogdarshan) of Patanjali -"Deshabandhacittasya Dharana.

   तत्र प्रत्ययैकतानता ध्यानम्–3/2

   Tatra pratyayaikatāntā dhyānam. -3/2

   "The practice of centric-ceaseless flow of the mind circuit." The key benefit of meditation is to be more patient in relation, more serene at office and happier is solitude with better life-partners, parents, businessmen and friends. Further our creativity and intuitive knowledge are seated at the higher level of the mind. The super consciousness, being a part of mind is seated above "middle mind" (yogic term). The whole vista of potentialities, seated in a phychic body, is very closely associated with many benefits to mankind viz –

(a) Arising above the animal nature
(b) Gaining vitality and energy
(c) Divine manifestation of love
(d) State of blissful intoxication
(e) Acquiring power of intuition

Thus with the practice of Yoga meditation, the youth can lead an active and conscious life of creativity void of tensions & fears.

8. समाधि (Samādhi) – Perfect absorption of thought into an object of meditation i.e. Supreme Spirit or devotion to penance or submersion to penance. It is of 02 types –

   (a) सविकल्पक (Savikalpak) – Optional – the state of distinction between the subject and the object or the knower and the known.

   (b) निर्विकल्पक (Nirvikalpak) – Non-optional –No distinction between knower and the known or the subject and the object.

Here the latter 03 stages (Dharnā, Dhyān and Samādhi) are meant for self-enlightenment and not in general life. And the former 05 stages, if nurture with care, would prepare the body, the mind and the sound intelligence to serve as a fit vehicle for sound growth in life.

Thus the 08 yogic manners or procedures can remove social evils. The individual consciousness working at the level of the mind, is made to journey through yogic meditation for higher goal of the mind. Further yogic practices help to establish harmonious relation to the external world combined with auto-suggestive techniques of meditation which enables an individual to flow with life rather than fight with it.

In view of Yoga, the stages may vary but the truth is one. It ensures not only physical pleasure but also emotional stability together with firmness of intellect. It, further, develops the character so as to ensure the unity and the harmony of the body, the mind and the soul culminating into a well integrated personality. In the long run it helps one to achieve a perfect understanding of the intellect and the body based on experience. For example – brain may be sure of sirshasan (upside down pose). When it comes to the factual knowledge of Asan, one realizes that one has to understand the use of arms, the neck and the correct position of the spine; again how to support legs, where exactly the weight should be and how one should balance one's own self without pulling strain on the arms or the neck. In this way one gradually masters the art of keeping energy in "zero position i.e. observing that the energy of the body is not dissipated but adjusted and retained within the body. Through this training one learns that the body and the mind attain immediate perception known as legitimate knowledge.

In Yogic hygiene, there are 05-life-wind mechanized with arteries and veins of the body purposely termed as –

1. प्राण (prāna) – heart region – breathing for life. It moves through mouth and nose pervading from the upper part of the nose up to the heart region.
2. अपान (apāna) – breathing out downwards – Anus region – pervading through the nucleus to the sole. It moves downwards to the lower orifice of the alimentary canal.
3. समान (Samān) – friendly digestive – Navel region – it has friendly motion around the cavity of the navel to make shift digestive chyme or juice within the whole body.
4. व्यान (Vyān) – veinal diffusion – whole body- it diffuses through the tubular organs of the body. Here tubular vessels are termed as Ida, pingala, susmna, Amolmbuja, kuhoo, sankhini etc.
5. उडान (Udāna) – breathing upwards – throat region- it rises up the throat and enters into the crown of the head. This life-wind helps to escape from the subtle body (Self) through skull aperture at death time.

Here it is to be noted that out of 72 thousands Nadis (channels) in the body the more important ones are IDAA, PINGALAA & SHUSUMNAA through which the flow of the mind, the prana and the Self move respectively. Gradually there comes a moment in yogic life when we begin to realize that the body is not final; the body and the spirit is controlled by the mind; it is the Self (Atma) which controls the mind and the body.

So when we become the master of the Self we would be the master of the mind and the body to avoid ailments. Thus the full knowledge of thought and action can. alone, strengthen the harmony between the creative thinking and dynamic pursuits to achieve the highest goal of life.

It is worthy to note here that the Science of HATHA YOGA (physiological balance and physical purification) is, also, based on these twin (Mind & Prana) forces.

Further I should specify that Yoga is a mystical Science in which Kundalani power (serpentine power to release trauma from energetic body through meditation) is generated to attain Super Consciousness or realization of the Spirit. This power rotates around the static centres of the body.

The micro-substances within SUSUMNAA vessel (between Ida & pingala) are chakras (wheel shaped centers). Each center radiates thousands of Nadis (transmitters for soundings) enforcing in varied directions throughout the whole body. Now it entails relevance to explain 03 Nadis (transmitters) as –

(a) IDAA (nervous system) – earthly sound associated with the Moon ending in the left nostril.

(b) PINGALAA (nervous system) – this sound associated with the Sun ending in the right nostril.

(c) SUS.UMNAA (central nervous system) – a hollow passage or vessel running through spinal cord and ends in Brahmanānda (an aperture at the crown of the head) through which the soul is said to be escaped from the body and the hollowed vessel is Kundalini Being (lotus having spiral flower) in consciousness.

Further the mass energy stored in Mulādhar Chakra (between anus & penis), begins to pass through SUSUMNA with great force drawn to the static force in SAHASRAARA CHAKRA (thousand of spokes of steering wheel) which has occult power to qualify divine spirit. In this process the CHAKRAS get pierced and the major amount of OJAS (virility) gets transmitted to the spiritual energy stored in the brain which enables the seeker to experience divine vision. Lastly the standard value of yoga is to keep our body and mind hale and healthy in homeostasis. This SAHASRARA CHAKRA in the physiology of the body acts as a dynamo which causes to release many important electric and energetic lights being the gate way of salvation.

Further 07 CHAKRAS are being illustrated again in sequence –

Sl. No.	Location of Chakras	Name of chakras	Phase of self-discovery
1.	Anus	Mulādhār	Self-preservation
2.	Genital	Swadhisthān	Self-gratification
3.	Navel	Manipur	Self-definition
4.	Heart	Anahad	Self-acceptance
5.	Throat	Visudha	Self-expression
6.	Brows	Agni	Self-realization
7.	Crown (mid-centre of skull)	Sahasrapadma	Self-vision

One deal has been left to focus on psycho-physiological aspect of Yoga is of more importance correlated between the mind and the body in the following facets –

(a) Withdrawal or control of sense

(b) Concentration or exclusive attention to one object or idea

(c) Mind – the most mystic component of the body, the cause of pleasure and pain. So who to harness the mind is taught in yogic practices.

(d) Meditation – It helps to wipe out past experiences and avoid pile of new ones. It is a sound strategy to rescue against material shocks which hinder self-realization. This is the essential tool for righteous practice to repeal peacelessness resulting positive attainment.

(e) The Science of forced meditation – practised in an unusual mode through hexa-karmas –

I. Neti (नेति) – Nasal cleaning

II. Vasti (वस्ति) – Stomach cleaning

III. Nauli (नौलि) – Abdominal cleaning

IV. Trātak (त्राटक) – Purification of the cranial region or kapalbhati

V. Dhauti (धौति) – Internal cleaning

VI. Mudrā (मुद्रा) – Inner attitude or gait

Now our sweet and sour experiences in life warrant brain compression & concussion accountable for nervousness.

As there is the correlation between the mind and the body. So 03 chambers of the brain gets disturbed due to bruises and each of the 03 chambers has the following activities-

(a) Cerebrum (proper brain) – Which controls mental activities. It being the center of consciousness, reasoning, memory and intelligence. acts for visual hearing, inhaling and speech measures.

(b) Cerebellum (hinder brain) – It controls, harmonizes and adjusts locomotive system

(c) Medulla oblongata (Marrow) – It controls heart-beat, B.P., sneezing, vomiting and treats digestive fluid.

So the only Yoga practices play vital role in harmonizing life-vehicle.

On the other-hand, Micro-biologists hold that each cell contains total potentialities of the evolutionary part and yogis say that the infinite potency of the knowledge exists within the individual who is "miniature version of the universe". The consciousness of the mind through yogic practices, if allowed to soar high, transcends the higher level of the Mind-the seat of Super Consciousness where one can observe the real "I" who reveals divine entity void of pains due to Nescience egoism, attainment, repugnance and instinctive clinging to mundane affairs as sage Patanjali says in Yogadarshan –

अविद्यास्मितारागद्वेषाभिनिवेशाः क्लेशाः–2 / 3

Avidyāsmitārāg dveṣābhiniveshāḥ kleshāḥ./2/3

"Here Avidyā (Nescience), Asmitā (Egoism), Rāg (Attachment), Dweṣa (Repugnance), Abhiniveśa (clinging to mudane affairs) are pains in life.

Besides scientific approach to yoga, it is the philosophy of righteousness which has backing of centuries' of experience. Yoga Philosophy states that with the practice of regular SADHANĀS one can rise out of pains and miseries of ignorance into the bright Sun of inner illumination, awareness and wisdom. Without awareness or inner knowledge one cannot steer one's vessel properly in order to lead a full & healing life.

Some fellows take pains in the form of mental agony out of unfulfilled ambition, fear and inscurity, while the other fellows may rack the body caused by indiscipline and bad habits of life style. Whereas Yoga Philosophy ensures healthier & fuller life.

It is, also, an Art which disciplines and develops the body, emotion and intellectual faculties of the individual and its purpose is to hone human beings.

Latin proverb – "Mens sana in corpore sano" means – a sound body has a sound mind. So if one hopes to live one's life completely, one should treat body to be a temple in which sacred activities are done. So at least save life – span with yogic exercises (even subtle ones) in lieu of letting life – span for ailments.

Yoga indicates laughter therapy also. Because it is a psycho-neural vitalizer to poise the mind and the body. That is why William James, American psychologist speaks – "We do not laugh because we are happy; we are happy because he laugh. So reconnect to our playful or fun part and enjoy the wonders of deep bellied laugh".

Further there are 8-supremo felicitous faculty power to enjoy macro-micro character or state of the body prone to lightness or heaviness at will through marvellous skill –

(a) अणिमा (Aṇimā) – Atomic nature of the Super human power. The Chief monkey (Hanuman) of extraordinary strength and prowess entered into the mouth of demon Surāsa enroute to Lanka territory in an atomic form as depicted in the Val. Ramayan. -1/156, 2/47

(b) लघिमा (Ladhimā) – Successive lightness or levity at will. The power to ramble in ethereal arena as depicted in Yoga Sutra. – 3/39

(c) महिमा (Mahimā) – Power of increasing size at will – As the Chief monkey increases His body size before a demon surasā as depicted in Val – Ramayan. (SundarKand). – 1/154

(d) गरिमा (Garimā) – To make oneself heavier at will. The Chief monkey weighed heavier to impede the route of Bhimsen as depicted in the Mahabharat (Vanparava). – 146 – 147

(e) प्राप्ति (Prāpti) – Obtaining power of anything at will – to obtain anything at mere solemn will or wish.

(f) प्राकाम्य (Prākāmya) – Freedom of will or power of Nature's enterprises – irreisistible auto-fulfilments of will for anything.

(g) वशित्व (Vashitva) – Authoritative subjugation – to subduce of 05 elements and allied substances.

(h) ईशत्व (Ishtwa) – Superiority of governance – The authority to rule over all physical elements in production.

In the university of Barcelona, (Spain), doctors and philosopher have produced extra-ordinary results from their researches into the effect of Shavāsan or yoganidra (psychic sleep state between sleep and consciousness) on the human body. Medical investigation has shown that it is not hypnosis but an entirely different technique. It is a practice where we are allowed to relax but not to sleep. One must know that the sleep is not true relaxation which occurs definitely in awakened state. During the practice of savāsan, we may see Delta wave appearing in few tunes when the subject is tired; sometimes Theta waves appear also. Whereas Alfa waves predominate essentially. Thus with the practice of Yog-Nidrā, we have been able to alter and harmonize the pattern of the brain waves with certain prānāyāma and chanting of Mantras. Doctors of the said university exposed people to medical investigation with sophisticated instruments and found that "Zero" was being tonned, Alpha (α) brains were predominant; and 'M' was being tonned to the extent of Theta (θ) waves. Thus if one is suffering from hypertension and blood pressure, one feels permanent relief on chanting 'AUM' for a short time. Regular practices of yoga also, cure diabetes, cardic disorders, kidney ailmets, amnesia, dysmenorrhea, arthritis and other psychosomatic complaints.

Further Medical Science discovered that within each individual lies the key to relieve physical, mental and emotional pains –

(a) At the purely physical level – the brain produces its own Narcotic Agent called "Beta Endorphin" secreted from the Hypothalamus in the mid brain which contains Enkephalins (pain soother). These have been demonstrated to control pituitary gland and the entire hormonal system of the body. American scientist and psychiatrist or psychopharmacologist, N.S. Kline of Rockland State Hospital (renamed- Nathan Kline Institute of psychiatric research (U.S.A.) & Canadian psycho – pharmacotherapist Heinz E. Lehmann of MCGill University, Canada obtained remarkable results from Endorphin treatment of the patient suffering from various psychotic and neurotic conditions. There hormones are involved helping to soothe the brain and the mind during trouble period. They are released simultaneously with ACTH (Andreno-Cortico-Trophic-Harmones) which triggers the release of stress-handling harmones i.e. Cortisone. This implies that Enkephalinase represents an action by the brain to encounter physical effects of stress in itself.

Like electro-stimulation prescribed to lure deadly diseases, Yoga, also, increases the electrical activity of the brain with technique such as Kriya yoga, Kunjalni, Banda and Prānāyām. These techniques tend to eliminate corroding elements eating into the vital of our body. They exert direct effect on the Limbo-Hypothalmic Endrophin system. By soothing the turbulent mind, emotion and physical structure (metabolism) enable us to regain consciousness and control our inner process. Again the mysterio-internal workings of the brain find their natural tranquility and powerful rhythm to flow with life. Now India which is rapidly industrialized, is heading towards arena of speed, strain and stress. Such life on wheels makes heavy demand on our nerves which are the invisible branches of brain. When nerves collapse, anxiety and neurosis of one kind or the other set in. further when the life is devoid of composure and cohesion, we are destined to create feelings such as self-pity, depression and lack of self-consciousness. However Yoga, on the other hand, unifies all our dissipated energy to achieve the highest goal of life. Our sanctified yogis have explored and understood the course of avowed observance of silence (Moun Vrat) through which all types of anguish and avarice vanish away, if practiced for, at least, 30 minutes. Through steadiness of mind a poise is maintained between cerebral hemispheres to transfrom even criminal career of terrorists into lovely one. Regret to mention here that we have been indifferent to such useful and rare endowment. Whereas much interests have been given to Integral Discipline in European Countries.

We all know that prevention is better than cure. So the Yoga is prevention which ensures strong yet elastic nerves that face a good deal of hectic activities, equanimity & poise. It has been discovered globally that most cancer patients suffer mental depression whereas yoga, through many ASANAS, Pranayam, Bandas (locks) Prtyāhār (Sense withdrawl) Mudrās (Gesture) Kriyās (cleaning techniques) and Dhārnā (Concentration) can provide tranquility of mind. Thus when stillness in the mind pervades creative calm and smile bloom within.

It is through yogic practices which are natural tranquillizer for developing countries even in hardship we can enjoy sound life at lower cost. In a nut shell its utility lies in –

I. Transforming our superficial way of living into deep and wide consciousness.
II. Converting over fragmentary experience into an inner and outer harmony.
III. Transforming our Hitlerian ego into universal spirit of Adi Shankracharya, Buddha, Vyas, Patanjali, Christ, Mohammad, Guru Nanak and etc.
IV. Transforming ordinary life into a life in Supreme Being.
V. Transforming the selfish mind of the leaders of the land into public benefits as suggested

न त्वहं कामये राज्यं न स्वर्गं नापुनर्भवम्
कामये दुःखतप्तानां प्राणिनामार्तिनाशनम्

Na twaham kāmaye rājyam na swargam nāpunarbhavaṃ,
Kāmaye dukhataptānām prānināmārtināshanaṃ.

'I do not long for sovereignty, heaven and salvation, but I long for the relief of the afflictions and suffering of the living beings.'

Their motto should be Yeoman service at all cost and not power at whims. Such harmoniously well-grounded leaders would chalk out healthy and welfare plans to the wide interests of the Nation geared for cosmopolitan spirit.

Thus I have reiterated that the Yoga is the holistic Science of therapy opposed to medical therapy. Because Yoga therapy is a "whole" treatment of the ailments. Whereas Allopathic medicines only cure the afflicted organs. Yogic techniques exert very positive effect on the illed organs.

Unlike allopathic treatment, it is within easy reach of each and every being of any Nation, caste, creed and sex.

4(B) – Ritual Science & Eco-Care

Firstly we should be aware of the fact that our surroundings shape our moods, thoughts and dreams. In every room of my little house, I have bouquet of fresh flowers. So we have to start to improve the quality of our personal environment which is an investment and not an expense. So let me invest my mind to know about Biosphere and its plight.

The Biosphere is formed of 03 compositions –

(a) Lithosphere – sound pollution, ultrasonic sound

(b) Hydrosphere – dust particles, thermal water sewage

(c) Atmosphere –

  i. Fossil fuel – petroleum, natural gases, coal and etc.

  ii. Air pollution – burning of coal & wood, factory, automobile, railways, aero-plane emission, exhaust gas, smog and heavy metal – Pb, Cu, Ag, Zn, atomic explosion, pesticides & bio-magnification

Besides, we have the device to assess the atmospheric effect of moisture & vapour density by Psychrometrics minutely.

These types of pollution cause decay and damage of the Nature's phenomena due to external interference as hinted by Maharshi Yaska thousands of years ago. When Nature's infrastructure gets injured, we do fall prey to ill-treat and ill-threat under environmental pollution. Our Rishis (Seers) were conscious to preserve and love for Nature under Vedic culture. They used to maintain greenery to perform sacrificial rites with wild-herb for climate hygiene.

Due to the whimsical trends of lavish life, Earth's climate has been damaged on global & regional levels since pre-industrial era-partly as increase in the atmospheric concentration of aero – soils and partly the global mean-surface temperature risen above 0.6+_0.2 degree Celsius in the current era. The non-polar glaciers have been retreated and Arctic (North pole) Sea-ice-extent & thickness have decreased majorly.

On the other hand, we are confronted with global pollution damaging the Biotics in many spheres as –

1. Air Pollution – It ranges from dust, smoke, Suspended Particle Matter (SPM) to CO2, carbon mono Oxide, Sulphur dioxide, Benzene and etc. which are highly injurious to the lungs and the whole body. The major sources of these pollutants are manufacturing process, power generation based on fossil fuel, automobile exhaust, forest fire and etc. CO2 gas, hydrocarbon and carbon emission from fossil fuels burning in many industries being the source of CO2 emission and options for reduction, have long term environmental and economic effects. The mass of fossil is not observed through geothermal energy to cleanse ecosystem.
2. Water pollution – Aquatic contamination can be caused in 04 ways –
   (a) High growth of biotic community in water
   (b) Poisoning the mass of water by toxic chemicals
   (c) Domestic sewage going to rivers and pools causing high growth of micro organism in water unfit for mass use.
   (d) Heavy industrialization, deforestation, carbonization and navigation are mainly responsible for dangerous level of toxicity in water.
3. Cacophonical pollution – Due to over-crowding, traffic noise, industrial activities, loud speakers effect on physical and mental health.

   Further we have twin catastrophes from the accumulation of Carbon in the atmosphere –
   (a) Depletion of Ozone layer mainly due to –chlorofluorocarbons
   (b) Green-house effect due to methane, chlorofluorocarbon and most of all CO2

Although the bigger concern over the linkage of climate-change with biotic activities entailed scientific researches and International conventions on policy options to address such issues. So there has been the need to ponder over Anthropogenic environment.

In order to tackle such global problems, the UNEnvironmental Program (UNEP) was established in 1972 to provide effective measures for global corporation to review abiotic ecology. During 1992 the Govt. all over the world agreed "Earth Summit" on United Nations Framework Convention on Climate-Change (UNFCCC). Since 1995 to 2003 Conference on Parties 01 to 09 captioned under (COP-1to9) Convened summit in Berlin to Italy. Wherein negotiations with trial &error reports of action on Environment convention decided to launch as –

COP – 8 to 9 –

(a) Clean Development Mechanism (CDM)

(b) Global Environment Facility (GEF)

Here it is worthy to note that the COP-8 was convened at Vigyan Bhawan, New Delhi in 2002. Where Indian credentials on global environmental statesmanship were applauded to have created great awareness regarding climate-change issue across the country. Wherein almost 05 thousand participants from more than 170 countries took part in the Meet against Murky climate.

Now I come forward to point out oriental measure to minimize such eco-problems through the Science of sacrificial rites as –

1. Since Rigveda period our seers of yores suggested multi-ritualistic procedures for biotic benefits to restore positive change in atmosphere. Traditionally such rituals are meant for ascetic reasons confined to limit community of the world. But Modern scientific researchers have divulged life care measures to cosmic comforts as we find their love for trees, herbs and allied Nature's phenomena prone to environmental hygiene in the Atharvaveda. Wherein anti-virus-cum-medicinal trees and herbs were nurtured with life vehicles. Some of them are being illustrated for awareness –

   I. अश्वथ (Ashvatha) – Ficus Religiosa (pipal tree or Baniyan tree) – It may be used to treat kidney and various blood-circulated problems as supplier of O2 gas, anti-bacterial, anti-diabetic and skin diseases.

   II. शमी (Shami) –Prosopis cineraria of the pea family. It is used to treat respiratory system, leucorrhoea, bronchial asthma and stomatitis.

   III. वरुण वृक्ष (Varun Vriksha) – Crataeva Nurvala (quoted in Sushruta Samhita). Its leaves and barks are useful in urinal problems, headache, heart-diseases and etc.

IV. अजश्रृंगी (Ajashringi) – Rhus Succedanea or Gym-Nema Sylvestre. It has anti-periodic and stomachic values. It is used to treat in leprosy, wounds, bronchial, asthma, cure cough & fever.

V. अपामार्ग (Apāmārga) – Achyranthes Aspera or prickly chaff flower used to treat in cough, bronchitis, Rheumatism dysentery, malarial fever, hyper tension and anti-inflammatory feature of aqueous extracts.

VI. औदुम्बर (Audumber) – Ficus Glomerata (fig tree). It is used to treat as anti-diabetic, anti-oxidant, anti-diarrheal, piles & infections, anti-pyratic menstrual disorders and etc.

VII. दार्वी (Dārvi) – Berberis Aristata. It is used to treat fever, diarrhoea and etc.

VIII. जरीगड़ (Jarigada) – Ziziphus Mauritiana. It is a tropical fruit-species belonging to Rhamnaceal family. In India it is known as carrot grass or may be parthenium hysterophorus.

IX. शतावर (Shatāvar) –Asparagus Racemosus. It is used to treat female reproductive system, breast milk in nursing mother, sexual health, female fertility, for the nourishment to both mother and the foetus.

X. गुगुल (Gugula) – Commiphora wightii. It produces fragrant resin to spread incense and is a Vedic medicine. It is not an edible herb. But someone suggests to use its extract to improve hypo-thyroidism.

XI. करीर (Karila or Kerada) – Capparis Decidua. It is drought resistant. It provides assistance against soil erosion. It is used in reforestation and afforestation. Its shoot in just like bamboo thorny plant in desert. It causes rains by oblation to the Fire.

XII. पलाश (Palāsha) –Butea Monosperma. It has enchanting sight in full bloom. It is used to root out worms from the stomach to manage diarrhea as its antimicrobial property and liver disorders due to its antioxidant properties. It is used to colour clothes. It may be called flamboyant or Royal Poinciana. It is anti-pollutant.

XIII. लाक्षा (Lākshā) -Laccifer Lacca. It is a reddish brown colour resin secreted by the female lac insect. It is used for bone fracture healing and bone strengthening.

XIV. हरीद्रा (Haridrā) – CurcumaLonga or Zingiber officinale. It is antioxidant, anti-allergic, anti-septic and blood cleansing. It is banned for one who has gallstones or slow blood clotting.

XV. हरीतकी (Haritaki) – Terminalia Chebula or Chebulic myrobalan. It promotes digestion and eases constipation. It has great therapeutic value. It is anti-allergic. It is famous for rejuvenating herb. It is used as a lotion for sore eyes.

XVI. हरेणुका (Harenukā) Vitex Negunda Linn. It is called – Nirgundi (which protects the body from diseases). It is used to treat rheumatoid Arthritis (Amvata). It collides with accumulation of impurities in the joints. It manages cough disorders. It is anti-spasmodic, convalesant, rejuvenating and antiarthritic.

XVII. प्रियन्गु (Priyangu) – Aglaia Elaeagnoidea or callicarpa Macrophylla. It is used to treat diarrhea mixed with blood (ulcerative colitis), general dibility, pain in joints, skin diseases, tumour, diabetes and in obstetric disorder.

XVIII. तगर (Tagur) –Tabernaemontana Divaricata or pinwheel flower or crape jasmine. It is used to treat in sleeping disorders, hysteria, nervous unrest, emotional troubles. It is a mild sedative-hypnotic herb. It is called sugandhavalā in Ayurveda also. It reduces vat & kapha. It is used in epilepsy as Apasmara – loss of consciousness.

XIX. कुष्ठ (Kustha) – Saussurea Costus. It prevents the growth of cancer cells. It has anti-inflammatory and antioxidant properties. It is antacid to improve digestion. It is of hot nature to fight against gastritis.

XX. दालचीनी (Dālchini) – Cinnamomum verum – it belongs to Lauraceae family. It is antioxidant and helps to relieve of chronic diseases - heart, diabetes & cancer.

XXI. चन्दन (Chandana) – Santalum Album or Genus Santalum. It is of white and red also. Its scent is used to calm the mind, nervous system, and it awakens intelligence, strength and happiness. It is a cardiotonic used for haemostatic – disinfective, gonorrheal and bronchial problems. It pacifies pitha in the body. It manages fatigue weakness, blood impurities. It is used in gastric ulcers, skin cancer, leukemia, prostate cancer and etc.

XXII. पर्वत (Mountains) – Our seers were not needed to explode or implode mountains being guards of biological diversity in tropical and warmer temperate latitude. Rocky mountains are important habitats for wildlife. They sustain global or regional climate. They pose barriers and bridges for species. Most rivers flow in their cradles. Montane forests are responsible for heavy rainfalls. They confirm the pure water and air for bio-life. Mountains are useful guards against soil erosion and landslide. They are helpful to maintain cultural diversity and spiritual values to the extent of solace to the mind and the body. Collectively they confirm ecological balance and green landscape.

Thus the range of environment is extended from village, town, state, island, solar system and the Space. That is why our Vedic Rishis invoked for peace and prosperity from individual to the Space to maintain poise in all biotic-components, water components, the Space, the plant, herbal endowment, all resources and human minds. Because whatever phenomena viewed in the Nature compose environment collectively viz. water, air, soil, trees and beings.

2. Now Sacrificial rite's function-we may avail soothing relief in the vicinity of ritual Fire where hot air moves upward to fill in the gap beneath the cooling one.
3. The evaporated aroma of freshly fumes filled with the essence of healthy herbs oblating to the Fire are inhaled by human beings to cure of ailments through our body pores. They convert inorganic compounds into organic solid compound for purification.
4. The Yajna flames emit O3 colourful rays-yellow, red and blue. wherein huge yellow or golden rays have nitrogen, phosphorus, carbon, oxygen, barium, calcium, strontium, manganese, titanium, aluminium, chromium, iron, nickel, copper and zinc of which micro –rays are absorbed through sense organs to increase RBC, immune fuctions glucos – carbohydrates breakdowns, oxygen, haemoglobin, lipid metabolism, cell growth & cardiovascular cures. Besides minute red – blue radiations help to intake nutrients to our cells, boost up circadian rhythm to cognitive functions and pacify mental excitement en route to the pressure on navel circle of the body. They amalgamate different types of negative neutral and positive energy to control bio- components against anti-bodies Collectively. They work as anti – pollutants to maintain ecological conservation.

5. The heat of the Ritual Fire kills worms and insects and the Ritual ashes flown into water cause saner & rhythmic sensation in our life.
6. The sacrificial rituals cause rains because of the incensed air, being weighty, remains on the earth and the scentless air goes up to the sky through thermal layers to form clouds for rains. Besides the negative charged molecules in the smoke due to lit- medicino-herbs absorb moisture to form clouds for rains.
7. The vapour of cow –ghee (clarified butter) oblated to the Fire covering voluminous space on the earth spoils poisonous or harmful insects as aldehyde and phenyl agents.
8. Afforestation (plantation yajna) I find the accounts or descriptions of Green Nation – Madhu Vidya (The Science of Forestry) in the Vedas for environmental hygiene against unhealthy hazard. Earlier I have discussed about 10 trees being treated as sons in the Matsyapuran.Now trees and plants provide pure air to all jivas and purify environment. We all jives are alive due to Botanical kingdom. Our Atharvaveda established the importance of herbs and plants as medicinal assets. In order to enrich and respect afforestation Indian wives worship the Great Divine banyan tree (Ficus benghalensis) of moraceae family as Vatsāvitri festival for long life of their husbands. Also we worship Mango tree (Mangifera Indica), Mahua tree (Madhuca Longifolia) for fruitful life, and Neem tree (Azadirachta Indica) to word off chickenpox & variola viruses).

   Here the motto hints at the preservation and propagation of forestry. So reforestation is essential to minimize organic dacay of the plant and animals defying inorganic chemical for heavy metals. Now the Ministry of Environment and Forest has legislative responsibility to maintain ecological balance and good environment as vouchsafed by the Constitution of India. Although massive afforestation programmes are being carried out across the country. Further the forest ecotourism to include energy water conservation, water disposal and awareness to education and training is being monitoring the inflow and impact on forest life.

Thus sacrificial rituals cause to have medicinal knowledge for bio-life with Nature's care and thereby tend to rescue from biospheric hazard on global level.

4(C) Lord Shiva Code & Global Mode

The Shiva kingdom is attributed to Tantra Philosophy obviously. Many of us get frightened at listening to the word –"Tantra" which is the way of global life. Because it seeks to synthesize the monistic concept of the Advaita Vedanta with dualism of Sānkhya and enriches global knowledge with devotional charms or feelings.

St.Sarvānand Deo Nath, Tantric St. of west Bengal, has agreed with the Advait Philosophy as hinted in Sarvollasa Tantra (Tantric compendium in 64 chapters)

एक देवं विना देवि नास्ति देवो महीतले
एक सूर्य विना सूर्यो नास्तीह जगति यथा–13
बहुपात्रे स्थिते तोये बहुसूर्यं यथा प्रिये
बहुभावे तथा देवं बहुरूपेषु दृश्यते–14

Ek devam vinā devi nāsti devo Mahitale
Ek Suryam Vinā Suryo nāstih Jagati yathā – 13
Bahupātre sthite toye Bahusuryam yathā Priye
Bahubhāve Tathā devam Bahurapeṣu dṛsyate – 14

"There is no other deity except Herself. we acknowledge the deities in different faces as the one Sun looks to be separate in many bowls with full water…

The Tantra is highly rational in its approach. It asks for no faith in advance. It is a self verifying science to develop natural energy into supernatural terms leading to Cosmic enjoyment in life through spiritual consciousness. It is the highway of immunity; it is a technical method to expand esoteric practice for self-defence through Shaiva, Vaishnava & Shākta mode.

This Tantrology has 04 sections

1. शैवागम (Shaivāgam) as the following figures
   - (a) Pranava shiva
   - (b) Yoga shiva
   - (c) Chitya or deepti shiva
   - (d) Kāran
   - (e) Ajit (umesh, Achyuta)
   - (f) Sudiptaka (trimurti, Hutāshan)
   - (g) Sukhsm (Bhava, Bhangam)
   - (h) Sahasrā (kali, khaga)
   - (i) Suprabheda (Vigyanesh)
   - (j) Anshumān (Ravi)
2. Rudrāgram
   - (a) Vijaya- Anādirudra, Parmeshwar
   - (b) Nihshwāsa- Dasharna, shailata
   - (c) Parmeshwar-Rupa, ushaṇā
   - (d) Prodgeeta- shuli, kacha
   - (e) Mukhabindu- prasānt, Dadheechi
   - (f) Siddha- Vindu, chandeshwar
   - (g) Santān-shivalinga, hansvāhan
   - (h) Narsingh-Saumya, nṛsingh
   - (i) Chandrahāsa-Ananta, Bṛhaspati
   - (j) Veerbhadra-sarvatma, veerbhadra Mahāgaṇa
   - (k) Swayambhuva-Nidhan, Padmajā
   - (l) Virakta-Teja, prajāpati
   - (m) Kauravya-Brahmnesha, Nandkishor
   - (n) Mamuta or Mukuta –EEshān, dhwajāshraya
   - (o) Kirana- Deopitā, Rudrabhairava
   - (p) Galit-Aalaya, Hutāshan
   - (q) Aanjaneya-Vyomshiva, strota
   - (r) Saurbheda-Visar, Vimala
3. Bhairavāgam
   - (a) Bhairavāstaka-08 (swachhanda)-chanda, swachhanda, krodha, Unmatta, Ashitānga, Mahochha, kapalish & Shuru
   - (b) Yamalāstaka-08 (-yamala, brahma, Vishnu, swachhanda, Ruru, Arthvam, Rudra, vetāla)

(c) Mattāstaka-08 (Rakta, lampata, laxmi, Chalika, Pingala, utaphullaka, Bimvaddyamal Shreegal)

(d) Mangalāstaka –08 (Bhairavi, tantra Bhiravi, Brahmi, kalā, vijayā, Chandrā, mangalā, Sarvamangalā)

(e) Chakrāstaka-08 (Mantra, Varṇa, shakti, kalā, vindu, Nāda, Guhya, churṇa)

(f) Bahurupāstaka-08 (Andhaka, Rurubheda, Aja, varnabheda, Yama, Vidanga, Mātrirodan, jāmil)

(g) Vānishāstaka-08 (Bhairavi, chitrikā, Himsā, kandanvikā, hṛllekhā, Chandralekhā, Vidyālekhā, Vidwatmātā)

(h) Shikhāshtaka-08 (Bhairavi, Veenā, Vināmani, Sammoha, Dhāmas, Ahavaka, kabandha, shiraccheda)

4. **Todal** - tantrakali, mundmala, Tara, Tanarvāna, Shivasāra, Veer. Nidshān, latārchan, Tawula, Neela, Rudra, vidyāsār, Bhairava, Bhairvi, Siddeshwar, Matribheda, Samayā, Gupta-shodhaka, Māyā, Māhāmāyā, Akskyā, Kumari, kulālarnava, kālikā, Kulsarvaswa, kālikākalā, Vārāhi,

   Yogini, Yoginihṛdyā, Sanatkumari, Tripursāra, Yoginivijayā, Malini, kukkutā, shree Ganesh, Bhuta, Uddisha, Kāmdhenu, uttarā, Veerbhadra, vāmkshwar, Kulchudāmani, bhavachudāmani, Gyānārnav, Vadrā, Tantrachintāmani, Virunivilasi, Hanstantra, chidambartantra, shwetvāridhi, Nitya, Nārāyani, Gautmiya, Tanrutar, Garjan, kubjikā, Tantramuktāvali, Brhadshreekran,

   Swatantrayoni, Mayākhyā. It entertains about their worship and information on yogic science.

   This Todal Tantra has 03 ways....

   (a) Left hand ritual

   (b) Right hand ritual

   (c) Middle hand ritual

Now the Tanra Discipline is derived from the Atharvaveda. It is a mystical science with conciliation of 04 kinds...

1. Tantra conciliation to enhance physical energy
2. Mantra conciliation to correlate metaphysical forte
3. Yantra conciliation to geometrical progression in the Space
4. Yogic conciliation

Out of Trinity I have chosen Tantra-lord shiva who has queer attires suited to all cults and culture of the world. His attires have symbolic significance in round about ways as.

(1) **Trishul (trident) represents Tri-Time** – viewer, Tri-world, Trinity, Tri-properties, Tri-state of the universe as well as commanding and controlling device.pervading to the Jews.

(2) **Bṛṣabha (Great Bull)** – A symbol of procreative potency under regulation. Twin culture of violence and peace. Controller of global herd and spreading in Asian countries mostly.

(3) **River the Ganges** – prompt to expiate or repent for evil or sinful actions

(4) **Bhujanga (Black Cobra)** – a symbol of tortuous motion in life. It may be symbol of assimilation and dissolution of the word's cycle. When it uncoils cosmic creation takes place and when it coils the world is dissolved.It is the symbol of spirit/energy and is worshipped globally.

(5) **Bhasma (RitualAshes)** – Hindu ritual and symbol of aversion of miserable and sensuous enjoyment to the extent of wordly decay. It is the transformed admixture of 05 Gross Elements (fire, water, earth, air and ether).

Here tri-icons infer recess, repose and restage on His forehead. Further these tri-icons stand for inerrable illumination, illusionary force and incorporeity.

(6) **Mundakapal (cranial bowl)** – begging for own livelihood and not accumulating for progeny. It indicates the Ravages of the Time.

(7) **Pinākа (actruated weapon)** – to punish the evil spirit resembling up to Christianity and sikhas.

(8) **Vyāghra charm (hide of tiger)** – The Time devours even the fierce creature and leaves none but symbol of valour.

(9) **Chandramā (bicorn Moon in concave shape)** – it soothes and lessens our anxieties resembling to Muslim's mythology also.

(10) **Dhusar ranga (neutral or grey colour)** – for purification and power of naturality or simplicity to have concavo-convex experiences of life.

On the other hand, His character is renunciative and benevolent for global goodwill and yeoman service.

Because-

(a) lord shiva, being sovereign of infinite multitude is adorned with ashes

(b) He being wanderer in crematory avenues, rules over tri-world.

(c) He being Knight Commander of Yoga is Hermaphrodite.

(d) He being embraced with His beloved is Cupid burner.

(e) He being the cause of all is causeless.

(f) He being unmanifest is manifest.

Now the Tantra Discipline covers conversational discourse between lord Shiva and lordess Parvati. Whereas the Vedas are the voice of the Supreme Being- as Purushasutra whereas Rudra sukta, Shatarudriya are invocational texts to lord Shiva.

The Tantra has 03 branches mainly

(1) Shāktaagam –questionnaire between Shiva and Parvati penned by lord Ganesh-77 shaktaagam.

(2) Āgam-questionnaire by lordess Parvati and answer by lord Shiva and the texts are Shaivagam, Pashupatāgam etc including 28 Shaivāgam.

(3) Nigam Tantra-questionnaire by lord Shiva and answer by lordess Parvati.

Furthur-

(1) **Āagam** – narrates Cosmic Creation, Dissolution, divine worship, positive conciliation, repetitive rites of deistic formulae and hexa-conciliation.It consists of 03 kinds

  (a) Shaivāgam

  (b) Rudrāgam

  (c) Bhairvāgam

  He has 05 heads being symbols of:-

  (a) Power of accomplishment

  (b) Power of bliss

  (c) Power of will

  (d) Power of cognition

  (e) Power of Action

(2) **Yamal** – here all mysteries of lord Shiva and lordess Parvati are dealt at mid-night or conversation between the two deities. It narrates creative elements, Astrology, regular rites, formulas, alphabetical differences, Era character. It has 08 phases-

  (1) Brahmayāmal

  (2) Vishnuyāmal

  (3) Shaktiyāmal

  (4) Rudrayāmal

(5) Arthavarnayāmal

(6) Ruruyāmal

(7) Vetaliyāmal

(8) Swachhandayāmal

(3) **Prime tantra-**narrates Cosmic Creation, mystical formulas, holy channel, class-conduct, sacred rules, Astrological institutions, (planetarium or planetary), fasting tale on fasting, purity, impurity, symptoms of male female royal rules, charitable rules and metaphysical rules.

Like Vaiśeṣic Philosophy as innate relation between Matter and their character, so here is innate relationship between Shiva and Shakti also.

In Skandpurana both are counterparts of the whole state of dynamic energy and stupor. Furthur Shiva is –non consequenty Shakti is-consequenty.

Lord Shiva and Parvati are condensed like word and its meaning as Great poet kalidas penned in Raghuvansha Mahākāvya.

वागर्थाविव संपृक्तौ वागर्थ प्रतिपत्तये
जगतः पितरौ वन्दे पार्वती परमेश्वरौ–1/1

Vāgarthāviva samprktu vāgartha pratipattaye
Jagataḥ pitarou vande pārvati parmeswarou.

Again Shivapurana says-

Yatha shiva ....

यथा शिवस्तथा देवी यथा देवी तथा शिवः
नानयोरंतरं विद्याच्चन्द्र चन्द्रिकयोरिव

Yathā shivastathā devi yathā devi tathā sivah
Nānayorantaram vidyāccandra candri kayoriva

"lord Shiva and lordess Parvati devi are interpersonified. The Both have Parity as the Moon and its moonlight inseparable."

Again Vishnupurana says-

न शिवेन विना शक्ति न शक्त्या विना शिवः
शकरः पुरुषाः सर्वे स्त्रियः सर्वा महेश्वरी–1/8/32
Na shiven vinā sakti na saktyā vina shivah
Sankaraḥ purusāḥ sarve striyaḥ sarvā maheswari-1/8/32

"here the vastitude of the Both has been hinted at the oneness effect of Shiva and Shakti-without either, there is neither.All men are Shiva and all women are Maheshwari (lordess Parvati)

Again ShreeMaddevibhagāvata says…

स्वयं पुमांश्च प्रकृतिस्तावभिन्नौ परस्परम्
यथा वह्नेस्तस्य शक्तिर्न भिन्नाऽस्त्येव कुत्रचित्–9/38/288

Swayam pumāmsca prakrtistāvbhinnou parasparam
Yathā vahnestasya saktirna bhinnāstyeva kutracit

There is mono –manifestation of prima Puruṣa and prima Prakṛti as the fire and its flaming force.

In Mundakopnishada- lord shiva –Inert character

Lordess- shakti (energy) Alert character

Again in shiv-shava is corpse

And +aspirated "EE" (+) - Electronic power

Total = shiva

further-

(1) shiva- observer and subject
shakti- observation and object

(2) shiva- spirit or soul
Shakti- Matter or substance

(3) shiva- establishes-artificial values
Shakti- establishes Nature's phenomenon

(4) shiva- establishes divine within all blessings
Shakti- establishes around all blessings

(5) shiva- establishes Reflection of the Self
Shakti- establishes the mirror and the world

(6) shiva- establishes inner Reality
Shakti- establishes outer Reality

(7) shiva- establishes Aum
Shakti- establishes shree

(8) shiva- establishes Male (biologically)
Shakti- establishes Female (biologically)

(8) shiva – establishes Ash (minerally)
Shakti- establishes water (minerally)

(9) Shiva – Triangle upward pointing
Shakti – Triangle inward pointing

(10) Shiva – Right Direction
Shakti – Left Direction
(11) Shiva – White Colour
Shakti – Red Colour
(12) Shiva – Banyan Tree (Botanically)
Shakti – Banana
Tree (Botanically)
(13) Shiva – Mountain (geologically)
Shakti – River (geologically)
(14) Shiva – Turtle
Shakti – Serpent
(15) Shiva -dot (.) – Geometrically
Shakti – circle (O) – Geometrically

Again Shvetāshvatara Upnishad (Atharvaveda) by Tyāgisānand Swāmi writes –

त्वं स्त्री त्वं पुमानसि त्वं कुमार उत वा कुमारी–4/3

Tvam srtee tvam pumānasi tvam kumāra uta vā kumāri – 4/3

You are the female, you are the male.

You are the virgin, you are the lad.

Elaborately the lord Shiva is genderless (transgender) – inseparable from His Energy.

Both are identical in the character of hermaphrodite.

Wherein male in the right and female in the left.

IdaChannel is feminine & Pingala channel is masculine and both channels are balanced to ever activate Susumna channel.

His composite gesture or character is mechanized to diffuse global Energy. That energy has triangular (vulvic) and passionate enforcement of infinite power in which the accomplished and to be accomplished are identical. It is intelligent, light discharger, light- dark and I- Shiva × Shakti.

In this vein Kularnava Tantra says:-

जीवः शिवः शिवो जीवः स जीवः केवलः शिवः
पाशबद्धः स्मृतो जीवः पाशमुक्तः सदाशिवः–09/42

Jeevaḥ shivaḥ shivo jeevaḥ sa jeevaḥ kevalaḥ shivaḥ
Pāshbaddhaḥ smrto jeevaḥ pāshmuktaḥ sadāshivaḥ – 9/42

The living entity is Shiva and vice versa being called merely Shiva. The entrapped living being is observed as jiva and unentrapped living being is ever Shiva."

Further we know Lord Shiva is in 03 perfections:

(a) The Absolute Reality – unmanifest, unchanging & transcendent.

(b) Pure Consciousness – Manifest, primal substance, pure love and light flowing through all forms, existing everywhere in all Times and Space as Infinite Intelligence & Power.

(c) Primal Soul manifested as

   i. Brahma – the creator – Rajas property

   ii. Vishnu – the preserver – Sata property

   iii. Rudra – the dissolver – Tamas property

   iv. Maheshwar – the Veiling lord

Besides such perfections His Energy has wide will power to accomplish cosmic pursuits in 03 characters:

(a) The left ritual – creators

(b) The Eldest excellence – sustainer

(c) The Violentess – dissolver

Further the Femino – Cosmic Energy for Creation is symbolised is a vertex – angle triangle pointing downward as Water and Earth Elements attributed to feminine cavity and vulva. Because water is downward oriented. and the vertex-angle triangle pointing upward as Fire, Air & Ether elements are attributed to masculine dominance (Shiva). These both triangles are crossed upon each other for creation with a dot (.) balance in the centre by Shiva + Shakti being Purusa + Prakarti – (Bhuvaneshwari or Mahatripura Sundari).

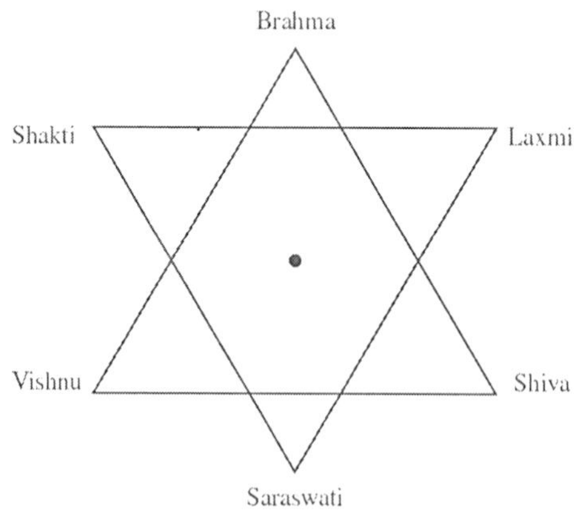

Such Spiritual union of Purusa + Prakrti

Shiva + Shakti

Vishnu + Laxmi

Brahma + Saraswati

Is geometrically symbolised here. Here the Puruṣa is – consciousness

Prakrti is – Nature.

Further out of 05 Gross Element:

Feminine evolvents are – Earth + Water

Masculine evolvents are – Ether + Fire + Air

Nature nurtures – The world

Prakrti protects – The world

Further lord Shiva resides in Sahasrārar Chakra (crown of the Head being Conciousness) of the living entity and The Shakti resides in the Mulādhāra chakra (around navel area of the body) of the living entity.

When Puruṣa + Prakrti unite in the Sahasrara chakra, the Consciousness and an object of the Consciousness become one. In this state of the Absolute Consciousness, there are no polarities for pains and distress resulting eternal love and bliss. So spiritual or divine love springs up under Cosmic Consciousness. Here I want to clarity that material love occurs between male and female objects. But spiritual love occurs between human & divine consciousness. At the same time conventional meaning of the term "Maithun" out of 05 MS in Tantrology is invalid instead of joining the Kundalini power with Shiva – Sahasrar in Jivas.

Thus The Tantric fusion is a special Science based on religion & philosophy. Where the idea of the term" Vipulānarthān" (expansive or co-extensive) corresponds to multi- sidedness and the least sided figure is the square& dot.

This square or dot in the centre is made by the motion in rotation in which one point rotates around the else dot. This point or dot has natural or innate motion being the symbol of sagacity for the Infinite Space, and such square or dot due to Whirling motion causes Whirlwind. Further the Whirl-wind combines with conceptual fire in the vertex angled triangle upwardly and begins to rotate with the conceptual water in the vertex- angled triangle inwardly. And the both triangles crossed upon each other in up & down mode is intelligible by the dot or point.

Further the circular dot within cluster of hair on the head (crown tail) has 23 petals of lotus circle as a token of the Moon. And the lord Shiva is annexed with the Moon as crescent to His Head. Where the dot circle setting on His Head enhances emotional peace and internal balance with concentration of the Mind. Such meditation generates the honey of immortality and relieves atrocities as well as heart -curbing.

The cut-fall organs of lordess Sati's burnt body above the heart centre as Right Cult and those of below the heart centre of Her burnt body as left – cult wholly affirm the Theory of Monism. Such Tri – landed Belle (female beauty) pervading in 8+1 (mono) triangles (vulvas) is known by 9 features as –

1. Tripurā
2. Tripureshwari
3. Tripurasundari
4. Tripuravāhini
5. Tripurasti
6. Tripuramālini
7. Tripursiddhi
8. Tripurāmbika
9. Mahātripur sundari & Bhuvaneshwari

Here the 1st one lordess resides within tiara point (forehead above eye brows) where "AUM" pervades. And the last one resides within head or crown tail where 23 – petals of blue and transparent lotus are cherished.

Here it is worthy of note that the above 23 petals of lotus correspond to 23 Matters assemble simultaneously by the spell of the Time (Kal) and again dissolve in course of the Time. So the Timeless – Kāli – (quintessential consort of feminine prowess as the sheer force of Nature or feral image of the Universe), being the Energy of lord Shiva, acts in Her own way at His directions.

As the Ganges was accepted to hold on His Head with great honour and Her 08 issues (Vasu) were blessed by lord Shiva to oversee the whole world designated as-

i. Dhar – The Earth God
ii. Anal – The Fire God
iii. Anil – The Air God
iv. Aapa – The Space God (water)
v. Soma – The Moon God
vi. Dhruva – Star (Soul) god in billions
vii. Pratyuṣa – Sun God
viii. Prabhaṣa (Bhismapitāmah) – The Ether

So Great poet, Kalidasa has screened 8-character of Lord Shiva by dramatis personae at the outset of his masterpiece–"AbhigyānShākuntalam." Wherein Kālidas entreated the vast potent – cum – Controller Lord Shiva to save the mass and paragon – cum – loyal wife "Shakuntalā" being adopted daughter of Rishi "Kaṇva" and queen of King Dushyanta in a bid to condense the theme of the play:-

या सृष्टिः स्रष्टुराद्या वहति विधिहुतं या हविर्या च होत्री
ये द्वे कालं विधत्तः श्रुतिविषयगुणा या स्थिता व्याप्य विश्वम्
यामाहुः सर्वबीजप्रकृतिरिति यया प्राणिनः प्राणवन्तः
प्रत्यक्षाभिः प्रपन्नस्तनुभिरवतु वस्ताभिरष्टाभिरीशः!

Yā shristih srasturādhyā vhahati vidhihutam yā havirjyā ca hotri
Y dv kalam vidhattah srutivisayagunā yā sthitā vyapya viswam
Yāmāhuh sarvabeejaprakrtiriti yayā prāninah prānvantah
Prātyaksabhih prapannastanubhiravatu vastābhirastābhireesah

Here the matter under elaboration is concerned with lord Shiva who is attributed to 8- manifestation ocularly (The Water, The Fire, The Ether, The Earth, The Air, The sun, The moon and The Soul). Further the 8 digit is also concerned with 8 siddhi (complete attainment of super human faculty) as an epithet of lord Shiva.

Further "EEsha" (word) may be defined as:-

ईकारः परमा शक्तिः
शकारः परमः शविः

Eekārah parmā sakthi
Shakāraḥ parmaḥ shivaḥ

That is - EEKĀRA is The Great Power & SHAKAARA-is the Great Shiva.

"Further such 8-manifestation of lord Shiva has been elucidated in "Mahimnastotram"- (a derived collection from Shiva purāna, Skund Purāna, Nardiya Purāna, Kurma Purāna & Matsya purāna also) as;

त्वमर्कस्त्वं सोमस्त्वसि पवनस्त्वं
हुतवहस्त्वमापस्त्वं व्योम त्वमु
धरणिरात्मात्वमिति च। –26

Tvamarkastvam somastvasi pavanastvam
Hutavahastavamāpastvam vyom tvamu-
Dharanirātmātvamiti ca

Here the Sun, The Moon, The Air, The Fire, The water, The Ether, The Earth and the soul-all are attributed to lord Shiva.

Now Lord Shiva is manifestation & Embodiment of renunciation Itself as in MahimnaStottram-

महोक्षः खट्वाङ्गं परशुरजिनं भस्म फणिनः
कपालं चेतीयत्तव वरद तन्त्रोपकरणम्
सुरास्तां तामृद्धिं दधति तु भवद्भ्रूप्रणिहिताम्
न हि त्वात्मारामं विषयमृगतृष्णा भ्रमयति–8

Mahoksaḥ khatwāngam parsurjinam bhasma phaninaḥ
Kapālam ceteeyattava varada tantropakaranam
Surāstām tāmrddim dadhāti tu bhavadbhrupranihitām
Na hi tvātmārāmam visayamrgtrisnā bhramayati

Here His total 07 belongings are aged- bull, a staff with fixed skull at the top for begging, a battle - axe, tiger-hide, ashes, Serpent and skull which are offensive, inauspicious and useful for Tantric instruments. At the same time all items are suitable to a beggar.

But all gods enjoy SUPER affluence by the graceful movement of His eye-brows; And He being the Supreme Spirit enriched with legitimate knowledge, need not wander in worldly affairs for sensual delight as mirage views.

Although out of 33 catgories of the deity, Lord Shiva is the concomitant of 11 Rudras as:

Rudras – 11
Vishnu – 08
Brahmas – 01
Surya – 12
Indra – 01
Total-33

Now I should clarify the terms "Tyāga" (renunciation) & Sanyas (Complete Renunciation). People believe that renunciation is forsaking all endowments. They are not ready to feel the ecstasy and enchantment of pure remunciation. Whereas it is to dispose off the useless things & negative ideas and get things more useful to oneself or the society. The significance of remunciation lies in growth of higher dimension and dropping of lower fascination. It is to dive deeper and more fulfilling aspects of our personality. When we elevate forward to cognitive delight, our – emotional thrills fade away into insignificance. So when we feel happiness within our spirit, all mundane enchantments drop up. Although sublime joy is subtler to be felt in solace. But our heed rests with lower affairs in distress due to Ignorance or Illusion only. Mind that this Ignorance causes 04 impressions-

1. Anger
2. Vanity
3. Greed
4. Infatuation

In order to get rid of such rude passions or impressions, we ought to know that all living organisms are his manifestations and graces and not mine. So enjoy the Nature's product by renunciation. Do not torture others, do not be greedy of other's belongings -being the path of prosperity.The 1st Mantra of Ishāvasyophishad (Shukla – Yagurveda) – Advocates –

ईशावास्यमिदग्वं सर्वं यत्किंच जगत्यां जगत्
तेन त्यक्तेन भुञ्जीथा मा गृधः कस्यस्विद्धनम्।

Ishāvāsyamidagvam sarvam yatkinca jagatyām jagat
Tentyakten bhunjithā mā grdhaḥ kasyaswiddhanam

The Supreme Being has sovereignty over the life assets of the world: So foster yourself by renunciation: do not be greedy of anybody's assets."

St. Ali Emran, also, says in THE QURAN-

व विल्लाहि मा फिस्समावाति व मा फिल्
अर्जि व इलल्लाहि तुर्जुअुल् उमूर–4/6/109

Va villāhi mā phissamāvati va mā phil
Arjiva ilallahi turj ua -lil Umur/4/6/109

All things in the universe belong to the Almighty: so their credits & consequences rest with Him"

Our enjoyment to mundane affairs depends on His will or unwill. So while utilizing them it should be borne in mind that they are not mine rather those of God's. So those who claim and want to claim their illegal ownership or sovereignty over some body's assets, have to suffer penalty of innumerable miseries out of Ignorance.So the cure of such long chains or fetters is possible only when we would disclaim Ahantā and Mamatā ('I' and mineness).

Lord Budha teaches (as also mentioned in "The Light of Asia" by English author. Edwin Arnold) that we are the cause of our griefs; we have been reluctant to Nature; we are infatuated to the object of temporal delight and happiness. Under the spell of Nescience we are managed to be whirled in mundane circuit of painful nature like an ox keeps on moving round to oil-press device. Here an ox keeps on moving around in the mirage of appeasing its appetite or avarice with grass hanging before it. but it goes on moving out of avarice and lastly only the oil is pressed and squeezed purposely.

To me such types of miseries are the outcome of our copied syllabus and the deprived norms of teaching in educational or technical institutions which prepare person fully starved of spiritual integration. As a result of which is lingering tediously in the morass of Nescience or Illusion.

(1) I reconnect 'sanyās and tyāga' issues as not desertion or negation of action but assertion of action. Because while giving up negative actions positive fruits springs up by virtue of benevolence. Such actions of renunciation free one from attachment and fruit- intent grows into higher dimension; and lower infatuation for mundane affairs drops up. Such positive properties enrich our deeper personality to procure mental and emotional pleasure. When such pleasure comes within the spirit, all mundane luxuries drop up. At this stage we must have insightedness to enjoy spiritual sanctum.Such type of typical analysis of non existence or nothingness in Indian philosophy helps us to identify our inner potency to our true solace. So the Theory- "out of nothing, nothing comes ' (Ex Nihilo Nihil Fit) is irrational in the light of the highest goal of life.

It is remarkable to note here that lord Shiva's renunciation or sacrifice for the emancipation of the world in peril due to emergence of the fatal venom churned out of the milky ocean – is the prime prowess of His life. He staked His life to let the Cosmos terror – free by quaffing or swallowing deadly venom (burning property) lifting on His palm and He was called as Fondler or Foster -Father of human, divine, inanimate entities and jeevas.

His acquiescence to engulf the venom is a magnum bonum to the universe as Shreemadbhāgvata purāna speaks—

तस्मादिदं गरं भुञ्जे प्रजानां स्वस्तिरस्तु मे–8/7/40
ततः करतली कृत्य व्यापि हालाहलं विषम्।
अभक्षयन्महादेवः कृपया भूतभावनः–8/7/42

Tasmādidam garam bhunje prajānām swastisrirastu me - 8/7/40
Tataḥ kartali krtya vyāpi hālāhalam visam
Abhaksyan mahādeoḥ krpayā bhutbhāvanaḥ - 8/7/42

The virulence of the venom may be assessed as its fallen drops swallowed by snake, worms and herbs pose deadly consequences even today.

Now let me discuss about the Mantras –

(2) Mantra (sacred formula) – It being the incantation of verbal sound through meditation which stirs multiglands of the mind. These glands have their own special sounds. Some sound waves to the center of of the head through IDA (Capillary tub – track from left testicle to the left nostril behind which pituitary gland is located to the hypothulmus by a stall like structure in the brain), which optimizes the mind as the lunar energy to change feelings. Some waves have special sound through Pingalā(tracking from right testicles to right nostrils symbolizing solar energy to stabilize intellect). This IDA seated around the navel center or belly button tends to shake its allied region with sound waves. The force or frequency of such sound waves should suit the frequency and force of the body, so that on meditating such fire element (Mantras), the dot circle as conductor of special sound may get unlocked to assist the incantation for consciousness through Susumnā tube (runs through the central channel of the spinal cord). So balancing through anterior and posterior lobes of the pituitary gland secreting different hormones helps to poise between the Sun and the Moon traits, and the body causes healthier and happier mind.The Mantras are to create wave velocity which depends on the elasticity and density of the medium between devotee and divine spirit.

The Mantras have 02 parts –

(1) Wisdom which as 02 sub-division

A – adorable in-rites

B – adorable out-rites customary Science and Yoga

Here we get wisdom with the grace of lord Shivas as Smriti says GYANMICCHANMAHESWARAAT - ज्ञानमिच्छन्महेश्वरात्"

(2) Scienc which has 02 subdivisions also –

A – Psychological Mantra Science

B – Action and Medical Science supporting livelihood.

Certain Mantras are being explained as follows-

(1) नमः (Namah-Neuter gender) – the manners of modesty to normalize the terrible and hurtful forces.

(2) स्वाहा (Swāhā) – feminine gender – the devotees apply all stamina or strength in benevolence and sacrifice to appease the consort of the Agni for expulsion of ill-will. Further the devotees vow to ward off the present and imminent obstacles.

(3) वषट् (Vaṣat – Masculine gender) – it aims at the internal circle to defeat the evil design of the enemies to the extent of life curbimg. Further release and relaxation of confinement or womb to deal Obstetrics by the rays of the Sun in stead of midwife.

(4) वौषट् (Vouṣat-feminine gender)-it teases the malice between enemies to be extinct.

(5) हुम् (Hum) –it indicates the wrath to ward off one's enemies and their strength.

(6) फट् (Phat masculine gender)---- it works as missile against enemies. it tallies fat-fat sound as exploding the rocks with dynamite.

Now I put up descriptive character of some of the Mantras to one's understanding –

(1) ह्रीं (Hreem) H – luminous Shiva –corporal Body

R- Nature pro

wess – subtle Body

EE -the Great Energy-causal Body

M- crescento-lunar power – oneness with the Spirit.

(2) श्री (shreen) Sh-Mahālaxmi

- R - Riches
- EE - Gratification
- M - As above

(3) क्रीं (Kreem)— K- Goddess kali to calm down calamilities

- R - Brahma (shiva+kali)
- EE- The Great Maya (conjuror)
- M- As above

(4) ॐ शिवोऽहम (Shivoham) – explains –

ईश्वरोऽहं महादेवि केवलं शक्तियोगतः
शक्तिं विना महेशानि सदाहं शवरूपकः
शक्तियुक्तो यदा देवि शिवोऽहं सर्वकामदः।

Iswaroham mahādevi kevalam shaktiyogatah
Shaktim vinā maheshāni sadāham shavarupakah
Shaktiyukto yadā devi shivoham sarvakāmdah

O Great goddess ! I am theAlmighty due to Her union.Without Her Energy I am reduced to a corpse.When the Energy is connected to Me, I start working to fulfil all wishes for prosperity.

Lord Shiva says in Sarvollasatantra

स्त्रीरूपं ब्रह्मरूपञ्च त्वयोक्तं वरवर्णिनि
अभावे स्वस्त्रियं देवि कथमुक्तं सदाशिवे।

Stripupam brahmarupanca tvayoktam varvarnini
Abhāve swastriyam devi kathamuktam sadāshive

O Devi Parvati ! Female or spouse is Brahma Itself having divine – golden complexion. Further She is presumed in 02 forms –

(1) Brahmadutta—oblative to the Fire

(2) Rudradutta— Femino performer in Shiva affairs. In the absence of family spouse, own wife is deemed to be Brahma in two forms as above

(5) ॐ नमः शिवाय (Aum Namah Shivāya) - Here 05-M corresponds to 05 syllables of the Mantras as –

न (Na) – is the lord concealing grace – The Earth.

म (Ma) – is the world – The Water.

शि (Shi) Is for lord shiva – The Fire.

व (Va) – His revealing grace—The Air.

य (Ya) – is the soul—The Ether.

Thus Mantras are life, Action and love and the recitation of the Mantras burst forth the Wisdom or Cognition out of light or Enlightenment within.

Now feminine Mantras are called Vidya numbering – 10 as –

Mahākāli, Tārā, sodasi, Bhuwaneshwari, Bhairavi,, Chinnamastā, Bagalā, Kamlatmikā, Mātangi, Dhumāvati. Here Tripursundari and Shreevidya are excluded from the above group on sundry opinions.

Now let me decipher their significance –

(1) Mahākāli – Superior among 10. She gives protection against odd influence of planets and fulfil all wishes of human beings. Further She gives Astasiddhi, cures of diseases, tantric obstacles, destroy enemies, solves misunderstandings and provides knowledge.

(2) Tārā – She gives power of speech, pleasure and salvation. She cast off evil effect of planets.

(3) Khodaṣi (Tripursundari)—since She possesses supernatural power, She has 04 hands and 03 eyes. She is seated on lotus which is placed on the body of Shiva lying in a peaceful posture. She also cast off malefic effect of planets.

(4) Bhuwaneshwari – one may obtain Her grace through righteous deeds controlled by Gurus.

(5) Bhairavi – She saves devotees from all sufferings and negative karmic pressure.

(6) Chinnamastā – Her devotees are blessed with long life, financial prosperity and stability. She helps to get rid of distress and pains.

(7) Banglāmukhi – She protects from all sorts of legal problems, adverse, accidents, She also imparts an ability to create a strong influence over others.

(8) Kamala – She can help to get rid of misfortunes.She cast off malefic effects of planets.

(9) Mātangi – She bestows perception, learning reasoning, natural ability and quality or skill. She has repository of 64 kalas (Arts).

(10) Dhumāvati – She is the goddess of those who are utterly crushed by events.She gives a particular strength to widow to pass on present and future life peacefully.

These goddesses can bestow one everything that one longs for health, riches, beauty, happy wedlock, children, prosperity, fame, power and position.

Such Femino-mystical Science (vidya) has 03 properties—

(A) दुरितक्षय (Duritakshaya), ward off calamities

(B) ऐश्वर्यप्राप्ति (Aishwaryaprāpti) – procuring the occult power which renders the performer invincible.

(C) क्रममुक्ति (Kramamukti) – successive release by wisdom or meditative exercise. the devotees to receive the effective grace of these Mahavidyas through tantric channel should observe nocturnal rituals in the prescribed mystico – ceremony. Because pin drop silence in the Chief Chamber or Bower of the performer is must for tantric rituals.

(3) यंत्र (Yantra) – Amulet or Talisman – it is the mystical diagram to restrain from the evil effects by enchantment – a static form of highly dynamic consciousness. Fatal weapons like Pashupatāstra, Brahmāstra, Nāgapash, and etc. were made on demand through Tantric devices in which physio – electrical energy of human body gets mechanized or specified to transmute atomic particles of Nature as when and where to operate upon at operator's will under warrant of the situation. These Tantrology is the source of subjection, magical incantation (enchantment) and supression of aggression and odium. it is extended to india, china, Tibet, Thailand, Magnolia, Combodge, Nepal, and in most Asian countries.

4(D) – Karma Philosophy & Immune Meditation

The Karma is a transcient quality which appears only at the boundary taking place within a system with a change of state.

It has been proved that one cannot do without Karma even for a moment. Extrenal & internal actions are being done all times as Respiratory system, blood circulation and etc.working on even in a deep sleep.

This ever working conception has been dealt in the Geeta-

नहि कश्चित्क्षणमपि जातु तिष्ठत्यकर्मकृत्
कार्यते ह्यवशः कर्म सर्वः प्रकृतिजैर्गुणैः– 3/5
Nahi kashcitkshanmapi jātu tishthatykarmakṛt
Kāryate hyabashaḥ karma sarbaḥ prakritijairgunaiḥ – 3/5

so none can decline duty or action for a moment subject to the law of the Nature. Again in the Geeta-

नियतं कुरू कर्म त्वं कर्म ज्यायो ह्यकर्मणः
शरीरयात्रापि च ते न प्रसिद्धयेदकर्मणः– 3/8
Niyatam kura karma tuwam karmajyāyo hyakarmanḥ
sharirayātrapi ca te na prasaddhayedakramanḥ – 3/8

Better to do pious duty regularly than idleness or inactivenss. otherwise yourlife-journey would not be fruitful or useful.

Further fortune never smiles on the lazy whose ends would prove Pandora's box only. The Deity, the demon, the evil spirit, the demi-gods, musician, attendants of Kuber (divine rich men) and human beings – all are distined to moral duty, business or task.

The effect of karmas plays vital role in one's life. Even the major portion of the Vedas cover ritulism as classified out of 1131 off shoots and 01 lac sacred formulas (Mantras) of the 04 Vedas-

(1) The section of ceremonio- sacrificial rites - 80 thousands

(2) The section of sacred meditaion & service - 16 thousands

(3) The section of the divine intelligence - 4 thousands

Total – 100 Thousands(01 lac)

So all rites and services are meant for divine serenity and global grandeur. The precept- oriented final Beautitude supports Supra- stoic Action; and those having engaged century- life in pleasure, do not mingle with human body rather do mingle with the Absolute as Ishāvāshyapnisada (shuklaYaguvada) affirms

कुर्वन्नेवेह कर्माणि जिजीविषेच्छतं समाः
एवं त्वयि नान्यथेतोऽस्ति न कर्मलिप्यते नरे।–ईशाव–02–शुक्ल–40 / 2
Kurvanneveh karmāni jigeebishachtan samāh
Evam twayi nānyathetoasti na karmalipyte nare – isha.-02
Shukla–40/2

So wishing to live for century and nothing else than everlasting or non-ending nature of the karma has been hinted at. Further a persion wishing to live for hundred years should perform actions throughout his life in a balanced perspective. Works are in thee and there in no otherway in which the Actions be deleted or besmeared.

Here the Ishāvāsyapisada assured us that the life on the Earth has no significance in weeping, wailing and tormenting in amoral display. So attempt to live in positive activities for full span of 100 years as the Vedaś wish-

शतायुर्वै पुरूषः
"Shatāyurbai purushaḥ"

This idea of 100 years span is the accepted tradition of India. After marriage ceremony the couple pray together to live for 100 Autumns in amity and safety. Otherwise longlife is a mere quantity and not quality of human life. Life must not be in years but be rich in quality, true knowledge and pleasuree- being the product of disciplined life & Action. All works must be done in the light of divinity. A mortal man must have the mentality of immortal instinct. There is endless hope in works.

In Taittiriyopanisad, while investigating into the nature of bliss and joy in terms of calculus of happiness does not find calculus of bliss in heaven as its units rather it finds in unit in a youngman with refreshing and positive outlook as-

युवा स्यात्साधुयुवाऽध्यापकः
आशिष्ठो दृढिष्ठो बलिष्ठः
तस्येयं पृथिवी सर्वा वित्तस्य पूर्णा स्यात्
स एको मानुष आनन्दः./II/8

yuvā syātsādhuyuvādhyāpakaḥ
āshishtho dridhishto balyshtah
tasyeyan prithivi sarvā vittasya purnā syat
sa eko mānushya ānandah – /II/8

Let us take a youth! a good mannered youth, well educated, full of hope, firm in mind and strong in body; let him has dominion over the earthly unit of human bliss. Here any youth, simply because he/she is young, can not serve as multiple of happiness. Many of the youth look senile even they are young in body. They look like old before they have started to be young. So they cannot serve as unit of human happiness. The young must have command our ethical assets to make their may-hey in the world. So we should optimise the youth with vim, vigour and vision to come forward to the renaissance of missionary operation as The Mission of Lord Krishna for National desideratum-

क्लैब्यं मा स्म गमः पार्थ नैतत्त्वय्युपपद्यते
क्षुद्रं हृदयदौर्बल्यं त्यक्त्वोत्तिष्ठ परन्तपः।–2/3
Klaivayam mā sam gamh pārth naitavyyupapdyate
kshudram hridaydourbalyam tyaktwottiṣta parntapaḥ – 2/3

O Partha (prince) Arguna! yield not to such debility or despair for it does not suit thee, cast off little faintheartedness and arise to foil the foes.

So sublime Action is the main subject of the Vedas as wise King JANAKA and the like attained संसिद्धि (merger with the Absolute Being by Supra- Action) as in the Geeta-

कर्मणैव हि संसिद्धिमास्थिता जनकादयः
Karmanaiva hi sansidhimāsthitā jankādayh -/3/20

Even Scottish Philosopher & satirical Writer Thomas Carlyle says-
The end of man is action and not thought,
though it were the noblest"
The smallest of action is always better than the boldest
of intentions"
or
Do the Duty which lies nearest thee, which thou knowest to be Duty.

Such Action is of 03 types in view of the pre-post life cycle

(a) Sanchit (the sum total of the past Action) accountable to sweet or bites actions in pre-life and yet to reap or enjoy.

Even Shree-Devibhagavata coins-

अवश्यमेव भोक्तव्यं सुकृतं दुष्कृतं तथा –/10/10
Avashyameva bhoktavyam sukṛtam duskṛtam tathā -/10/10

But one's life is not sufficent to endure and experience the taste of all Karmas.

(b) Prārabdha- Action to be experienced in current life as a part of ripened accumulation.

(c) Kriyamāna- (Action on duty) which is currently creating on duty or in possession to shape our future from birth to death.

Further the status of living creature is subject to Action as averred in the Shreemaddevibhagavat-

जननं मरणं दुःखं सुखं प्राप्नोति चावशः –/10/29
Jananaṃ maranaṃ dukhaṃ sukhaṃ prāpnoti cavashḥ -/10/29

"One recieves dawn, decay, distress & destiny of life in pursuance of one's Action. One must enjoy and suffer the corresponding fruits of one's Karmas in next life proportionate to the deposit of noble and anoble activities in one's life series as ShreeMadhabhagvata puran says-

येन यावान् यथा धर्मोऽधर्मो वेह समीहितः
स एव तत्फलं भुङ्क्ते तथा तावदमुत्र वै /6/1/45
Yen yāvān yathā dharmodharmo veh sameehitḥ
Sa ev tatfalam bhunkate tathā tāvadamutra vai -/6/1/45

King Dasharatha of Ayodhya (India) while addressing queen Kaushalya, suggested in valmiki ramayan (Ayodhya kand)

यदाचरति कल्याणि! शुभं वा यदि वाऽशुभम्
तदेव लभतेभद्रे! कर्त्ता कर्मजात्मनः /63/6
yadācarati kalyāni shubham vā yadi vāshubham
tadeva labhatebhadre karttā karmjātmanḥ

O Blessed or Beloved! one does reap the fruit of action as one does good or bad. A doer has to reap the fruits of his own activities.

Further we should take to all tragedies or problems of life and overcome them with legal and linking persevereance. No great goals can be achieved wihout Zeal and Zest. So feel the pains and savour satisfaction- but mind to avoid inferior or defective or faulty actions for fear of failure as the Naiyayikas (logician) says-

"कर्तृ क्रियादि वैगुण्य"
"Kartṛ kriyāda vaigunya"

But do not dishearten yourself and does pave the mistaken paths for better consequences.

Generally we understand that any crime or offence or malpractice or intrigue or evil design which you operate in darkness or solitude, gets unknown to the public resulting care free of its dire or dark punishment. But mind that there are Nature's witness to detect our heinous activities also all the time as Shreemadhabhagvata says-

सूर्योऽग्निः खं मरूद्गावः सोमः सन्ध्याहनी दिशः
कं कुः कालो धर्म इति ह्येते दैह्यस्य साक्षिणः /6/1/42
Suryoagniḥ kham marudgāvḥ somḥ sandhyāhanee dishḥ
Kam kuḥ kālo dharma iti hye daihyasya sākṣinḥ

The Sun, The Fire The Sky, The Air, God or demigod The Moon, The Evening, The Day, The Night, The Time or The Space, The Water, The Land and The Supersoul Himself-all are great judges or witness of Actions of the living beings to confer decrees for atonement. So always mind to get rid of this clandestine judgement against malicious designs or actions

Now let me explain positive and negative Karmas to some extent as follows-

(1) Positive karmas- Selfless service, devotional deeds, meditation, romantic love, yeoman service, pardon, harmony ruth, unity and the like

(2) Negative karmas- jealousy, grudges, hatred, passion, egoism, selfishness, torture, kidnapping, usurpation and the like.

The Karma Philosophy reiterates that each action returns to its original nature-state for consequence due to intervention of interaction sooner or later. So the Cosmic Law of the Karma coincides the Third Law of Motion by Scientist Isaac Newton. We do karmas atleast in 04 ways-

(1) Through thoughts

(2) through words or speech

(3) through actions that you perform yourself

(4) through actions that others do under your instructions.

Thus everything you have thought, spoken, done and abeted or commanded to do- all are karmas.

So exercise positive thoughts and excrete negative ones to design your destinity and awesome potentials. So do not miss the precious events of life and do practise mental and physical sanity to merge with Divine Light.

In order to achieve such goal, we have to dissolve difilement through 05 – sheath in our body as follows-

(1) cereal case (ceres as Roman goddess of Agriculture) - to devolop our physical nourishment with lacto-vegetarian diet instead of alcohol and drugs = physical body

(2) Life energiness- we should inhale natural 0_2 which radiates our ambience= Astral body

(3) Mindness- we should imbibe good thoughts from the Nature to have balance in life through yoga practice = Astral body

(4) Intellectual body - we should apply logical discretion for truthful judgement and innate impression void of egoism = Astral Body

(5) Blissful body - we should cultivate unconditional cognition or wisdom to liberate from the nucleus of our existance = causal body

Only the legitimate knowledge can help us to be freed from such sheaths.

In other words one of the timeless secrets to a long and happy life is love for your noble work or actions. Hours will slip away as quickly as they come. So go on playing with work. Works should be treated as fun. But the art of living makes a little difference between work & play, labour & leisure, mind & body, information & creation, life & religion. Hardly we know which is which...........

My motto is to open karma- Account. Thus more ease to life the more balance to coin business of life. All are distined to work as by-product of Nature - Action for Action -sake (Niṣkām karma)

Now there are 05 types of Action in Hindu mythology-

(1) Nitya karma (daily duty)

(2) Naimitika karma (occasional duty) - in birth, death, marraige, holy bath etc.

(3) Kāmya karma (optional duty) to acquire assets, sacrifice and divine cultivation.

(4) Nisiddhakarma (prohibited duty)not to amoral duty

(5) Prāyascita karma (rites to atone for sins or expiation) to lessen the evil effect of unholy results

Further the mind is a part of the body. It is the charioteer of life- chariot. It wanders in the whirl pool of our mortal life.

In Nyāya philosophy it is an intergral organ of the cognition or instrument (dravyas) by which the sense- objects affect the soul and is distinct from soul.

Worthy of note that the mind is not the brain rather resides in the forehead of the brain. There are 03 levels of the mind.

(1) Conscious

(2) Sub-conscious

(3) Unconscious

But in Modern Age- The brain is all in all as the controller of the body. Such body- consciousness in exposed in lust, anger, egoism and attachment. So in order to delete such diabolical diameter we should install high optical fiber to communicate pulses of light for total internal reflection.

So when one practices meditation, one's mind is made free from horrible pains and thereby one becomes intelligent spiritually instead of indulgently in mundane affairs. It acts as a rocket which flies to infinite Space by pushing out of the gravitational field at Earth circle. Such gravitational field may be treated as bondage and worldly lust and we are to cross above with high voltage of Super-natural power or light. We ought to know that all nuclear weapons are assembled with rational intelligence power of the conscious canvas. So right emotion and meditation dynamize to develop deserving device for divine Deliverance (salvation).

Unlike several concepts, we ought to know that meditation is an action to relax the body and the mind. Humming sounds linked through meditation will aid one in finding inner peace, helping to reduce stress and falling in psychic sleep. It is a self-healing science to bring spiritual, physical and mental happiness with well-proven tips and techniques.

Meditation is apt to practise amidst mountains, rivers, waterfalls, plants, pyramids, prayers. There are many types of technique of meditation in the world. Such as-

(1) Tibetan Mediation
(2) Mantra Meditation
(3) Happy Songs Meditation
(4) Positive energy Meditation
(5) Nature's surrounding Meditation
(6) Sleeping sounding Meditation
(7) Relaxing tips Meditation
(8) River brim Meditation
(9) Top-guided Meditation
(10) Top sleep Meditation
(11) Yogic Meditation
(12) AUM-Calm Meditation
(13) AUM-Mantra Meditation
(14) Healing Meditation
(15) Chakra Meditation
(16) Deep-healing Meditation
(17) Anxiety Meditation
(18) Night Meditation
(19) Rain-forest Meditation
(20) Summer-rains Meditation
(21) Tropical Beach Meditation
(22) Depression-ultra-sound Meditation
(23) Storm Meditation
(24) Thunderstorm meditation
(25) Music Temple Meditation

Lastly meditation is an age-old technique that was developed by global Seers to gain complete control of the mind. It is a method to train the mind with the functional design of the way of life. Its key benefits are-

- Peace Tranquility
- Good relationship
- More serene and happy at office and in solitude

It makes better parents, life-partner, business person and good-mate or friend. That is why mere indulgence in books or philosophical treatises does not suffice to attain eternal pleasure which entails spiritual fondness charged with self-luminosity of knowledge-

"ज्ञानस्वप्रकाशत्वम्"
"Jnānasvaprakāshatvam"

Chapter - 5

Global Terror & Oriental Canon

5(A) – War-weevil & world peace

In modern times we praise warriors and soldiers for their renowned victories and triumphs; we are amazed at the strategy of battles, conquest of Nation powerful and proud. We boost much of the pride, pomp and daring of admirable war. But we neglect the destruction, miseries and griefs of the millions. Military forces are succumbed to injuries. So such bloody victory stains the soil of the Nation. Now biological warfare damages the condition of the survivals. Whereas victories are parallel to worthiness which brings health and happiness, wealth & prosperity and freedom & justice to the mass.

The effect of war may have the following vicissitudes-

(a) Destruction of wealth and the living beings

(b) Economic crunches

(c) Ruin of great empires or sovereignty

(d) the origin of new states and sovereignty

(e) the rat-race of armaments and artilleries.

The horrors of war may be summed up in the following consequences–

Death, destruction & carnage,
loss of life and orphanage,

Burnt cities & villages,
Wailing, weeping & wreckage,
Dead bodies littered everywhere,
fathers bury their young sons,
Elders mourn for their ones
Missiles boom, whiz & zoom
wounded crowd in hospitals' room
let us avert this horrible hazard.

Even History is replete with wars and battles since the dawn of civilization- such victory of war started from Imperialism and Colonialism to rule over the sub-continents for sovereignty. So when the maximum parts on the earth were made colonies, a revolt erupted due to injustice done to the defeated parts that resulted the Ist world war (1914-1918) between the Central Powers (Australia, Hungary, Germany and Turkey) and allies (Britain, France and Russia). Wherein the loss of about 10-million lives of combatants and injuries of 20-million human beings were incurred. An unknown number of death occurred from cancer in between these years.

As a result of which the world realized the need to establish a machinery to avert international conflict in future and maintain global peace to the extent of the establishment of the league of Nations in 1920.

Hardly after 20 years of the 1st world war, the 2nd world war broke out in 1939 causing great human hazard again. It lasted for 6 years and at the end of which the UNO was established in 1945 and proceeded for good ends.

In between its establishment 1941- Franklin D. Roosevelt 32nd U.S. President and Winston Churchill former P.M of the United Kingdom signed Atlantic Charter for global peace and harmony among the Nations.

1943- The Representatives of 50 countries met in San Francisco (U S) with aims to maintain peace, eradication of illiteracy, poverty, and chronic ill- health and breaks. Further a ceasefire agreement by Indo- U S Defence dealing final warning of reducing emissions and Ballistic Missile Defence (B M D) for cooperation and Robotic arms controlled by brains were chalked out.

Further we have suffered Israel- Palestine war, Gulf War, Indo- Pak war, Kargill War in 1965, 1971, & 1999.

Someone says that war is to end war. But the gap between ceasefires causes chaotic events and random casualties. Although the Treaties are signed for pseudo- peace for some-times. The overwhelming plight after war may maintain peace against the degree of disasters and ruins. But the time gap may help to prepare for next war to regain Bossism which one has lost in the last war.

So the cycle of war works as a fuel for next war-cycle. War answers to the question of war and nothing else. Perhaps it does not mean for peaceful environment but lament for peril and pains of humanity. In German novelist, Paul Thomas Mann's words- "war is only a cowardly escape from the problem of peace". So it is only the euphoria to invade So the approaches to warfare should be sincere from both sides based on mutual benefits as stated by St. John the Faster (John Nesteutes- Roman Bishop) "The world will never, have lasting peace so long as men restore for war" -akin to Gandhian perception of non-violence and truth applied in Indo-British movement.

Many legislations & Treaties were signed for nuclear curtailment and disarmament as-

(1) POTA & POTO (prevention of Terrorist Act or Ordinance)

(2) NDT (Nuclear Disarmament Treaty)

(3) NPT (Non-proliferation Treaty) and etc.

Besides there have been Cold war in which arms and artilleries are not operated but wars with arrows of itching words. Further the sovereings hatch secret plots with friendly states to weaken the hostile ones in the exercise of nepotism. So certain Military Treaties were enacted to disfavour such intrigues.

The above circumstances notify that the declaration and declension of war correspond to the inevitability and exigency to the situation under trial. Although war cannot be ignored against injustice, infidelity and infraction; rather to proceed for war for righteousness uncaring for its consequences as the Geeta says-

सुख दुःखे समे कृत्वा लाभालाभौ जयाजयौ
ततो युद्धाय युज्यस्व नैवं पापमवाप्स्यसि–2/38

Sukha dukhe same kṛtvā lābhālābhou jayājayou
Tato yuddhāya yujyasva naivam pāpmavāpsyasi–2/38

Here exhortation of war to damn consequences for profit or loss, win or defeat, sin or sacred, etc is suggested.

Normally try to tolerate the tyranny to some possible extent; and at last bridle the unbridled foes through surgical strikes. Because imminent defamation excels demise of the sovereign as the Geeta says-

अकीर्तिं चापि भूतानि कथयिष्यन्ति तेऽव्ययाम्।
सम्भावितस्य चाकीर्तिर्मरणादतिरिच्यते-2/34

Akirtem cāpi bhutāni kathyisyanti tevyayām
Sambhāvitasya cākirtirmarnādatiricyate -2/34

Here lord Krishna advised Arjuna to unflee uncaring fear of his life: better to die in the battle that would save you against ill-fame or losing dignity in the society. Because disgrace is worse than demise.

Now I have discussed on the devastating effect of war. Afterwards I would like to skim over the accounts of war mgt. in Vedic literature of which the people, in general, are bereft.

We find the military strategies in the Vedic- remembered- literature on verbal transmission (Smrti).

We find the accounts of the subtlest units of military mgt. regarding kings, the Ministry, The Army and etc. So whatever strategies on military mgt. are being taken into operation were, already, chalked out in India thousands years ago. As we find such illustrations in the Vedas, the Puranas, the Smrtis, the Ramayana and the Mahabharata. where imprisonment, punishment, squadron, troops, military array resembling a wedge, communicative capability, Garuda- typed military-array and lotus like troops were used to have deployed as the situation warranted. Further we find the narrative of the duty and responsibility of the Commander-in- Chief in YāgyaValkya Smriti, Narada Smriti, Buddha literature, Lohit, and Manusmrti. The Commanders-in-Chief should maintain peace and harmony for the public by adopting the policy of conciliatory negotiations, cordage punishment, dissension, etc.

The eligibility of the Chief Commanders

The Rigveda states-

यः सेनानी यो वः सेनानीमहतो गणस्य
Yah senāni yo vah senanimahato ganasya

The Chief Commander was the General Commander of the military group. He was prone to shoulder the security and peace of the Nation. According to Manusmrti- he was the caretaker of O7 organs of the military strategy such as – the king, The Military of Defence, the public, the Forts, LAC or LOC, the passionate pursuits, punishment and friendship----7/65

There were O6 types of troops as

War- chariots

Elephant troops

Horse troops

Boat troops

Infantry or foot soldiers

Carriage soldiers

And each faculty was controlled by the Commander of the Army and the military groups were called the troops consisting of 45 foots, 27 horses, 9 chariots and 9 elephants.

Military Merits

1. Equipped with arms and ammunitions
2. Ample funding for military pay and perquisite
3. Loyal to the Nation
4. Emergency medical service
5. Shelter facility
6. Healthy physique
7. Hale and hearty

Older or Oriental Types of Troops

1. Standing Army –famous for ancestral bravery and royal faith and fixity.
2. Army of alien origin- as mugal, Turky, Arabic, Arab, Hunas, Aryan outcast (non- Aryan) as in Kaurava Army.
3. Trained in war- tactics and co-opted on demand at irregular pay.
4. Demanded troops from friendly states at paternal state maintenance
5. Leaving own state and join the other one as a treachery.
6. Troops enlisted in wild tribes and interested in usurpation or killing.

Rules of War- Fare

Our oriental stalwarts, after chunring debates, discussion and exercising logics, elucidated monarchy, military mgt, national policy, national or international meet, states- administration, foreign policy and etc. Where foreign policy included 06 expedients or models-

1. Treaty of peace
2. Hostility or disfavour
3. Marching against hostility
4. Maintaining or resection of military posts at border lines.
5. Dual state of policy and keeping friendly with neighbour countries and countries beyond apparently. Dividing troops to encounter with tactical shrewdness.

6. Seeking protection or shelter with power states or leaguing together for mutual security.

The Chief Marshal was expert in arraying of troops and squadrons as classified in Nitiṣāra (Element of polity and State craft) by Kamandaka or Kamandakiya Nitisār-

1. Mandal- A circular array of troops in the central Monarch with O5 sub kings whose dominions were in the front and O4 sub kings whose dominions were in the rear of his kingdom and the intermediates with different sub kings.

   According to someone the Circle consisted of O3 –sub kings only-
   - (a) Natural enemy
   - (b) Natural array
   - (c) Natural–neutral sovereigns whose dominion lies beyond those of the natural array – a particular position of foot in shooting.
2. Asamhat- (a) Semi- circular shaped or crescent shaped
   - (b) Fire place
   - (c) Adamantine kind of military array (vajra)
   - (d) Crab- Horny
   - (e) Crow feet shaped
3. Bhoga-Carriage of military array resembling
   - (a) wedge
   - (b) Crocodile- shaped array of troops
4. Danda-
   - (a) Dispersion of Army
   - (b) Tough array of troops
   - (c) Intolerant array of Army
   - (d) Bow caved Army
   - (e) Haunting enemy with trained hawkys troops
   - (f) Troops of triumph
   - (g) Try for peaceful settlement
   - (h) Piercing mode of Military array
   - (i) Pillar or post vigilance
   - (j) Division army or warrior consisting of 729 elephants, many cars, 2187 horses, 3645 foots
5. Jumping array of troops

6. Ring like array of troops

   Archery

   (a) Missiles
   (b) Handling weapons
   (c) Cannon balls through tanks
   (d) Weapons prone to return to the attacker after attacking the enemies
   (e) Super natural missile –Narayanāstra, Indrāstra, Vāyavyāstra, Brahamāstra, Vaishanavāstra, Āgneyastra, Varunāstra, and etc.
   (f) Pashupatāstra – by Arjuna(Mahabarat)

Tantric Missiles-under the training of Dronacharya (son of Rishi Bharadwaja and royal precepter of Kauravas and Pandavasas as sub-Commander-in-chief in Kurukshetra Battle).

We are known to Mahabharat war in Kurukhetra, where war was waged for righteousness under prescribed rules and mid-arrangements. But Rules were broken several times as in the slaying of Abhimanyu, Ashwathāmā, Bhurishravā (Commander in Kaurava side) Jayadrath (King of Sindhu Kingdom), mace- combating and etc. Such Rule breaks might have been the exigency of fire – feelings of revenge reeled in hearts.

Lastly I cannot help saying to quote that war strategies must be adopted tactfully as Lord Krishana adopted to foil the terror of demon Kālyavan as thrusting terror on Mathura (India). Lord Krishna shrugged or uncared His stigma of being called Ranchhoda (war- shirker) to let burn demon Kālayavan to ashes by the firing eyes of sage Muchukund (Ikshvāku dynasty-Suryavansha) who was reposed in the cave for meditation.Here the incidence occurred as Lord Krishana flew away to that cave and the chasing Kalayavana kicked off Seer Muchukund who got enraged to burn the demon to ash-heap –Shrimadhagavata-10/51

World Peace

We have been off oasis of Nature and our life runs in din and bustle of Metro-cities. We have been aloof from our walking in the woods and listening to the chirping of birds to feel quiet and normal. We have been deprived of sylvan life.On the other hand Commune to Nature is an excellent way to unlock our creativity and generate lofty ideas. A deep sense of inner quiet floods our entire body and thus creativity flourishes. The leaves reflect the soothing sense of serenity away from the uproar of cities. Many questions about life remain unsolved under the crush of our daily humdrum. But while enjoying Nature with the complexity of flowers some questions get solved with healthy fruits.

Great scientist Newton, under an apple tree, discovered the law of Gravity. So Nature's surroundings stir our brilliance for global benefit. Mahatma Gandhi observed-

"When I admire the wonder sunset or the beauty of the Moon, my soul expands in worship of the Creator." So we should soak up the beauty of the Nature around us as nothing complicated but completely fun for solace.

Mind that our society is made up of our outer and inner integration of personality. But when you give more importance to monetary success for social appraisal, we get disinterested to other's care for sympathy and indiscrimination. Human values are on trial for market competition and accountancy. Recently the advertising enterprises appointing large number of psychologists affect our cultural and spiritual strength in cognitio to prepare social spinners. Cash mgt. is a tool to change our mind and heart impatiently as proved by psychologist of almost 70 countries of the world. So slow the race of foreign policy framed by the political leaders preferring outer values. Lastly we have to change ourselves to monitor mental peace in family life and fraternity with global gamut.

That is why Manusmrti states-

संतुष्टो भार्यया भर्त्ता भर्त्रा भार्या तथैव च
यस्मिन्नेव कुले नित्यं कल्याणं तत्र वै ध्रुवम्–3/60
Samtuṣto bhāryaya bharttā bhartrā bharyā tathariva ca
yasninneva kule nityam kalyānan tatra vai dhruvam–3/60

"When husband is heartily satisfied with his wife and vice versa that family is prosperous and happier."

Mind that (Manusmriti)-

न कश्चित् कस्यचिन्मित्रं न कश्चित् कस्यचिद्रिपुः।
व्यवहारेण मित्राणि जायन्ते रिपवस्तथा।
Na kashcit kasyacinmitram na kashcit kasyacidripuh
Vyayahārena mitrāni jāyante ripavastathā

None is friend or foe to anyone. Friend or foe grows on nature of behavior or action.

What I mean that the universal mind excels the universal body and the universal soul excels the universal mind and the individual body is the counterpart of the universal soul. Thus both are identical. Now again the question poses that the universal soul, being infinite and eternal, may not be divided into creatures to ensure its eternity and infinity. Further we may think of the multiformity of the soul. But it is puerile to think like this. Because the sunlight reflects on lacs of bubbles, there is the reflection of the total image of the sun in every bubble. In similar vien the individual soul abiding in all creatures is the embodiment of the totality of the Supreme One, being the manifestation of light.

St . Rumi tells in the Quran-

शमसे–इ–तब्रीजि "Shamse-I-Tabrije"

"Who is the Absolute light- The Sun and its ray of the Supreme Reality .The Sun stands for shamse light –Tabreji- such symbolizes the eternal relation of individual–universal-consciousness

So the intrinsic nature behind the multiformity of the universal soul is the Supreme One. That is why the expounders of the non-dualistic Philosophy proclaim that life is the manifestation of the embodiment of the existence –wisdom-bliss (Sachhidānand).

However the senses, the mind and the intellect are said to be the seat of eternal foe of the wise and insatiable (Duṣparenānal) in the force of wicked desire which disintegrates the embodied soul from the Universal One. So it is in the fitness of things to control the senses through renuniciation of Action and unveil the bliss (zero point) through 5-layer of chambers in the inner body.

Like the Third law of Thermodynamics in Physics elucidating how orderliness in a system can be improved by reducing the state of the excitement, the level of individual and collective consciousness can terminate violence and as a result of which peace reigns even to the most disturbed regions of the world .Such happens due to the fact that when person's consciousness dives deep into the very source of thoughts and attains transcendental state, the whole being is charged with new vim and vigour causing psychological changes in the brain, heart and even in the blood.

Consequently enemies or crimes disappear, alcoholics become teetotaller, drug addicts free themselves from its fatal group and bad temper; uneasiness, depression and other corroding elements vanish. Thus the harmony of the inner and the outer life begets musical soul and the blessed mind remains absorbed in the transcendental state of divine rapture–individuo-universal fusion. These practices help us to transmit our urges for lust, anger and sensual pleasure into the perfect tranquility of the consciousness towards the possibility of world peace.

As the world is engaged in sacrificing material energy to develop education, social status, economic condition and plans for mass upheaval of humanity. So the people, in general, are bothering about peace of mind. But such peace is received through sacrifice for satisfaction of the third person either in the form of family, society, community or entire biotics. At the same time we all want to attain peace in parts and not in intergrity.One preaches religion, the other teaches morality, and still other advocates for socialism. So the idealistic world peace, capitalistic world peace, undisarmed world peace of developed and under developing Nations are propounding unfathomable and unbelievable unrest through hasty efforts for world peace. Human sensibility has been splitted and dissociating day by day.

We suffer from noveltic fever bent upon to cross all limits. Our soul is mad after ornate novelty whatever be the consequences.

We have cut pieces of life for own peace. Such self centered peace gets disturbed with surroundings under groaning segments. So, only the global peace stands for long pleasure, gravity, mobility, passion free imagitation, satisfaction, sinless performance and renunciation. Further we should be ready to sacrifice for fellow friends of God, where non bossism, impartial kindness, love, austerity, sweet heartedness and harmony are tips to enjoy true peace as the Geeta says:

भोक्तारं यज्ञतपसां सर्वलोक महेश्वरम्
सुहृदं सर्वभूतानां ज्ञात्वा मां शान्तिमृच्छति–5 / 29

Bhocktāram yagyatapsām sarvalokamnaheshwaram
suhrdam sarvabhutānām gyātwā mān shāntimṛcchati–5/29

Further we should realize that we are suffering from paranoia or psychosis due to violence and unrest. The root of violence is fear in multi-dimensions- political fear, economic fear, religions fear, moral fear and the likes. Secondly, the endless needs of life may cause violence. That is to say that fear and need cover every walk of life in particular and life on earth, in general. So the state of fearness and endless avarice tease world peace. Next the world is burning in to the fire of fierce and unrest due to violence. To explore satisfaction to endless demands in earthly life and more discoveries to satisfy mankind by Science and Scientists, the world are pushing step by step towards the verge of perilous fear or disaster. The quest to discover numerous secrets of Nature for all benefits to mankind might have harnessed the forces of Nature in proper or improper care because a man is essentially a part of Nature. As a precautionary measure Dr Bhabha (Indian) presided over the "Atom for peace conference" sponsored by UNO in Geneva, 1955. later on "the Agency for international Atomic energy" was also established for peaceful purpose in july, 29, 1957. But the tenacity of purpose was lost in pandemonium and neutrality. As a result of which the Atomic Diplomats are tending towards the 3rd global conflagration to achieve political ends. It would mean destruction of the entire world and the scientists would weep for its improper use. So the Brahmos are assembled to control the situation and not to crush.

At the 7th meeting of the non-Aligned movement in 1983, New Delhi, the late Hon'ble P.M. Indira Gandhi reiterated- "development, independence, disarmament and peace are concomitants and -----". However we fear the concomitance of nuclear arms and living beings. It is a false co-life with the Bomb, wherein we are trying to exist peacefully at times of human crises.

The Non-Aligned movement, being the most powerful institution of the world, could be a great resort against the intrigues of big powers engaged in pushing the world into furnace of thermo-nuclear blast. So now, it has been high time for Brave Theory to ensure cosmos without chaos neither by inspiring exploitic power and high handedness nor by upholding injustices but by watering the human root with induction of the creative potential to foil evil forces.

ON MY 3RD ANGLE OF VISION -----------

In order to foster the world with peace and attachment and keep pace with the scientists for the most valuable aspect of the Cosmos- the struggle for life of the Cosmos Herself, let me turn to economic, commercial, political and diplomatic chaoses that are dissecting the world due to our stresses or thrusts on trivial parts of humanity and negligence of the paramount ones of the humanity. So we have to play a vital role in the canvas of global amity and cooperation. To make it effective in toto, we have to apply our learned and creative talent – being homely to the diversed people of the world – that the colour of skin and practice of cult or faith are but our superficial traits. Whereas that deep life within our heart flows the same blood and reigns the same spirit: The entire population of the world is a single race- that of homosapiens, mankind are brothers and sisters. Such fraternity would increase our happiness in prosperity and diminish our distress in adversity. Further it would cheer our dropping spirit, share our misfortunes and lighten the heavy burden of our mind. Such amity or fraternity is not like a summer companion which fades away in the frosty days of winter, rather nurtures with love and affection for good. When such feeling of universal affinity comes to reign supreme, life's final star would be safety and amity for real peace.

In order to end endless avarice we should exercise Pauranic dictum as in Shreemadbhagvatapurana---

यावत् भ्रियेत् जठरं तावत् स्वत्वं हि देहिनाम्
अधिकं योऽभिमन्येत् स स्तेनो दण्डमर्हति–7/14/8

Yāvat mriyet jatharam tāvat swatvaṃ hi dehināṃ
abhikam yobhimanyet sa steno dandmarhati–7/14/8

"Human beings have rights to enjoy their own quota for appeasement to belly, but those who mean or want more than quota as own are liable to be punished.

Again Ishavasyopanishad says-

ईशावास्यमिदग्वं सर्वं यत्किंच जगत्यां जगत्
तेन त्यक्तेन भुञ्जीथा मा गृधः कस्यस्विद्धनम्।

Ishāvāsyamidagvamsarvam yatkinca jagatyām iagat
Ten tyakten bhunjeethā mā gṛdhah kasyaswiddhanaṃ

The Supreme Being has the rights of possession over all life-assets of the world. So enjoy yourself by renunciation of greed against else assets or belongings i.e. quota-limit.

Now we may conclude that avarice, fear, hatred, conflict, rivalry disrupt free peace of mind which is essential to secure universal welfare-being the characteristic of Advait Vedant of Shankar. Global entity can be emerged through free peace of mind to satisfy the yearnings of billions in one hamlet. Vedantins' composite views may be translated as-

Stone walls do not make a prison
Nor iron bars a cage
Mind innocent and quiet take
that form a hermitage.

Moreover human mind can make a heaven of hell and a hell of heaven. It can supersede the influence of its environment. Destitutions, dangers and difficulties may assault it (mind) on all sides. But the mind has got the power to protect itself against them by upholding communion with its Innerself or God. Neither the iron bar nor the stone walls of dark dungeon can disrupt the quiet of human soul which turns the prison into a hermitage by virtue of meditation and abides peacefully in that sanctuary of mind. The Geeta deepens the very impression and Russian writer Leo Tolstoy's views-"The kingdom of God is within you, give it a permanent form".

So we should change ourselves before changing the world.

Now in order to operate upon negative ideas as attended to above, it is for we to cultivate positive ideas that are implanted in our tender hearts. Evil thoughts should be uprooted as unwanted weeds. Such noble ideas entail to elevate our cosmic consciousness which does communicate through our integrity proportionately as French Scientist B.Pascal's law-

"The pressure applied" to an enclosed fluid will be transmitted without a change in magnitude to every point of the fluid and to the walls of the container. The pressure at any point in the fluid is equal in all directions. For example-

Take a hollow rubber ball and make numbers of pin-holes at different places on the surface of the ball. Pour water into the ball through a wide hole. After closing the wide hole with fingers and squeeze the ball, we see that the streams of water from the pin-holes reach up to the equal distance in air indicating that the increased pressure in water has been equally transmitted in all directions.

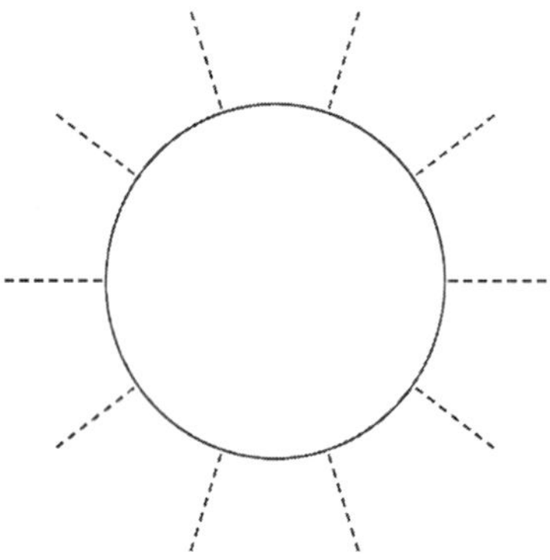

Earlier I have discussed about violence and fear in varied forms which can be averted with Gandhian Philosophy also. These two phenomenona are based on his "Truth" which is neither material nor spiritual but of third type. His truth is the unification of experienced (religion or faith) and experimented (Science and technology) touch. His Theory of Truth and Non-violence enunciated the ideal of "Sarvodaya" (welfare to all) after the practical transformation which brought about in his life through the study of English critic John Ruskin's famous book "Unto This last" as a Common heart aerial.

Further This non-violence is a positive and dynamic force towards biotic realm through real love and charity. It does not mean submission to the will of evil doers but to rule over evils by good deals. He opines that human spirit, when hit by divine fire, is stronger than the mightiest armament. His Ahimsā is based on Truth loaded with philosophical and ethical overtones. Whereas his Truth is the confluence of material and immaterial life open to equality, prosperity and uniformity from the grass root.

Lastly without peace, prosperity, pleasure and cessation of war, the world would be utterly ruined by the typhoon of global temper which can be neutralised by the exercise of oriental thoughts & intents.

5(B) - Terrorism and oriental Tenet

We live in the bog of crimes and terrors. Politics has been the roaring ground of the notorious criminals. Separatists provoke shelter of evil designers against peace and progress of Nations. Gone are the days when our patriotic leaders sacrificed for Nation's cause. Most of our countries or states are suffering with escalating violence and hurling of missiles. The more disturbed regions are Islamic states which are censured for manoeuvring terrorism. The Islamic State of Iraq and Al-sham- Islamic states of Iraq and Syria (ISIS) incites followers for attacks whenever they are located or travel to ISIS- help territories in Iraq and Syria to recruit as foreign fighters. Whereas some Heads of the Islamic States express grave concern or condemn terrorism from time to time as-

(1) Imam Ali Raza (Descendant of the Ismalic prophet, Muhammad – 766 CE(1) to 818 CE or BC)-

"Be like the honey bee

It eats in clean

anything it drops is sweet

The branch it sites upon does not break."

(2) The Hon'ble Malasian former P.M., Mahathir bin Mohammad (1981-2003, 2018 to 2020), while addressing 03-day meet organized by OIC (Organisation of Islamic countries) in Kualalampur, April 01, 2002, condemned & said- " I would like to suggest in view of the deteriorating situation in West Asia, here that armed attacks or other forms of attacks against Civilians must be regarded as act of terrors and the perpetrators of such attacks regarded as terrorists. So Muslim, everywhere must condemn

terrorism, one it is clearly defined, that terrorizing people is not the way of Islam."

(3) Hon'ble Nursultan A. Nazarbayev, secular minded president (Former) of Kazakhstan (1990-2019) convened the meet by CIACA (Conference on Inter-Action and Conflict-building Measures in Asia) in Almaty in june 2002, where treat of security, terrorism and other concerning issues were discussed amicably.

(4) Former Hon'ble president Gen. Parvez Mussarraf vowed to crush terrorists in the 57th Anniversary of Independence.

(5) George W. Bush, former Hon'ble President of America pointed out simply as unconventional nature of conflicts.

 (a) Now the world has suffered gruesome murder of humanity by terrorists for decades together. So the term "Terrorism" has posed a wide coverage to define it. To me it is unlawful use of violence against civilians or any segment thereof for political ends. Further it is a political violence designed to impose Psychic fear through vehement victimization and massacre targeted. So anyone who coerces the community by intimidation until final defeat is called – Terrorist.

 (b) Because the purpose of terrorism – is to explore the media to obtain maximum publicity by amplifying forces of fear to rejoin for royal goals. In other words it acts as a device of forceful forfeiture that to achieve political or visionary goals.

 (c) Further the cause of terrorism – argues that ethnic stigmas, destitution, lack of education, and political crunch impel people to take in terrorism. Youngman, monopolised with awkward circumstances, are made easier to be deployed by terrorists organization. Whereas we the people, suffer cacophony of life trimmed up to offend faultlessly.

On the basis of causes and purpose of terrorism. I may divide it into following categories-

(i) Revolutionary group – here terrorists rebel against their Govt.

(ii) Sub-revolutionary group – terrorists work for political ideology.

(iii) Established terrorism – terrorists are at work in crimes and criminal advantage.

The above 03 categories fall under 03 dimensions –

(1) Domestic terrorism – domestic crimes are committed by individuals or groups for ideological ends erupted out of social,

racial, faiths and political revolts. Such threats are on for years together to meet cruel targets.

(2) International terrorism – since 2000 such terrorism has been posing a serious threat conspired with associated groups or States sponsored organisation entitled foreign terrorists .

(3) Lone offenders –they are challenging to trace out, investigate and thwart their plots of large group hatching for lone offender attack. Some times they commit violence without clear affiliation to groups or organisations .Besides Extremists use Internet for messaging platforms, on-line images, videos, pamphlets & bills.

These measures help to mould their brains into violence and vengeance for hostile attacks. They are bent on using chemicals, biological, radiological and nuclear explosives.

How to identify and prevent them from their activities which cover a complex range of threats being the bare needs of the time. Such threats are imposed by orgainsed terrorism in conflict zones, foreign terrorist fighters focusing on social media and other digital channels.

So now it is high time to curb or neutralise terrorist cells and operatives through multi – devices as follows-

(a) The defenders are deployed to deter, detect and disrupt terrorists incidents.

(b) The people should be vigilant against motive, methods and money sources through information sharing, intelligence analysis, capacity building and operational support.

(c) Supporters are member countries in preventing & responding to random attacks. A coordination among agencies with police,customs, border controls, health professional, military intelligence service and environmental mgt. be ushered.

(d) Exchange of operation-zones between the Police and Military and use of biometric data to identify and prevent from crossing borders.

(e) The world's police enforcement may share intelligence and alerts on transitional terrorist network to arrest suspects through INTERPOL (International Criminal Police Organisation).

(f) Tracing out terrorists' financing.

(g) Counter terrorism – which includes military tricks, law enforcement and intelligence agencies to fight against terrorism.

(h) Protection of people both on-line and in person ,and report any suspicious activity with which they encounter.

(i) Noticing a change in behavior to mobilise violence through resources such as –

 (a) Suspicious activity reporting

 (b) Community preparedness Tool

 (c) Home-ground violent Extremist Indicators

 (d) Terrorist Explosive Device Analytical Centre

(j) An advisory on terror financing to investigate high quality of forged currency notes. In 2019, on OSAKA summit, India along with BRICS (Brazil, Russia, India, China & South Africa) condemned terrorists' attack in all forms and began to tackle all techniques and channels of terrorists in order to fight against terror-financing for the land. Besides TFFC (Terror Funding Fake Currency) Cell has been formed to monitor terror-funding and fake currency cases.

(k) Strengthening high security at international borders by surveillance-technology and observing intensive patrolling. Additional personnels be deployed for round-the-clock surveillance.

(l) Stop Drone assassination of innocent civilians.

(m) Stop imperial victory for Arab oil. Because much of war on terror is a fight for Natural gas really.

(n) Stop supporting Dictators who fund for brutal terrorists.

(o) Avoid too much torture which may turn terrorist into more vulgarity of rudeness.

Under oriental perspective such evil or mischievous spirits were called demons. Wherein the people were frightened with demoniacal tremor as we reap today. So whatever measures, motives and strategies were taken with available devices for combating should be conceived now. In this context Hindu mythology allows none to let terrorists free for their heinous targets: rather they should be forfeited against devastation by hook or by crook.

Further the citizens hatching conspiracy for self ends against the Nations are called Separatists. Such evil doers are liable to be exiled from the land as Acharya Manu says in "Manusmrit"-

यो देश ग्राम संघाना कृत्वा सत्येन संविदम्
निसंवदेन्नरोलोभात्तं राष्ट्राद्विप्रवासयेत्–8/8/219

Yā desha grāma sanghāna krtvā satyena samvidam
Visamvadenna rolobhāttam rāstradvipravāsayet–8/8/29

The man who solemnly promises to nurture the interest of the village, society or organisaton or Nation and later on does against the mass out of selfishness or greed or temptation is liable to be exiled from the land.

Further the Rigveda delineates thc validity of cursing Action by Lord Indra to rend the skulls of he-she-demons indulged in noxious conspiracy and slay them before sun-rise-

इन्द्र जहि पुमांसं यातुधानमुत स्त्रियं मायया शाशदानाम्
विग्री वासो मूरदेवा ऋदन्तु मा ते दृशन् त्सूर्यमुच्चरन्तम्–7 / 104 / 24
Indra jahi pumānsam yātudhānamnut striyam māyayā shāshadānām
Vigri vāso murdevā rdantu mā te drshan tsuryamuccarantam–7/104/24

O Lord Indra! do kill tyrannical demons and even frauding she-demons or deceptive women against Vedic Ethics, and one who sports with heinous crimes, be void of organs of perception (eye-sight) so that one would not see luminous sun-rise.

Again The Sāmveda teaches-

यो नः स्वोऽरणो यश्च निष्ठयो जिघां सति
देवास्तं सर्वे धूर्वन्तु ब्रह्म वर्म ममान्तरं शर्म वर्म ममान्तरम्–21 / 24
Yo nah svoran yashca nistayo jighānsati
Devāstam sarve dhurvantu brahma varma namāntaram sharma varma namāntaram–21/24

"those who feign friendship and hatch our ruin in cognitio, let our deity should ruin them with Vedo-mystic arm & armour."

Again The Sāmveda is grave for massacre of quisling foes-

कंकाः सुपर्णा अनु यन्त्वेनाम् गृधाणामन्नमसावसतु सेना
मैषां मेच्यधहारश्चनेन्द्र वयांस्येनाननुसंयन्तु सर्वान्–26 / 16
Kankāh suparnā anu yantvenām grdhānāmannamasāvasatu senā
Maiṣām mocyadhahārshcanendra vyānsyenānanusanyantu sarvān–21/26

Let arrows be hankered after quisling foes towards the ravage as corpse-heap and carnivorous vultures should feed on foemen lest no foemen should be left uninjured

O god Indra! quisling foes or traitors should not be saved: carnivorous birds be clustered on them.

Again the Sāmveda delineates that seer-made missile and air-fighters were stationed to rend hearts of hostile spirits in toto, even to the farthest spot- how much far away-

अवसृष्टा पराशत शरव्ये ब्रह्म शंशिते
गच्छामित्रान् प्रपद्यस्व मामीषां कंच नोच्छिषः–25 / 15

Avasrṣtā parāshata sharanye brahma shanshite
Gacchāmitrān prapadyasva māmiṣām kanca nocchiṣah–25/15

In order to impose righteousness and peace over the land, We are free to operate guerilla tactics or strategies against demoniacal designers. As Lord Krishna cared a fig for being called Himself as war-shirker for the cause of the Mother land. He succeeded to kill terrorist Kalyavan who was burnt to ashes by seer Muchukund in a mountain caves as The Bhagvatpuran says-

स तावत्तस्य रूष्टस्य दृष्टिपातेन भारत।
देह जेनाग्निना दग्धो भस्मसादभवत् क्षणात्–10/51/12
Sa tāvattasya ruṣtasya dṛstipaten bhārat
Deha jenāgninā dagdho bhasmasādabhavat kshanāt–10/51/12

Further

The Time is on vigilance to deploy Super Power by impersonating to destroy evil doers and re-instate righteousness for Ages as Lord Krishna bodies forth in every Era-as The Geeta says-

परित्राणाय साधूनां विनाशाय च दुष्कृताम्।
धर्मसंस्थापनार्थाय सम्भवामि युगे युगे–गीता–4/8
Paritrānāya sadhunāmvināshāy ca duskrtām
Dharma sansthāpanarthāya samabhavāmi yuge yuge–Geeta-4/6=8

Again Lord Krishna incarnates Himself to save and secure the living creatures in hazard as The Mārkandeypurān affirms-

इत्थं यदा यदा बाधा दानवोत्थाभविष्यन्ति
तदा तदावतीर्याहं करिष्याम्यरिसंक्षयम्–दुर्गा सप्तशती–11/54–55
Ittham yadā yada bādhā dānvotthābhavisyani
Tadā tadāvatiryāham karisyāmyarisankshayam–Durgā sapashati–11/54–55

Whenever barriers occur due to the dawn or advent of demon or devil, I incarnate Myself to rescue The Universe or The Land.

Islamic scholar Shah Waliullah Dehlawi (Indian) reiterated in his book-

'Hijjatullah Allah-AL Balighah'- In the moment of hazard to humanity, Lord incarnates Himself in different figures to lessen the load of lawlessness on The Earth.

Irish poet Y.B. Yeats proclaims the very theophanism in " The Second Coming".

Mere anarchy is loosed upon the world
The ceremony in innocent is drawned
The best lack all convictions which

the worst are full of passionate intensity
that the 20th century of strong sleep
were vexed to nightmare by a rocking cradle
slouches towards Bethlehem to be born....

Here one may interpose as to how and how much can one keep mum or on wait for incarnation when onslaughts on humanity are continued to vex the land? So I am to clarify that we dare to undertake operational strikes with counter strategies without fail and The Time would conjoin the Herculean Personnels with zenith, zeal and mystic spirit to rescue the land and the Public.

Our Oriental tenets have been elucidated in previous chapters with which Swiss Psychiatrist, Carl Jung agrees-

"we are one in supra-spirit indirectly or minutely"

So Lord Krishnite zeal should be uptaken by human-states to tread down terrorists. Furhter Lord Krishnite alacrity to arouse Arjuna for Holy war-trade is cited as in the Geeta-

हतो वा प्राप्स्यसि स्वर्गं जित्वा वा भोक्ष्यसे महीम्।
तस्मादुत्तिष्ठ कौन्तेय युद्धाय कृतनिश्चयः–2/37

Hato vā prāpsyasi swargam jitvā vā bhoksayase nahim
Tasmāthuttistha kounteya yuddhāya kritnishacayah–2/37

You would fly straightway to the heaven as martyr or would enjoy/ govern The Earth as victor. Do uprise or keep up for arrow shooting certainly.

5(C) - Vedic canon & cannon ball

The Vedas (spectrum of global Google) which came into existence- 1960853000 years ago, postulate the chemistry of Nature's coincidence and coherence. They are conscious to collate its inner mgt for war-free life in peace and harmony.

So I look into the vast vision of the Vedas precisely. Because the elaborate illustrations would take a huge deal.

They unveil the vast vision of valuable knowledge for global harmony and humour. They treat the trauma of thoughts tending to physical & mental troubles. They convey the conception of विद्ययाऽमृतमश्नुते vidyayāmṛtmaśnute (ishopnishada-11). Divine wisdom causes divine life world beyond. Such type of nectarian notion rests in The Rigveda

आ नो भद्राः क्रतवो यन्तु विश्वतः–1/89/1
ā no bhadrāh kratavo yantu visvatah

"let noble thoughts come to us from all sides"

Such nobility of thoughts entails to tame the excellent & executive trait of the mortal world in terms of the earth & the like by the will of The Divine Architect (vishwakarma) as in Yajurveda.

अदभ्यः सम्भृतः पृथिव्यै रसाच्च विश्वकर्मणः समवर्त्तताग्रे
तस्य स्वष्टा विदधद्रूपमेति तन्मर्त्यस्य देवत्वमाजानमग्रे–31/17
Adabhyah sambhrtah prthivai rasācca visvakarmanah samavarttatāgre
Tasya svaṣtā vidadhadrupameti tanmartsya devatvāmajānamagre–31/17

At the outset of the world's Creation Viswakarmā (divine Architect) generated fruit guice for trees and the Earth through non-copulative creation. But their divinity by birth got polluted with worldly lure which led to infernal favour. As a result of which they were divided into divine and devil spirits called noble and evil beings. Here The Vedic Mantras stood or stand for divinity lest they should be devilish. Today the creation of beings is done with intaking of juice like semen in the fair sex passing through 5 step of solemn oblation of hydro particles which cause analogical figures or images with the parents' couple normally.

Again the Vedas convey the homolytic chemistry of congruity and cohesion to see oneself in all beings and all beings be seen in oneself to avoid disgust and distress as in the Yajuveda(EEshāvāsyophishad).

ईशावास्यमिदग्वं सर्वं यस्तु सर्वाणि भूतान्यात्मन्येवानुपश्यति
सर्वभूतेषु चात्मानं ततो न विजुगुप्सते–40/6
Ishāvāsymidangvam sarvām yastu sarvāni bhutānyātmanyevānupasyati
sarvabhutesu cātmanam tato na vijugupsate–40/6

So we should not kill or slay jeevas for taste for a moment. As the Yajurveda enjoins to follow Ahimsā (non-hurt)

मा हिंसीः पुरुषम्–ग्टप्.3
mā hinseeḥ puruṣam–XVI-3

"Do not murder human being."

Again Yajurveda

इमम् मा हिंसीः द्विपदं पशुम्–XIII-47
imam mā hinscch dwipadaṃ pashuṃ–XIII-47

Do not murder biped being.

Further fraternity and affinity be cultivated so that I ought to view all with genial eyes and all ought to view me with friendly eyes i.e. be friendly to one another as coined in the Yajurveda.

मित्रस्याहं चक्षुषा सर्वाणि भूतानि समीक्षे
मि॒त्रस्य चक्षुषा समीक्षामहे–36 / 18
mitrsyahām caksuṣā sarvāni bhutāni samikṣe
mitrsya caksuṣā samiksāmahe–36/18

The Atharvveda defends the same sort of conception of affinity and amity which ensure bravery or fearlessness in all times & aspects alike

अभयं मित्राद् अभयं अभित्राद्
अभयं ज्ञातात् अभयं पुरो यः
अभयं नक्तं अभयं दिवा नः
सर्वा आशा मम मित्रं भवन्तु–19 / 15 / 6
Abhayaṃ mitrād abhayaṃ amitrād
Abhayaṃ jnātāt abhayaṃ puro yaḥ
Abhayaṃ niktam abhayaṃ divā naḥ
Sarvā āshā mam mitram bhavantu–19/15/6

"Be safe or fearless from our friends
Be safe or fearless from our foes
Be safe or fearless from our known object
Be safe or fearless from our front entity
Be safe or fearless from days and nights
Be safe or fearless from all walks or aspects of life."

Mind that these dictums are based on reciprocal foot in which the wisher and the wished must have friendly fun of the mind and heart being integral personality.

Now The Vedas awaken the morale of marching and musing in constant relationship and togetherness. All activities should be done unanimously. So you, too, commune and cultivate the cause of conscience as the conduct of God adorable since time immemorial what the Rigveda (Sangyansukta) suggests-

संगच्छध्वं संवदध्वं सं वो मनांसि जानताम्
देवा भागं यथा पूर्वे सञ्जानाना उपासते–10/91/2

Sangacchadhvam samvadadhvam sam vo manānsi jāntām
Devā bhāgam yathā purve sanjānānā upāsate–10/191/2

Move, speak and think favourably as gods yeild or stand for. So avoid all isms and accept co-habitat globally in proper rhythm.

The Vedas advise us to avoid anti thoughts which erode the mind and body. They command us to let our ears hear good or friendly speech or expressions, let our eyes see all good & eco-affairs as in The Rigveda (Mudakopnishada, prasnopnishad and Māndukyopnishad)

भद्रं कर्णेभि शृणुयाम देवाः
भद्रं पश्येमाक्षभिर्यजत्राः।
स्थिरैरंगैस्तुष्टु वाँग्सस्तनूभिर्व्यशेम देवहितं यदायुः–1/89/8

Bhadram karnevih srnuyām devāh
bhadram pasyemāksabhiryajatrāh
Sthirairangaistuṣtu vāngsastanubhirvyashem devahitam yadāyuh–1/89/8

Evil thoughts do eat into the vitals of our body. So if one wishes to have long-long life, one should exercise positive thoughts to nourish one's organs of the body for longevity in sound health.

Further the Vedas wish to enjoy beyond centennial longevity to see, live, hear, and teach in cheers by the grace of God who ordained the Sun being His eyes, to rise in the East: And His grace should gear our life to complete and enjoy centenary autumns (years) as in the Shukla Yajurveda.

तच्चक्षुर्देवहितं पुरस्ताच्छुक्रमुच्चरत् पश्येम
शरदः शतं जीवेम शरदः
शतग्वं शृणुयाम शरदः
शतं प्रब्रवाम शरदः
शतमदीनाः स्याम शरदः
शतं भूयश्च शरदः शतात्–36/24

Tacaksurdeohitam purastācchukramuccarat pasyem
Saradaḥ satam jivem saradaḥ
Satagwam srnuyām saradaḥ
Satam prabravām saradaḥ
Satmdeenā syām saradaḥ
Satam bhuyasca saradaḥ satāt–24/36

Here mutual affinity for prosperity throughout centenary life has been taught.

Now the Vedas' will to have wellness and sweetness of Nature's phenomena for hale and hearty life has been expressed.

Sweet or favorable phenomena of environment have been portrayed wherein sweetened or incense breathing Air blows, Seas flow sweet or healthy or hygienic water, herbs be sweet or medicinal, enjoy sweet or favourite night and morning (day). The dust or earth of the Earth should yeild sweet and favourable cereals, herbal plants and trees be kept us well; the Ethereal father (sky) should provide eco-frienldy rain-falls, The Sun should radiate sweet or hygienic rays. and cows should produce sweet and nutritive milk as in The Rigveda-

मधुवाता ऋतायते मधु क्षरन्ति सिन्धवः।
माध्वीर्नः सन्त्वोषधीः मधुनक्तमुतोषसो।
मधुमत्पार्थिवग्वं रजः मधुद्यौरस्तु नः पिता।
मधुमान्नो वनस्पतिर्मधुमां अस्तु सूर्यः
माध्वीर्गावो भवन्तु नः।–1/0/6–8

Madhuvātā rtāyate madhuksaranti sindhavah
mādhvipnah santvosadhih madhunaktamutoṣaso
Madhumatparthivagwan rajah madhudyourastu nah pitā
Madhumānno vanaspatirmadhumām astu suryah
Mādhwirgāvo bhavantu nah–1/90/6-8

Here rays of reverence to Nature's phenomena have been focused on to wish for winsome life

Further the rest of Nature's phenomena are supposed to be sweet or favourable to hurt-hating such as herbs be filled with sweetness. The Earth be filled with sweetness, the Space or the Sky let fall sweet rains, the land lord or the peasant be meant for sweet affairs and we should be hurt-hating and favourable to mankind as in The Rigveda.

मधुमतीरोषधीर्द्याव आपो मधुमन्नो भवत्वन्तरिक्षम्
क्षेत्रस्य पतिर्मधुमान्नो उस्तत्वरिष्यन्तो अन्वेनं चरेम–8/4/97/3

Madhumati-rosdhirdyāva āpo madhumanno bhavatvanta riksam
Kṣetrasya patirmadhumānno ustatvariṣyanto anvenam carem–8/4/97/3

The Vedas exhort the global phenomena to let pervade and preserve pacification and exultation within the universe. They are personified as the pioneer of perennial peace and harmony. Because they wish Heaven, Space, Earth, Water, herbs, trees and plants god Vishwdeva (son of Vishwā-the divine Nature). The Supreme Brahma and the whole world be peaceful and graceful. Even the Peace by itself be peace giving as in The Yujurveda.

ॐ द्यौ शान्तिरन्तरिक्षग्वं शान्तिः पृथिवीशान्तिरापः शान्तिरोषधयः शान्तिः।
वनस्पतयः शान्तिः विश्वेदवाः शान्तिर्बह्म शान्तिः सर्वग्वं शान्तिः
शान्तिरेव शान्तिः सा मा शान्तिरेधि–36/17

Aum dyuo shāntirantrikṣagvan shāntih prthavishāntirāpah Shāntiroṣadhayah shāntih vanaspatayah shāntih visvedevāh shāntirbhrahm shāntih sarvagvam shāntih

Shāntireva shānti sā mā shāntiredhi–36/17

or

"Preserve the divinity of Nature
And Nature will preserve us
And help Nature thrive
With Space, Earth, herbs, plants
In watering for lubrication
To make the scenes and environs green"

But the present age is lamenting for peace which has been injured with the herrors of wars and terrors. All are obsessed with the idea that there has been the possibility of Nuclear War. Human race is made to sit on the heap of nuclear holocaust laced with lit-up tape and as such we are reminded of the vicissitudes of the Second World War. Wherein massacre, brutal murder, anarchy, ruthlessness, feud, barren land and the spread of blood cancer by the cruel effect of the radio-active fission were the results.

Now the arsenals of the Super Powers contain over 50000 nuclear war-heads and each of which has nearly 20 times above mortal or ruinous power of the Hiroshima Bomb. As the time is a great mischief monger so it might use H-bombs and harmful rays to operate under Brutal Force.

Under the circumstances worlds peace and harmony hang by thread. Every move to save Nature's phenomena from impending disaster is therefore, solicited. Pacifists all over the world are trying to resolve conflicts and explore to end the frantic arms and arsenals. They are anxious to solve the problem of peace and disarmament. Because the lives of the pros and cons are to stake to flames.

Consequently agriculture, industry, economic-structure, trade, commerce, culture and humanity all are in dangers of being waned. Is it the irony of fate with human being? That is why the people have begun to draw the idea that Science is disastrous and not spiritual. But I mean that there is nothing bad in the Atom. The evil is with human mind who has led to the design of ectronic equipment and warfare devices to meet the target. The cruel designs of terrorists warrant exercise of nuclear weapons to wreck mankind and ecosystem such as-

1. Nuclear weapon – Bomb explosion to spread radio-active fall-outs causing extensive heat and hazard to Biosphere.
2. Chemical weapons- easy to fuel social phenomena.
3. Biological weapons – to use dreadly microbes as offensive devices.
4. Super-sonic -cruise missile – to search out pirates.
5. Drones- act as aerial spies to survey potential target and assess battle field damages. They are remote-controlled pilotless planes called UAVs- (Unmanned Aerial vehicles)

Despite pertinent Treaties, Aggreements, Charters, BMD(Ballistic Missile Defence) to reinstate global peace and harmony we are vexed with conflict and crusades. Various Amendments to operate upon fissiparous trends such as – castes, Sexism, communalism cultural crises, untouchability, goondism and other mortal coil are being substituted but lagging behind. Also we are vexed with rape, tyranny suicide, malpractice, avarice and allied heinous crimes.

In view of such tumults and turmoils we must despise and condemn-

(a) Those who work for war and vote for military appropriation.

(b) Those who press for manufacturing missiles, nuclear arms and arsenals.

(c) Those who vote legislative bodies for further militarization of politics and arm-race.

To me the cause of the chain of problems lies in the lack of the exercise of the Vedic canons to vindicate at their roots with Creative Intelligence latent in everyone. As we are guiding missiles and misguiding men, so the chances of creating global affinity and amity correspondingly recede.

So it has been the crying need of the hour to lessen the load of artilleries over the billions through NPT (Non-Proliferation Treaty). Earlier the twin Super Powers (USA – USSR) Agreement in Washington to dismantle N- arsenals played a more effective role in the maintenance of peace and prosperity. But with the passage of time such tenacity went on trials to some extent.

So the biggest question, today, is how to preserve global integration, solidarity and oneness without which the orderly progress of every Nation is not possible. Further we have been reluctant to know-how to utilize the Nation's most precious resources – The Brain Physiology of every Nation.

Although Atomic Energy has universalized the achievements of Science and Culture which were framed in the myriad-minded Seers of yores. Science has been extended to promote talents and creative efficiency of human beings by overthrowing barriers between science and humanity to a remarkable extend; but we are not yet free of its perils. What does it profit a person if he gains the whole world and loses the serenity of life? So the Scientist and Noble prize Winners advocate –

> "humanity was threatened as never before by the so –called drastic extinction; society, now is organized to decay and not to have life with human values;

The Atomic energy has put humanity on the verge of pure disaster which has caused soil exhaustion, erosion and ecological damages. Whereas our Upnishadic Mantras and mentalities alluded earlier emphasize the unity of minds to mould healthy & powerful Organisation for prosperity & pleasure of all and promote fellow-feelings and righteousness on the basis of human rights. All are equal and share universal brotherhood for overall development of the society without discrimination between the superior and the inferior. We are all chips of the same block advancing together for common concept & conscience.

Therefore, it has been quite essential to exercise the pristine & perfect consciousness reposed in our Vedopanishadic compass caring for each trade of life in beatitude.

5(D) –Great pilgrim & Post – Mortem life

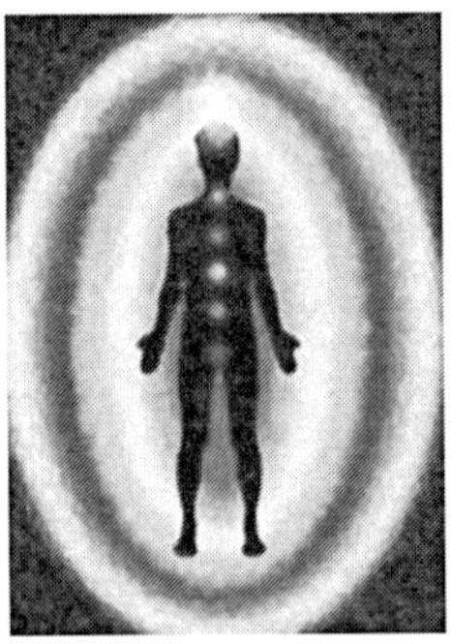

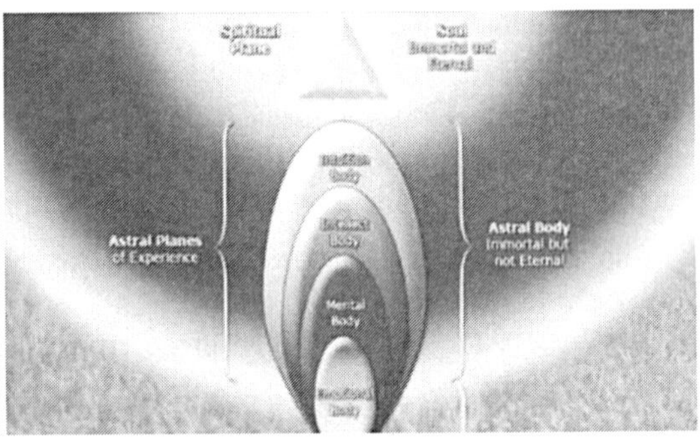

Great pilgrim tends to contrive transmigration from one life to the next one since time immemorial as lord Krishna says in the Geeta-

बहूनि मे व्यतीतानि जन्मानि तव चार्जुन।
तान्यहं वेद सर्वाणि न त्वं वेत्थ परन्तप।–4/5

Bahuni me vyateetāni janmāni tava cārjuna
Tānyaham veda sarvāni na tvam vettha parantapa–4/5

But the chain of living life to life is unknown to Arjuna and not to Him.

Let me review the following arguments under the topic –

(1) Rishi Gautama of Mithila formulated the concept of previous lives in his masterpiccc – 'Nyāyasutra" as

वीतरागजन्मादर्शनात्–3/1/45
Veetarāgajanmādarshanāt–3/1/45

i.e. all living organism are born with secular passion which is not possible without recollecting previous lives' impressions. Such impressions from the eternal chain of previous lives are carried forward through innumerable bodies. Wherein the concomitance of recollection through previous lives is effective due to the constancy of the Self dwelt or dwelled within.

(2) The Royal sage Indradyumna was cursed by sage August to have an elephant race/species . But when it was grasped by crocodile in the river and finding no way out, the elephant recalled its worship or ritual done in his past life to the God. Consequently, the elephant was released out of the morsel of the crocodile and marched for heaven. Such incidence proves the Theory of Re-Birth.

(3) In Arithmetical system once the digits from 01 to 9 exhaust, we transmit or reverse back to starting digit = 0 or 01 which justifies that when one cycle of life exhausts, the next exists or reverses.

(4) The Geeta affirms the inevitable life cycle of Great journey and Rebirth also. So lamentation is not needed for anyone –

जातस्य हि ध्रुवो मृत्युर्ध्रुवं जन्म मृतस्य च
तस्मादपरिहार्येऽर्थे न त्व शोचितुमर्हसि–2/27

Jātasya hi dhruvo mṛtyurdhruvam janma mṛtasya ca
Tasmādapariharyerthe na tvam shocitumarhasi–2/27

5) Again the Geeta confirms – just like a person puts off his clothes for new ones to put on, so the soul takes off the wearied body to take into the next one –

वासांसि जीर्णानि यथा विहाय नवानि गृह्णाति नरोऽपराणि।
तथा शरीराणि विहाय जीर्णान्यन्यानि संयाति नवानि देही।–2/22

Vāsānsi jeernāni yathā vihāya navāni girhnāti naroparāni
tathā sareerāni vihāya jeernānyanyāni sanyāti navāni dehi–2/22

(6) Any living entity does suffer total decay and the decayed or deceased does enliven to rebirth by virtue of Account – Audit of past Actions with warning – Shreedevibhagwat says–10/17

कर्मक्षये जन्मनाशः प्राणिना–10 / 17

karmkṣaye janmanāshah prāṇinā–10/17

(7) There is no discrimination in assimilation or exemption of such consistent recycling until our fusion with the Supreme Being as Great English playwright & poet, Shakespeare affirms in recycling mode also-

Further uploading of heaviness is alike to all Jivas because-

If thou art rich, thou are poor
for like an ass whose back is ingots bows
thou bearest thy heavy riches but a journey
And death uploads thee
All things are taken from us and become
portions and parcels of the dreadful past.
If there any peace in climbing the climbing ware.
All things have rest, and ripen towards the grave." - **Shakespeare**

So such process is a transition from physical world to the astral plane. As a caterpillar creeping on the end of a grass – blade withdraws itself to take next step. So the Self strikes off the consumed body in the process of transmigration.

(8) The Vedic philosophy advocates that we (The Soul) keep back our corporeal body through micro atomic one deserting our corporeal body due to consequences of Actions – streams from time immemorial. This atomic or subtle body is just a luminescence to overview and regulate our past, present and future status.

This subtle body reruns (recalls, explains, remembers, understands, notes) the performance of the present body with pre-features imbibed through reflection, devotion and action of our pre lives. On trial and audit of the pre lives' Account the validity of the plight of re- birth is conferred as

(a) The Supreme Being delivers judgment on virtues and vices of our pre – lives to avail weal and woe in our next life

(b) We may not avail high middle or low body without the evaluation of virtues & vices of our pre-lives

(9) according to "Yoga Sutra" by sage Patanjali we might not have impressions & fears or frights of death without its bitter experience faced with pre lives. We are let involved in life- death cycle until emancipation due to righteous rites, sacred meditation and due understanding is undertaken.

Now let me explain the term "emancipation"

मुञ्चन्ति पृथग्भवन्ति जनाः यस्यां सामुक्तिः

Muncanti pṛthagbhavanti janāh yasyām sāmuktih

Emancipation or salvation or final beautitude may be achieved through legitimate knowledge in isolated state.

(10) whereas bondage or Nescience may occur in irreghteosness or immaterial ignorance misleading constancy, righteousness, self-pleasure in impure, non-eternal and miserable body as – defined in "yoga darshan" by st Patanjali

अनित्याशुचिदुःखानात्मसु नित्यशुचिसुखात्मख्यातिरविद्या–2/5

Anityāshucidukhānātmasu nityashucisukhātmakhyātiravidyā–2/5

Further "Yoga Darshan" of st Patanjali argues –

भवप्रत्ययो विदेह प्रकृतिलयानाम्–1/19

Bhavapratyayo videha prakṛtilayānāṃ–1/19

It's the worldly–life experience in which a perfect absorption of thoughts into abstract meditation is the mere cause of transmigration spontaneously or effortlessly. To untie the Theory, we feel that a man who has got rid of the gross body in his past life through good yogic practices mindfully and the man who has reached a certain state of mind-scope in yogic philosophy but yet to unite with the Supreme Spirit due to intervention of death – both conceive quick and perfect cognition in re-birth (present life) smoothly and amazingly. The phenomenal reason is to fulfil the rest paraphernalia which was left half-done in his pre-lives to be accomplished as the Geeta says –

प्रयत्नाद्यतमानस्तु योगी संशुद्धकिल्विषः
अनेक जन्म संसिद्धस्ततो याति परां गतिम्–6/45

Prayatnādyatamānastu yogi sanshuddhakilviṣah
Aneka janma san siddhstato yāti parām gatim–6/45

(11) According to the Thermodynamical conception of physical body, human body is made up of molecules which are in random motion and each molecule exerts a force of correlation or attraction on other molecule. Thus molecules possess energy and the body is the external energy of the molecules. So when the body is burned/burnt or decayed or rotted on handing over or resigning or returning all its Elements to the earth; The chemico thermal energy of the molecules of the body is let radiated from negative to positive energy being constant for next life of embodiment based on qualitative state in fluctuation of the Karmas.

(12) According to modern Physics – The Matter is a condensed - Frozen-form of energy.

Actually, when physical matter of the existence dissolves, we pass on to next energy level of our existence at successive stages-

(a) Physical gross body – That is perceptible to our senses. This is condensed form of energy of a certain frequency and wavelength

(b) Subtle body – The matter of high frequency and wavelength not perceptible to our senses being out of the range but a compile of past properties and pursuits

(c) Causal body – Matter of still higher frequency when the corpse gets cremated and the skull is cracked open, this soul or Self and the causal body (mobile chip) takes off to Manes land for judgement based on Account of past records of the deceased.

The Great pilgrim takes away toll Of youth, beauty and glamour. But positive and negative or true and untrue Actions chipped to the Self go alone being stripped of regal robes within the fading moment of starry globe. The causal body let stand in a queue for next state of life as our past Actions confirm. So when our astral, mental and causal bodies continue to exist after death, only cognition and feelings remain but the mobility of the Actions does not exist. Besides our material assets and status are left behind. Whatever level we get in the Cosmos depends on our Karmas entirely. The soul is guided on the astral level by audible and inaudible vibration of the Mantras leading towards realization or resurrection and judgement by the Divine Authority.

To some extent we generally use two elements in cremation -

(1) Fire – Which stands for remission from penalty, sins, debts, pardon

(2) Water – For creation (re-birth) as epithet of Brahma

In other words, past records of deeds, Karma-Accounts & debts incurred in the life span are judged in the astral dock for next sequel of progression or declension.

So, debts and equities are being classified for the purpose as follows –

(1) Debts incurring Actions – Selfish Actions that demand and indulge the egos.

(2) Equities earning Actions – Selfless Action where ego sacrifices pleasure for the sake of the world

(3) Debts Actions – The Manes world orders to replay mundane circuit by forcing to re-birth

(4) Equity earning – The Authority of death (Yama) liberates the Manes from the obligation of Re-birth under right earnings

But we are unaware of these 04 stages of commitment due to be entangled with physical impulses only.

Lastly my advice is –

(1) to live in full felicity under sobriety so that you may die happily

(2) to cultivate righteousness towards the twilight of life in order to enjoy post mortem Judgement as -

अन्तमत: स्वेव गत:

Antamataḥ sweva gataḥ

"The last urge of mind or memory is the momentum for next life."

According to our Oriental Mythology on The Theory of ṚṆĀNUBANDHA–The pledge of non-volatile memory surveillance based on the affinity of features, looks and describers is carried on from the present life to next one corresponding to anthropometrical karmas under The Cosmic Theory of debts cycle of responsibilities, duties and lusts left unpaid or unfrozen or unfulfilled. Such memory may be sensory, short-term, long-term, explicit, episodic, semantic, implicit and Testing (forensic science). In human body BM (Body Memory) or CM (Cellular Memory) involves the potential to preserve and recover traumatic informations what one experiences. So to achieve the ultimate goal of human life, we should neaten O5 Gross Elements of the body to pay off physical, mental and even emotional overdrafts of Karmic-Accounts debenture. The whole Karmic Accounts of past lives tagged with the astral body of the individual is adjudged by the celestial Judge authorised for next enforcement of reward or retribution. Here humanistic orientation of psychoanalysis on the concept of the Self-elevation adjoins behavioural science dealing with biometrical chemistry of Actions (Karmas) under–

(i) physical analysis

(ii) Ballistic analysis

(iii) fluid analysis

(iv) DNA analysis

(v) chemical analysis

(vi) gait analysis

Due to the aforesaid science BM or CM of debts' commitment, we, sometimes, hear or see around ourlife to let deny sesame oil or salt (Secured automated Landing Trauma) through skin or body touch. Because the word "salt" is derived from "salarium" or salary which inflicts liabilities

& indebtedness being precious commodity of life. Also with the case of sesame which is as precious as divine manifestation in cognitio to avoid body-indebtedness.

5(E) – Finishing Touch

The holy work is brimful of useful treasure of oriental wisdom with ultra-modern devices more than inventions to ease stress and strain in bio-life.

Its mission is to boost up crystalized cognition and fluid intelligence to solve global problem under specific system of life. It would change our whims of thoughts to blossom into positive consciousness under holy horizons. It acts as a shower of self-serenity and sanctity. As an advisory on human life it would turn and control the aura of the society under pristine propensity. Here 05-chapter of the work correspond to 05-Gross-Matter, 05 sense of wisdom, 05 sense of Action and 05-look or face of lord Shiva as Global – Saviour. As 05 elements are inevitable for proper origin and orbit of human life on global level. So 05 - chapter in the Work on human life has been explored for Bio bonanza as –

(1) The first chapter rotates round the sheer materialistic view of education system, human nuisance, oriental senses of human rights and havocs in material life on global level – all amendable on oriental devices.

(2) The 2nd chapter rotates round myriad mechanics of oriental geniuses, globo-oriental views on human community and democracy of cult, religion, culture and industrial re-enforcement- all emendable under oriental tenets.

(3) The 3rd chapter rotates round Nature – human harmony, Mono – metaphysical mentality, Anatomic – amplifier of AUM & ZERO (0) zenith and orient healing tips against women harrassment on global level

(4) The 4th chapter rotates round holistic therapy of human ailments, Vedic rites for eco-care, Lord Shiva – Character as Global Saviour and human plight on Karma Philosophy

(5) The 5th chapter rotates round Vedopnishadic tints and tips for terror – war aversion and post mortem life-soul appropriations and provisions.

Thus, the theme of the work – Oriental potential to gear the Bio-globe.

The work on Globo-natural philosophy (Metaphysics + modern science) for Bio-bonanza could be finished by virtue of single covalent energy no. 63 oriented to global commission and confluence in the teeth of global havoc due to Coronavirus (COVID-19).

Lastly the reader – cum –communicator is advised to entertain the work with global attitudes & impressions cherished in the holy Work.

Any suggestion is solicited on E.mail – drscmishra6@gmail.com

M- 9939984914 / 7667921138

Bibliography

The Vedas

1. Rigveda
2. Yajurveda
3. Sāmaveda
4. Atharvaveda

Upnishada

1. Kathopnishada
2. Brhdāranyakopnișada
3. Mundkopnișada
4. Chhāndogyopnișada
5. Swetāswataropnișada
6. Ishāvāsyopnișada
7. Māndukyop nișada
8. Rikprātishākhya Samhitā (k)

Smrti/Sutra

1. yāgyavalkya Smrti
2. pārāshar smriti
3. Manusmriti
4. Āpasthumbdharma sutra
5. yogavāsishtha of st. valmiki

Purāna/Brahman

1. Shree Madbhāgavata purāna
2. Shree Maddevibhāgvata purāna
3. Shree Madbhāgavata geeta
4. Matsya purāna
5. Padma purāna

6. Taittiriya Brāhman
7. Visnu purāna
8. Shiva purāna
9. Brama purāna
10. Mahabhārata
11. Rāmāyan of st. Valmiki
12. Vishnudharmottar purāna
13. Vāyū purāna
14. Mārkanadeya purāna

Scientist/Philosopher

1. Micro-physicist Āchārya Kanāda
2. Quanto- Metaphysicist Achārya Kapil
3. Astrophysicist-Acharya Aryabhatta-I
4. Astrophysicist-Acharya Aryabhatta-II
5. Astrophysicist-Acharya Vārāhmihir
6. Poly-mathematician Bhāskarāchārya-I
7. Poly-mathematician Bhāskarāchārya-II
8. Aeronautical Engineer Achārya Bhāradwāja
9. Electrical engineer Acharya August
10. Alchemist – Acharya Nāgār Juna
11. Medical scientist – Achārya Charaka.
12. Astrologist – Rishi Nārada
13. Plastic Surgeon & Beautician – Ashwini Kumar
14. Yoga Scientist-Achārya patanjali
15. Politician & codifier Achārya Kautilya ---
16. Sexor technician & Therapist – Achārya Vātsyāyana
17. King Vartrihari
18. Achārya Panini
19. Achārya Jaimini
20. Achārya Gautama
21. Achārya Kumārila Bhatta
22. Achārya Mandan Mishra
23. Achārya Vāchaspati Mishra
24. Maharshi Yāska (Nighantukar)
25. Achārya Udayan (Udayanāchārya)

26. Achārya Vasis.tha
27. King Bhoja
28. Swami Vivekānand
29. Acharya Gangeshopathyāya
30. Brahma Gupta

Literature/Philosophy

1. Yoga darshan - Palangali
2. Yoga Sutra
3. Shabda Kalpadruma
4. Vākyapadiya
5. Tarkāmrta
6. Brahmasutra Shānkarbhasya
7. Nyāya Sutra
8. Siddhānta Kaumudi
9. Ekākshari Kosa
10. Tarka Sangrah of Annam bhatta
11. Kāvya prakash of Mammata
12. Dhwanyāloka of Anand Vardhan
13. Swarnaprabhāsa Sutra (Buddism)
14. Param laghumangus.ā (Vyakaran)
15. Raghuvansha of Kalidas
16. Abhigyān Shākuntalam of Kalidas
17. Khandan Khandakhādya of Shree Hars.ha
18. Jain & philosophy
19. Buddha philosophy
20. Vaishesic darshan
21. Sāmkhya darshan
22. Qurān
23. Islāmic scholar – Waliullah Dehlawi

Western Scientist/Philosopher/Writer

1. The Bible
2. The Old-Testament
3. The New-Testament
4. German Theologist – Martin Luther

5. The Light of Asia – Edwin Arnold
6. Unto the Last – Ruskin
7. English Writer – Thomas Hardy
8. Russian Writer – Leo Tolstoy
9. Irish Poet – Y. B. Yeats
10. French Scientist – B. Pascal
11. German Novelist – P.T. Mann
12. Isaac Newton
13. English poet – P.B. Shelley
14. American Philosophy – R.W. Emerson
15. Modern physics
16. Bio-Chemistry
17. Organic Chemistry
18. Modern Zoology
19. Modern Botany
20. Canadian-Ken Galbraith
21. American prof. Clark Kerr
22. British T.S. Eliot
23. Willam Shakespeare – English Playwright

Tantra/Tantric

1. Madan Mohan Upādhyāya
2. Vishnuyāmal Tantra
3. Sarvollās Tantra
4. Kulārnava Tantra
5. Mantrayoga Samhitā
6. Shree Mahimnastotram by Pushpadantāchārya.

यतस्व रक्षितुं संसार जीवनं निरापदम्।
जयस्व रक्षितुं संसार जीवनं निरापदम्।
सहस्व रक्षितुं संसार जीवनं निरापदम्।
म्रियस्व रक्षितुं संसार जीवनं निरापदम्।

Jatasva Rakshitum̥ Sansār Jeevanam Nirāpadam̥
Jayasva Rakshitum̥ Sansār Jeevanam Nirāpadam̥
Sahasva Rakshitum̥ Sansār Jeevanam Nirāpadam̥
Mriyasva Rakshitum̥ Sansār Jeevanam Nirāpadam̥

Strive to secure global life against hazard
Surmount to secure global life against hazard
Suffer to secure global life against hazard
Sacrifice to secure global life against hazard

Patron (Mission) Smt. Kalpana Mishra alias Bachi- "Shastri"